OPERATION CODY
BEST OF THE WILD

WASHINGTON FISH & WILDLIFE DETECTIVE TODD A. VANDIVERT (RETIRED)

Printed by: **Create Space**
Distributed by: **www.amazon.com**

ISBN 978-1484148372

Cover created by: **Austin Suit, Graphic Designer- suit226@gmail.com**

DEDICATION

To my dad, Verl Vandivert, who instilled in me that job satisfaction is

far more important than pay.

WILDLIFE JUSTICE SERIES (FICTION):

POACHING SPREE

TO PROTECT A PREDATOR

A FALCON'S TALE

LETHAL REMOVAL

DEEP TROUBLE

FOR YOUR PROTECTION

HUNTING THE HUNTERS

FOLLOW THE WATER

POACHER'S PEAK

NON-FICTION:

OPERATION CODY

GAME WARDENS AND POACHERS

FICTION:

THE BLUE MOUNTAINS POACHER

"If you're going to be a bear,
be a grizzly."

-MAHATMA GANDHI-

PROLOGUE

Dictionary.com defines camouflage as: *"the act, means, or result of obscuring things to <u>deceive an enemy</u>, as by painting or screening objects so that they are lost to view in the background."* Game wardens worldwide are very familiar with camouflage, but perhaps not the type that Game Warden Jennifer Maurstad and I are attired in this day. For this undercover assignment, the camouflage of the day is what I refer to as "my good clothes" and requires me to pull on dress slacks, a nice polo shirt, and dress shoes, clothes that feel totally foreign to me. Jennifer and I refer to this type of camouflage as "dressing money." "Dressing money" is required today to deceive our "enemy", in this case, a millionaire illegal wildlife trafficker. We have portrayed ourselves as mid-level traffickers and must look and act the part. As we head towards the millionaire's home to trade in high-value illegal wildlife, we both already look forward to changing into our "trailer trash" clothes for the next stop.

Clothing changes are the least of our concerns as we meet with our clients, some of whom are heavily involved in illegal drugs and violent crime. With little support from our own agency, we travel across the northwest, buying and selling hawks, eagles, bighorn sheep, bear parts, caviar, and thousands of pounds of deer and elk meat. As our illegal wildlife business heats up, so do the attacks from within. Ultimately, we successfully worked our way into the wildlife black market to an extraordinary level, breaking up both domestic and international poaching rings.

INTRODUCTION

While the details in this book are facts, the names of the suspects, the federal agents, and some of the specific locations have been changed.

OPERATION CODY resulted in probable cause to arrest over 100 suspects across the U.S. Due to the enormous volume of case material, only a handful of the most interesting suspects and cases are profiled in this book.

I began my natural resource career with the Washington Department of Game in 1979, fresh out of college. At that time, the state of Washington had two similar natural resource agencies, the Department of Game (later changed to the Department of Wildlife) and the Department of Fisheries. The Department of Game (or Game Department as it was commonly called) was responsible for the management and protection of all the animals that walked, ran, crawled, or flew, as well as "Game Fish," which included trout, steelhead, and warm water fish (bass, catfish, crappie, etc.). The Department of Fisheries was tasked with all shellfish (clams, crabs, oysters, etc.) and all saltwater fish (other than sea-run cutthroat trout and steelhead). Most of the Department of Fisheries-managed species were available for commercial harvest and sale.

In contrast, very few of the Department of Game's species could be legally commercially harvested or sold. Department of Fisheries officers ("Fish Cops") commonly referred to the animals they were to protect as "product" (a result of considering the animals as commercial commodities rather than as wild animals), while Game

Department agents ("Game Wardens") never used this term when describing the animals, we worked so hard to protect. Two different philosophies existed- one driven by monetary value, the other driven by natural value.

In 1994, the two agencies were merged into the Washington Department of Fish and Wildlife (WDFW). I will not go into great detail regarding the merger, but suffice it to say that many senior officers never truly merged, while others did so quite successfully. Some officers held true to the priorities and philosophies of their former agencies and believed the responsibilities of the "other" agency were not essential, and refused to waste their time on the enforcement of the "other" agency's laws.

Soon after the merger, the new agency recognized the need to keep many of the officers in specialized positions. Thus, the uniformed officers were divided into two groups: land and marine, with land officers comprising about 80% of the workforce and marine officers taking up the remaining 20%. Most land and marine officers work well together and assist each other as needed. Still, the marine officers clearly took over the role of the former Department of Fisheries officers, while the reverse was true for the land officers.

Before the merger, both agencies had separate investigative units, SIU (Statewide Investigative Unit). With the agency merger came the merger of these investigative units. SIU is comprised of several detectives headed by a supervisor, who, in turn, answers directly to the DC (Deputy Chief). Uniformed officers spend much of their time answering calls regarding wildlife damage to crops, injured/orphaned wildlife, dangerous wildlife (bear and cougar conflicts), trespass, and anything else the public sector believes officers should be doing for them. Uniformed officers also conduct field checks of hunters and fishermen and, when time allows, conduct investigations of criminal activities in their patrol areas. WDFW detectives are solely responsible for investigating large-scale (major) fish and wildlife crimes.

In 2005, after more than two decades in uniform, I took a detective position in SIU. I had no idea what I was getting into, but I thirsted for major casework (while getting away from nuisance calls). At that time, the unit was made up of five detectives and was supervised by Captain Ed Volz. Only one other detective and I were former game wardens. Detectives ultimately answered to Deputy Chief Mike Cenci (a dyed-in-the-wool fish cop). At the time, I didn't realize just how important the composition of SIU's personnel would be in my future endeavors.

Soon after assuming my duties as a detective, I learned a few important things: First, a detective can't be effective without support and information from the uniformed officers. Second, many of our uniformed officers had a very poor impression of SIU and were reluctant to share information with detectives. Third, SIU (nicknamed by the uniformed officers as "The Clam Cops" or the "Shellfish Investigative Unit") had a reputation for only working geoduck (a high-dollar-value clam) cases and having no interest in anything else. Lastly, SIU deserved most of its reputation and did little to fix it.

Probably because I had worked so many years in uniform and took great pride in those duties, I made it my goal to do as much as

8

possible to bridge the gap between the uniformed officers and SIU detectives.

Detectives work cases both overtly (in the open) and covertly (secretly). Examples of overt casework include interviews/interrogations, taking witness statements, gathering forensic evidence, and conducting searches and reviews of business records. Covert work typically involves surveillance or undercover. I was promoted to detective to work covertly (while all the other detectives spent most of their time on overt casework). It is very risky to move detectives from overt to covert capacities, as overt work exposes the detective to the "bad guys," who could easily recognize that detective in a later covert capacity. Covert officers/detectives typically do not work out of a public office, nor do they make public appearances. That suited me just fine, as office environments and I do not get along, nor am I a fan of public speaking.

I have read more than my fair share of articles and books relating to undercover work (especially anything wildlife-related) and have found that some writers view the risks of undercover fish and wildlife work differently than I do. In my opinion, uniformed fish and wildlife officers face a far greater risk from criminals than do undercover operators, as long as the suspects do not learn the undercover investigator's true identity during the operation (discovery of our true identity in the middle of an undercover case could make for a seriously bad day). Undercover drug investigators are often victims of rip-offs and gang violence, two problems rarely faced in undercover fish and wildlife work, as our transactions don't normally require the large sums of cash common to drug operations, and we don't typically work inside gangs. Make no mistake, it is all hazardous work, and many officers have lost their lives protecting all of us and our natural resources. Still, I believe the real heroes are the men and women in uniform who confront and arrest criminals daily.

The last bit of information I would like to clarify is a couple of terms: undercover (UC) and plainclothes. It is not just the general public that doesn't understand the differences between the two terms, as many officers often confuse them. Simply put, plainclothes means an officer is wearing civilian clothing (and often driving an unmarked or personal vehicle) to blend in. They will typically wear department-issued equipment (such as a duty pistol, handcuffs, police ID, and/or a radio) under a cover shirt or jacket. They will take enforcement action and make arrests when a crime is witnessed. In plainclothes, the officer merely blends in with the hope of witnessing a crime or locating a suspect without drawing unwanted attention.

On the other hand, undercover officers/detectives work under fictitious names with none of the issued police equipment available. They assume a new identity and work "inside" a group within the criminal element, observing (and many times committing) crimes as they occur. Undercover officers/detectives must gain the trust of the suspects they are working to apprehend in an effort to learn as much about the criminal organization as possible. Many, if not most, officers have worked plainclothes assignments, but very few have worked true undercover assignments.

Editor's note- Text messages and emails within this book are exact quotes. These quotes often contain misspelled words and improper grammar, but are exactly as they were written by the people involved in this operation.

CHAPTER 1- JUST A THOUGHT

Once per year, a group of wildlife investigators from across the western US and Canada gets together for an informal meeting. At these meetings, we share information, brag a little, get to know our fellow investigators (valuable for interstate or international cases), and compare investigative techniques. It was at one of those meetings in the spring of 2010 that I met an investigator who had just completed a long-term "storefront" operation. A storefront operation is one in which the investigator(s) opens a legal business, secretly hoping to attract criminals. An example would be a pawn shop (very attractive to burglars and thieves). This investigator went into great detail about how he set up the business and how quickly the wildlife criminals (in this case, fish-related) came pouring in. At the conclusion of the operation, he had wrapped up some major fish and wildlife criminals and had them dead to rights. He explained how the "business" made it possible for him to simply sit and wait for the poachers to come to him, rather than the more traditional undercover, where the investigator seeks out the violators. The criminals caught up in this sting were charged with crimes that likely never would have been detected by any other method.

It all sounded like the best possible approach to address Washington's biggest poachers, except for one thing: the undercover investigator lived and breathed this case 24/7 for a very long time (well over a year). He could not go home to his real house, he couldn't interface with his fellow officers (the officers in the area he worked didn't know who he was), he couldn't see his family and friends, and he had to be available to open shop whenever the bad guys showed up with fish.

While I certainly took pride in the undercover work I had done thus far, I wanted more. I wanted more bad guys, bigger bad guys, and I wanted to take the biggest bite out of illegal wildlife trafficking I possibly could. On the other hand, I simply wasn't willing to put my personal life on hold for that long. I have a wife and daughter whom I love dearly, as well as other things in my life that I wasn't willing to give up. There had to be a way to conduct a storefront operation without the total commitment of time and resources this investigator had to dedicate.

In my opinion, illegal wildlife trafficking was running rampant in Washington. During my extensive tenure with WDFW, there had never been a long-term operation targeting illegal wildlife trafficking. I had worked on many smaller short-term trafficking cases, but wildlife trafficking had never been given the same attention as shellfish (many long-term shellfish investigations had been conducted). The "market" seemed ripe for the picking, but how?

For the next couple of days, all I could think about was how to work a storefront operation within my criteria….my way. Finally, one of the activities that took up some of my personal time proved to be the answer. For years, I have owned and operated an internet-based business on the side. It is a very small business taking a tiny portion of my free time, but it brings in a little play money for my family. My business is run out of my home, using a website for advertising, pricing, and ordering. That very same model seemed to be the answer for a wildlife storefront.

13

What started as a thought soon became a plan. I spent a lot of time covering all the angles and anticipating problems, but it seemed feasible to run a storefront business without the store. Like many businesses now, I believed I could run a wildlife business (specializing in wildlife parts) through the internet. I planned to open a legal business, offering to buy and sell wildlife parts, using the internet for advertising. It seemed possible to run such a business without a brick-and-mortar store. I would need a storage unit to keep "merchandise," a truck to deliver and pick up wildlife, a cell phone capable of internet/email and texting, and some standard business materials. The only opposition I anticipated from the chain of command would be related to the operating budget.

Knowing that one of the most critical factors in our command staff's decision-making process would be cost, I worked out a proposed operational budget. The monthly expenses would include storage unit rental, shipping costs, a cell phone plan, website maintenance, email, and cash for undercover purchases. I crunched the numbers and figured I could do a pretty damn good job for about $4,000 per month (or $48,000 per year), a figure I knew would raise significant concern, but I wrote that figure down in my proposed operational plan. In anticipation of a big "hell no," I was prepared with two counter-arguments. Washington law allows WDFW to forfeit (take and keep forever) any equipment used in wildlife violations, including vehicles. WDFW can seize evidence and proceed to the forfeiture of any equipment and/or vehicles used in wildlife crimes. Equipment forfeited becomes property of the state of Washington and is sold at auction. After the auction, the agency keeps the proceeds, meaning the forfeiture of a couple of nice vehicles would more than make up for the

14

expenses of the operation. My second argument was simply that each of our uniformed officers cost the agency well over $150,000 per year in wages, benefits, equipment, fuel, etc. I certainly expected this operation to do more damage to the poaching world than any single officer could do, making the operation cost-effective (at least in my opinion).

The next piece to consider was the operational duration. Since I wanted to get as many bad guys as possible, I wanted to run the case as long as I could. I also knew, from experience, that it takes several months (if not years) for a new business to really start rolling. The word has to get out, and you need time to build a customer base. Two years sounded like a reasonable timeframe, as the statute of limitations on gross misdemeanor crimes is two years in Washington, so we wouldn't have any cases go stale (Later, I'll go into more detail on the laws).

My next point of focus was to identify what wildlife to target. With thousands of wildlife species, I knew I had to specialize somewhat. Each state sets the laws regarding what is legal to hunt, kill, possess, buy, and sell. There is little uniformity between the states, making things very confusing for everyone. Still, I primarily had to be concerned only with Washington's laws (wildlife from other states would just mean a phone call to that state for clarification). Washington law prohibits the sale of edible portions of all game animals (including deer and elk meats), game fish (trout, steelhead, bass, etc.), bear parts, bighorn sheep parts, mountain goat parts, protected wildlife (including all raptors), and anything considered to be

15

illegal to sell or possess by federal law. Violations of these laws constitute felony crimes.

Since most of my experience and knowledge is in big game (deer, elk, sheep, cougar, mountain goat, and bear), they went on my list. While I know people collect and traffic in virtually all wildlife, I didn't have the know-how to bluff my way through a butterfly or lizard transaction, so they were out. In addition to big game animals, Washington (like most states) has suffered a great deal of raptor (eagle, hawk, and owl) poaching, which most officers believed to be commercially motivated, so they also went onto the list. Lastly, I added bobcats and lynx, as they are commonly poached and traded. With my target list complete, it was time to move to the next issue.

The next item to cover was manpower. In a properly executed undercover case, the team consists of the undercover(s), backup and surveillance officers, a case officer for case management (suspect backgrounds, gathering intelligence, and budget), and an evidence custodian. At this point in planning, I figured I would handle the undercover alone. I wouldn't need backup and surveillance officers (since I had never been offered any before and wouldn't know how to handle them if I had them), so I factored in only three employees for my proposed operation.

The last consideration was coordination with other states and the US Fish and Wildlife Service (USFWS). At that time, the relationship between WDFW and USFWS was pretty much dead. There had been some bad blood between the two administrations, resulting in virtually no communication or joint ventures for several years. Our relationships with adjoining states seemed to be reasonably

16

intact, but I believed the operation would fall short of its potential without the Feds on board. From experience in my sideline internet business, I knew there was virtually no way an internet business would stay in-state only. Since all interstate shipping of illegal wildlife is a federal crime, we badly needed the feds' buy-in. It seemed like a good time to extend the olive branch to the USFWS and put the egos in check. Fortunately for us, two of the USFWS Special Agents stationed in Washington were close friends of mine who had both previously worked for WDFW.

I spent a good deal of time and effort writing up my proposed operational plan, and once completed, I was very anxious to get going. Now, the only hurdle left to clear was obtaining approval from the administration.

Wanting to get this operation moving before the fall hunting season, I made an appointment to pitch the idea to the supervisor of SIU (Captain Ed Volz) in the late summer of 2010. I could barely contain my excitement as I sat down with the captain to give my pitch. Sitting across the conference room table from Captain Volz, I laid it all out.

"I like it. This has great potential," Volz said (just the response I had hoped to hear), shortly followed by, "**but** I think we need to focus on shellfish, geoduck, crab, and prawns."

The captain's "Fish Cop" colors showed through, but I was ready.

"Believe it or not, the reason I am opposed to involving shellfish is not any bias on my part, but rather logistics and costs," I explained, "Other than wild game meats, the merchandise I propose buying and selling does not require refrigeration, but shellfish must be kept alive, and that means refrigerated trucks, cold-storage, oxygenated saltwater tanks, forklifts and lots of manpower." I explained, "You want an undercover storefront shellfish operation, and I'll give it to you, but you better plan on forking out $20-25,000 a month, not the $4,000 I am asking for."

Volz gave it a little thought and said, "I agree we can't handle an operation that costly or involved right now, but how about at least including sturgeon?"

Washington's sturgeon suffer tremendous poaching loss, primarily for the eggs (caviar), which are extremely valuable. I knew breaking into the caviar black market would be tough, as it is primarily run by Eastern Europeans (Russians), who are not a very trusting and open group of folks, but I was willing to try.

"You got it; I'll be glad to add sturgeon and caviar to my business plan since a few jars of caviar won't take up too much room in the freezer," as if I was ever going to have to worry about a Russian criminal selling illegal caviar to this old American white guy.

"Who do you have in mind to work with you on this operation?" Volz asked.

I responded, "I would like to get Chris (Detective Chris Clarke) for the case management detective and one other detective of your choosing for evidence."

Even before Volz answered, his facial expressions forewarned me I wasn't going to get what I was asking for: "Chris is too busy with shellfish casework, but I could assign Brad Rhoden to work the UC with you and help out wherever you need him when he can fit it in."

Brad was a newly promoted detective with zero undercover experience, and he lived over three hours away from me. "Nothing against Brad, but I see three problems with using him as my UC partner," I explained, "He lives too far away, has absolutely no experience, and most importantly, I think it would be a tough sell to have two adult men driving all over the state together to pick up and sell relatively low value smaller items in a pickup truck. Why would it take two of us? That doesn't make sense?"

Volz explained that he wanted a team working undercover, but understood my concerns with using Brad and added, "It would be a good way for Brad to get some experience under his belt."

I made my last argument, "This will be a 2-year internet-based operation. If we get burned early on, it's all over. This isn't an operation for someone to cut their teeth on."

Volz shot back, "How about Jennifer (Officer Jennifer Maurstad)? She has a ton of UC experience, you have worked UC with her more than you have with anyone else, and she lives close to you."

"Great idea, but I doubt she would do it, and even if she agreed to, I am not sure her chain of command would allow her to," I replied.

While I knew Jennifer would be a perfect fit, I also knew she wouldn't be too thrilled about abandoning her patrol district for up to two years. Uniformed duties were near and dear to her, and she took great pride in cleaning up her area to the best of her abilities. Volz and I discussed the options again, and he agreed to ask Officer Maurstad if she would be interested. Another possible hitch in the new addition of a partner to my proposed operation was getting permission to "borrow" Jennifer from her supervisors. Since she was one of the top-producing officers in the region, I knew both her sergeant and the captain would be very opposed to losing her for that long, even if it was for the "greater good."

Once I had agreed with Volz's amendments to my operation, we set out to see if we could gain a part-time undercover partner. I told Volz I believed it would only be necessary to take a partner along on the actual deliveries and pickups, which I estimated could be done in 4 to 5 days of travel a month. I could easily work solo the remainder of the time, answering phone calls, emails, texts, shipping merchandise, keeping the books, etc.

A couple of days later, and ready for an "Are you kidding?" response, I called Jennifer, asked her if she had heard from Volz yet (she had not), and pitched the operation to her. To my surprise, her response was, "I'm in," with the caveat of "If you can get approval from my chain of command." I passed the news on to Volz (who had told me he would ask Jennifer but, for some reason, never got around to it) and asked him to set up a meeting to pitch it to the DC (Deputy Chief) before we went any further.

At this point in my career, Jennifer and I had worked together in uniform for a couple of years and had already worked undercover together (off and on) for about five years, with most of our work being on unlicensed guides and short-term wildlife trafficking cases (primarily bear gallbladder trafficking) with outstanding success.

The gallbladder from a bear is highly coveted by some Asian cultures for its medicinal value. Unfortunately, the only way to get the gallbladder is to kill the bear. The demand for bear gallbladder is astronomical, so the prices buyers offer can lead to increased bear poaching. Over the past couple of years, Jennifer and I had cut a swath through the bear gallbladder black markets, resulting in an unprecedented number of wildlife trafficking cases and convictions.

While I was cooling my heels (for over a month), waiting for the all-important blessing from DC Cenci, I worked on a draft website. I knew the more visual aids, the better my chance of success, so I put together a sharp-looking website draft and waited. Finally, the word came down from the deputy chief (through Volz), and it wasn't good. The operation would not be authorized unless we focused on shellfish rather than wildlife.

The second in command of Washington's Fish and Wildlife Enforcement had spoken, and the message was, "If you want to do this operation, then go with what I can sell to the legislature, geoduck, and abalone."

I was both furious and stunned. I knew Cenci's blood was saltwater, but I never thought he would shoot down an entire operation solely because it didn't involve the almighty shellfish.

21

I responded to Volz, "Abalone? Maybe Cenci is not aware of it, but there is no legal harvest of abalone at all in Washington, nor any sign of any black market activity involving them. We haven't even heard a rumor of illegal Washington abalone sales in over a decade, probably because they are damned near-extinct here. Could we convince someone to harvest and sell us some? Probably, but it would likely be entrapment, and you would spend a bunch of time trying to explain why WDFW encouraged poachers to kill the last remaining abalone stock just to make a case".

At that point in the meeting, Volz showed his true colors and sided 100% with Cenci, adding that if the operation was to go forward, it must focus on shellfish rather than wildlife. On my way home, I called Jennifer and told her she had just been involved in the shortest-term undercover operation in the state's history and thanked her for at least volunteering.

For me, it was back to short-term undercover cases (unlicensed guides, small sales, and purchases of fish and wildlife) and assisting other detectives with their shellfish cases. All the while, my mind kept coming back to the storefront operation. I had heard strong rumors of illegal trafficking in game meats all my career, but as far as I knew, only one or two Washington officers had ever made cases on it. I knew it was happening and believed it was likely widespread, but my best shot at addressing it was tubed before it started. The more I thought about it, the more I resented Cenci.

I first met Cenci when he worked as an assistant at a local fish hatchery. He begged to go for a ride-along with Officer Mike Johnson and me until we each finally gave in. I caught him lying to me on that first ride-along when I asked him about his past "experiences." I usually don't give people a second chance when I catch them in a lie, but Officer Johnson talked me into giving Cenci one more try....a mistake I greatly regret to this day.

Cenci's law enforcement career (he was eventually hired by the Department of Fisheries as a Fisheries Patrol Officer) was not what I would call stellar. While he was and still is a workaholic, his judgment left much to be desired. He worked a year or two for Fisheries, quit, and went to National Marine Fisheries, quit, and returned to the Washington Department of Fisheries. Cenci had a way of generally pissing off just about everyone he came in contact with. Within a year of his return to Washington, it was widely known that the only thing greater than his enormous ego was his love for himself.

The one thing Cenci had going for him was a knack for being in the right place at the right time. When a fisheries sergeant position came open in a part of the state, most officers would consider punishment; Cenci was already living there and got the promotion by default. Next came a marine captain promotion, more of the same. Why the chief (a former Washington State Patrol Deputy Chief) had promoted Cenci to be his deputy chief remains one of life's greatest mysteries. To this day, Cenci has only two administrative traits: an outstanding work ethic (often putting in over 80 hours per week) and no hesitancy to chastise even those who don't deserve it. He commands not by respect but by fear and bullying, and cannot be reasoned with. Blind arrogance is terrible enough, but it becomes outright dangerous when coupled with a lack of knowledge and understanding. I, like many others, consider Cenci to be a narcissistic cancer to Washington's Fish and Wildlife enforcement program, a cancer that was now making me sick.

Knowing I only had one rung up the ladder left to try, I emailed Chief Bruce Bjork asking for reconsideration of my storefront operation. On October 22, 2010, Chief Bjork offered to meet me in a neutral location to discuss the operation. What I expected to be a 30-minute meeting quickly passed the two-hour mark as the chief absorbed my plan's intricate details.

At one point in the conversation, the chief stated, "In the State Patrol, we used confidential informants for this kind of case, not undercover officers. Have you considered using informants to get to these groups rather than working undercover?"

I responded, "There are two problems with using informants. We simply don't have many informants right now, and I want to make this as far-reaching as possible," I added, "I don't just want to target one group of traffickers, but as many as we can."

Ultimately, the chief loved the idea and blessed it for up to two years of operation, just as proposed.

"We haven't run this kind of investigation for wildlife trafficking in the agency's history that I am aware of. It's about time. I'll tell Deputy Chief Cenci I approved the operation, but he will oversee it and work out the details", Chief Bjork announced. Chief Bjork had one last question: "Why did you name it Operation Cody?"

Just a few months prior, Chief Bjork had purchased a very expensive records management computer program (named CODY),

24

which all officers were forced to use. Officers strongly objected to CODY as they felt it was far too time-consuming, difficult, expensive, and they weren't sure they would get anything useful out of it (it is now somewhat accepted).

With a broad smile, I answered, "Well, chief, this operation is internet-based, expensive, opposed by almost everyone who has heard about it, and we are not sure it's even going to work. Sound familiar?" That got the only belly laugh from the chief I had ever heard. The chief asked me to set up another meeting with Volz and Cenci to discuss the details and budget.

A few weeks later, it was time for the last "Pre-Op" meeting. Volz, Jennifer, and I sat in the same conference room in Mill Creek, where I had been shot down not that far back. The three of us were sitting at the Mill Creek Office conference table when the DC came waltzing in, sat down, and declared he was ready to be impressed. I started with how I had come up with the idea, went into the nuts and bolts (including the budget), and finished with our expected outcome. This time it was different, as I knew the operation was a go. I was also pretty damned sure the temperature in the room would be a bit chilly, as nobody likes to be overruled, especially as a result of a subordinate end-running the chain of command.

Cenci started the meeting, "You have your operation. It will run for one year, with a review after six months. After a year, if things are going well, we may extend it for up to another year. You can use Officer Maurstad for undercover for 4 to 5 days per month, and we will clear that with her supervisors," adding, "Financial services will audit you regularly, Chris Clarke can handle evidence for you, but there is nobody else available to work on the operation."

Cenci and Volz picked through the website and other material I had prepared for the operation, making suggestions as they went. The last two items they made clear were "no working with the Feds" and "no doing business with Indians." Both Cenci and Volz had an unadulterated hatred of the US Fish and Wildlife Service, and they made it clear I was not to involve the evil Feds. I tried, in vain, to convince them the case could not possibly stay "in-state," and we would need the Feds, but they wouldn't budge (a battle I knew would come back up later). I had a monthly operating budget of $4,000 cash and the okay to get going.

After months of planning and pitching, we were finally ready to go. I still had the website in "non-public" mode with no real merchandise to fill in the blanks. I had a plan, a budget, and a team of three (actually two and a fourth if you consider my partner could only work the operation for 4 to 5 days per month). I chose to ignore the fact that we had no case investigator, no support/surveillance, no intelligence officer, and no backup. We had an operation and were bound and determined to make it work.

On November 2, 2010, just before the website was to go public, we had one last meeting in Olympia with the DC. At that meeting, Cenci was primed for a fight, and it wasn't minutes before the two of us were at each other's throats again.

Cenci couldn't help himself from voicing his opinion about our operation, "Nobody gives a shit about deer and elk! If they are so

26

important, then why do we give out kill permits?" (A line, the deputy chief has proclaimed more than once).

With those few venomous words, he had insulted every game warden in North America, shown his apparent prejudice, and expressed his desire to kill the best opportunity to capture significant wildlife traffickers our state had ever seen. My face must have been red as a fire engine since my blood was hot enough to need one.

After my blood pressure came down enough to keep my ears from ringing too loudly, I responded, "First of all, what nobody gives a shit about is geoduck. Only the buyers in China and the industries that harvest and ship the geoduck care, and only then, because they make money off them. Nobody has ever loaded up the family mini-van to go watch the geoduck spurt water on the beach, but when an elk or a bear crosses the road, traffic comes to a standstill, and everyone jumps out to snap a picture."

After my outburst, I was herded into the deputy chief's office, where I was told I was once again "on the brink of insubordination." Still, against his better judgment, the operation was a go but would be closely scrutinized by Cenci. Cenci told me the operation would only be allowed to run for three months (and admitted he had reduced the duration because he was mad at me), but backpedaled and said he would give it a year. Enough said.

CHAPTER 2- BAITING THE HOOK

Over 35% of small businesses fail within the first two years of operation. This was a terrifying statistic for some businesses, but from the outset, we planned for our business to fail financially. For one thing, any money spent on illegal wildlife was gone (at least until a judge ordered the suspects to pay it back). Secondly, courts seem to frown on the government profiting from illegal sales in sting operations. Moneywise, we planned on our business failing, but our real profits would be measured not in dollars but in bad guys brought in. But would it work?

In preparing for this operation, the pitfall I had to be most aware of was entrapment. Illegal entrapment is another widely misunderstood concept. Some members of the public believe undercover operations as a whole are entrapment, while on the other extreme, some believe anything goes as long as we catch the bad guys.

The Revised Code of Washington defines entrapment as *(1) (a) The criminal design originated in the mind of law enforcement officials, or any person acting under their direction, and (b) The actor was lured or induced to commit a crime which the actor had not otherwise intended to commit.*
*(2) The defense of **entrapment** is not established by showing only that law enforcement officials merely afforded the actor an opportunity to commit a crime.*

Basically, entrapment is when the idea for the crime comes from law enforcement, and it's just too tempting for an ordinary person to resist. The key to defeating an entrapment defense is a predisposition. Predisposition is when a person is either already engaged in the criminal activity or is ready to commit the crime before the undercover suggests or offers an opportunity to commit a crime.

So, in basic terms, if law enforcement offers an opportunity for a crime to occur (for example, leaving the key in a bait car) but doesn't suggest to a suspect they should go ahead and commit the crime, it is not entrapment.

In this operation, I wanted to defeat any entrapment argument well beforehand. To do so, I didn't want to offer to buy or sell anything illegal, and I wanted the bad guys to suggest it. This extra precaution wasn't necessary, but would undoubtedly make the prosecutions cleaner. I intended to walk right along the line but not cross it. We would offer merchandise that would be legal to buy and sell in Washington, but would imply (to a criminal) that we just might be willing to deal in illegal items. Considering those criteria, I began compiling a shopping list of merchandise or props for our website and "showroom."

The first order of business was to gather "intel" (intelligence) from the field officers. I knew all game wardens possess a lot of knowledge about who is doing what kind of illegal business in their area, whether they can prove it or not. I wanted to hear about every bit of information relating to wildlife trafficking that the uniformed officers across the state had stuffed away in notebooks, on the back of regulation books, or in their memories. I asked our command staff to send an email out to every officer across the state, asking for all information (no matter how vague) relating to possible illegal wildlife trafficking.

I began purchasing items for our business from other (legitimate) businesses and also found some in the warehouses (graveyards) of our regional offices. I loaded up on deer and elk antlers, hides, teeth and claws, trophy mounts, sturgeon caviar and meats, elk and deer meats (from out-of-state game farms), and birds. All the items I selected were legal to buy and sell under Washington law, but some would not be legal in adjoining states.

I photographed the merchandise, wrote descriptions about each piece, and added it to the website. After tossing around a dozen or so potential business names, Jennifer and I settled on *Best of the Wild.* We chose our undercover names as Tom and Tina Davis and decided the best place to claim our residency was nearby Everett, WA (a large population base to get lost in). With the assistance of the wife of one of our uniformed officers, I completed the website, including how to order, contact details, legal disclaimers, merchandise, and shipping costs. As I had no desire to conduct much legal business, I carefully researched the prices of the same merchandise on other websites and priced our merchandise about 15% higher.

Next, I designed and ordered business cards and brochures. These items would be our "eye candy" and would open doors for us and further help spread the word about our business. After the business cards and brochures arrived, I began setting up driver's licenses, hunting and fishing licenses, social security cards, bank accounts, credit cards, mail, and even a business license (we had to pay sales tax just like any other business), all in our undercover names. I even went so far as to get a dog tag, for my yellow lab, with our undercover names, address, and phone number on it…..you can't be too careful.

While I had set up undercover identifications many times before, this time was far more complicated since I had to assume the people we would be dealing with on this operation would be more computer-literate and a bit more careful (since we would be potentially taking away their livelihood). Our "back-story" had to be better and more reliable, so someone looking into us wouldn't discover any gaps or red flags.

Since 9/11, the protocol for obtaining ID (including social security cards and driver's licenses) has changed dramatically. To make it harder for criminals to get a fake ID, the government made it harder for undercover law enforcement officers to get one. We had to jump through a lot of hoops and exercise a great deal of patience, but we finally got it all in place. I found the new laws had made it much easier for an illegal immigrant to get "valid" identification than for undercover officers…. so much for making us safer.

Once we had a bank account, with the first $4,000 in place, we picked up some of the equipment we would need. In an effort to be extra careful, I didn't want to recycle any WDFW equipment in our operation and chose to go with all new equipment that could only be traced back to Tom and Tina Davis. We wanted to be sure there would be no WDFW property stickers or the potential of recognition from a suspect who had seen that item in one of our offices. We purchased freezers, a laptop computer, and the most challenging item of all, a cell phone.

31

I had decided I needed a cell phone capable of internet and email. I am certainly not an electronic gadget guy and don't know one phone from another, but I walked into a Verizon Cellular store in Everett with my fresh ID in hand. The young man at the counter was more than helpful in assisting this old, technologically challenged guy in finding a phone with the features I wanted, yet simple enough for me to understand. Then a problem arose when it was time to sign up for the plan.

Pushing a corded numerical keypad toward me, the young clerk said: "Just type in your social security number so we can run a credit check."

Crap, I hadn't thought of that. I usually take the time to memorize my new address, name, date of birth, and social security number, but on this day, the ink hadn't yet dried on my card. Reaching into my wallet and bringing out my Social Security card grabbed this astute young man's attention.

"You don't know your Social Security number?" he asked. I thought about telling him I had a memory disorder, but I forgot that excuse about as quickly as I thought it up.

"It's new; I grew up overseas where we didn't need it," I threw out, hoping it would fly.

"Oh yeah, where?" The kid wasn't giving up.

I quickly fired back, "New Zealand."

"Columbo" wasn't ready to quit. "I stayed there a few months. Where did you live?"

Now back in my comfort zone, as I have spent a fair amount of time in New Zealand, I answered, "New Plymouth on the North Island."

With one last effort to crack me, the future detective asked, "I always forget. What's the Capital of New Zealand?"

Forgot my ass; he was trying to break me, and not knowing how much more I could take before I cracked, I burst out with, "Wellington."

That did it; I passed. After the most intense interrogation I have ever faced, I finally got my cell phone! As soon as I got outside, I swore that when this operation was over, I would take that kid a job application and my letter of recommendation.

The last items I wanted in place were covert (hidden) cameras. From experience, I knew juries typically trusted officers in their testimony, but nothing was more compelling than having the jury watch the transaction on video. If a picture is worth a thousand words, a video is priceless. Unfortunately, Washington (by state law) is a "two-party consent" state. That means people (including law enforcement officers) can't audio record conversations without all parties' consent (hence two-party). There are exceptions, including court orders, none of which apply to fish and wildlife crimes, even if those crimes constitute a felony. So in this ultra-liberal state, audio recording of our undercover conversations was out. Still, we could video-record all of our contacts without the knowledge or consent of the suspect. Even without audio, this video evidence is very compelling and hugely beneficial at trial.

Micro video recorders have improved significantly in recent years. A few short years ago, we struggled to hide bulky battery packs and a cigarette pack-sized DVR (Digital Video Recorder), leading to a hidden camera. Today's covert video cameras can be hidden almost anywhere. My goal was always to have at least two cameras recording every minute of our contacts. The redundancy was desirable to provide two different views of the transactions and as a fail-safe if one of the recorders malfunctioned. I had decided to put a semi-permanent covert camera in the back of our pickup (which had a canopy enclosing the truck's bed).

When it came to mounting a covert camera in the bed of our truck, I turned to Detective Chris Clarke. He had been hand-selected by Volz to be promoted to detective (even when Chris didn't meet the minimum qualifications for the detective position) due to his expertise in digital video systems and photography. Volz had been so confident in Clarke that he (Volz) had announced to a crowd, including Chief Bjork, that Chris would be promoted to the next detective position even before the promotional opportunity had been announced.

Chris asked that I leave my truck with him for a few days while he decided which way was best to mount a covert camera to cover transactions that were bound to occur on the tailgate of our truck. Four days after dropping the truck off with Chris, my wife took me to the office to pick it up. When I arrived at my truck, the first thing I did was open the canopy to see how long it would take me to find the camera. After more than five minutes of careful inspection, I failed to find even a hint of a hidden camera. I was thrilled; if I knew it was there and couldn't find it, there was no way in hell the bad guys would ever spot it.

I entered the office and found Chris chatting with Captain Volz, "Alright, I give up. I couldn't find the camera. Where is it?" I asked.

Chris deflated my enthusiasm with eight words, "I couldn't find a place to mount it."

"You're kidding, right?" I hoped he was jerking my chain.

"Nope, I even asked around, and the only thing I have to offer is a fire extinguisher with a camera mounted in it. Maybe you could mount the fire extinguisher in the back of your truck?"

I couldn't believe it. With literally hundreds of micro-camera set-ups to choose from, the best we had to choose from was a fire extinguisher. Who carries a fire extinguisher mounted in the bed of their truck other than government employees? Four days with my undercover truck, and that was it, nadda?

Disappointed but not ready to give up on the truck camera, I drove home, called one of the nation's top law enforcement covert camera businesses, and ran my idea past them. They asked me to send them some measurements and photos of my truck, and a couple of days later, I received the camera system in the mail. After two hours of installation, I installed a fully functioning hidden color camera in the back of my truck. After hundreds of hours of video-recording suspects, nobody (including our officers, who were told a camera was in the back of the truck) had ever spotted it. It turned out not to be as hard as I had been told.

With all the props, cameras, and funding in place, it was time to fire up the business. I flipped the switch on November 19, 2010, and the website went public. As with any new website, I knew it would take months and some cash to work our way up the search engine ladder to the point where people could find it before giving up. I never really counted on doing a great deal of business by way of people finding our website by searching the internet, but instead planned on using the website to back up our claim of having a legitimate business. In other words, the website was just a big part of our back story. People tend to believe a business is real and more trustworthy if that business has a well-designed website.

With everything in place, it was time to begin sorting through the multiple referrals we had received from the uniformed officers in response to our request for intel. While digesting all the tips received, one thing became apparent: the intelligence was clumped in small geographic locations. WDFW divides the state into six regions, three on the eastern side of the Cascade Mountains and three on the western side. Those regions are broken into smaller work units called detachments. Captains head up regions, while sergeants supervise the detachments. As I ferreted out the interesting information from the worthless, I found some of the detachments had sent in a great deal of accurate intel on potentially useful targets.

In contrast, some detachments hadn't responded at all. This wasn't a big surprise, as I knew many of the sergeants strongly believed they didn't need SIU's help to make significant cases and could handle their own problems. Other, more enlightened sergeants realized that giving SIU intel would help them accomplish their goal of stopping poachers most effectively. It became a matter of ego (with a little resentment tossed in) vs. efficiency.

The intel we had asked for was specific to potentially illegal commercial wildlife operations, which consisted mostly of guiding businesses, meat-cutting businesses, taxidermists, restaurants, and fur dealers. Unlike the rest of the western states, Washington has virtually no regulations on hunting guides; however, taxidermists, meat cutters, and fur dealers are a bit more regulated. In any segment of business, you find cheaters. These businesses are no different, and most of the referrals we received dealt with suspicions of criminal wrongdoing by individual wildlife businesses.

I read through all the referrals, ran background checks on the suspects, and sorted them out by their criminal history and potential impact on the resource, regardless of where the suspects were or how difficult they might be to deal with. I automatically eliminated any suspects who might recognize us. Even after growing a beard and hair long enough to pull back into a ponytail, some people would recognize me from my uniformed days. Since Jennifer was still a uniformed officer, we also had to be very careful about her being recognized during what would be a very long undercover operation, knowing I always had the option of working solo in any area she might be known.

I put a list together, discussed it with Jennifer, and was ready to go out and spread the word about our new business. Meeting suspects with no introduction (such as an introduction from an informant) is referred to as a "cold contact" and has a much lower

37

success rate than contacts in which the suspect's trusted friends vouch for the UC officers. Cold contacts were nothing new for Jennifer and me, as we had conducted nearly a hundred of them in the past and had unprecedented success. I knew our first success in our new business would come from one of these cold contacts rather than someone just finding us online or by our feeble advertising efforts.

On November 22, 2010, Jennifer and I met and agreed to hit the road starting in the first week of December to see how well we could do. We were prepared to buy and sell a lot of legal merchandise (to gain the trust of potential bad guys) and hoped to hook a bad guy or two by Christmas. All the while, deep down, I had an overwhelming concern we would fall flat on our faces, and I would have to listen to Cenci give me the dreaded "I told you it was a waste of time."

CHAPTER 3- GAME TIME

NOVEMBER 2010

On November **23**, 2010, I received my first interesting phone call to Best of the Wild. The caller introduced himself as Brandon Clark. Brandon apparently didn't believe in foreplay, as he started right out by telling me how many deer he had already killed this year (the limit in Washington is only one per year). Brandon said he was a US Army soldier based at Fort Lewis. He stated he'd already killed three deer and sold them, but was willing to sell to us if the price was right.

I warned him that the sale of deer was very illegal, and his response was simply, "Do you want some or not?"

I told him I needed to meet him in person and talk, as I didn't even know who I was talking to. Brandon responded that he would be back in touch. When I ended the call, I wasn't sure if the call had been one of the worst attempts at an undercover sale (by one of our officers trying to set me up) or if there indeed was a Brandon Clark, and he was really that bold. On November **30**th, I found out. Clark sent a text message asking to meet me at the north end of the Boeing Field runway on Albro Road in Seattle (a less-than-stellar part of town) around 7:30 that night to sell me a deer. Jennifer was not available on such short notice, so I geared up to go solo on this first contact.

On a rare rainless night, I arrived at the agreed-upon spot where I waited only minutes before seeing a beat-up white Mazda pickup with no taillights pull in and back up to the rear of my truck. I got out and greeted my first "supplier" and, at the same time, noticed a dead deer lying uncovered in the open bed of his truck. Brandon had the looks of a street fighter, young, muscular, square-jawed, with arms covered in tattoos.

I opened the conversation with some advice: "Driving around with an un-tagged dead deer, during the closed season, sitting out in the open bed of a truck with no taillights is asking for a trip to jail."

Brandon's response was about as simple as he was, "I have a (deer) tag in my wallet."

"Look," I advised, "if we are going to do business in the future, you have to be a little smarter and a lot more careful."

With my "how to avoid getting arrested" lecture behind me, we settled down to pricing. As this was all new territory for me, I had no idea what an illegal whole deer was worth on the black market, and could only go by what game-farmed meat sells for (I later learned that game-farmed meat is <u>way</u> more expensive). We negotiated a price of $346, which I based on the total weight of the deer at $3.15 per pound. Brandon promised, "Way more deer where that one came from." We transferred the deer from his truck to mine, I paid him the cash, and off we went. Christmas had come early, and we had our first case, a felony, in the bag. I photographed the deer, took a DNA sample, and transferred the carcass to a uniformed officer to be cut and wrapped, a process I didn't know at the time would be repeated many more times in the coming months.

The next day, before starting my case report, I called Jennifer and told her she had missed the first Operation Cody illegal transaction. Her response was exactly what I expected from my Type

A partner, a bitter-sweet "Congratulations." With the first one under our belts, we were excited to head out on our first sales trip.

CHAPTER 4- DECEMBER 2010

On December 1, 2010, Jennifer and I started out on our first statewide road trip. The purpose of this trip was twofold: to make a few cold-contact stops and spread the word about our new business, with spreading the word as our primary goal.

Earlier, I stated that Jennifer and I had a decent success rate with our undercover contacts. Still, truth be told, we actually had a flawless record (100% of our undercover contacts had resulted in criminal cases) until about a year prior, when the DC (Cenci) had begun releasing details of our undercover cases to the media. This resulted in internet, television, and print media coverage, which included our methods, targets, and even our undercover names (which, for obvious reasons, we had since changed).

In my opinion, our undercover track record was so remarkable for two reasons. First, the illegal wildlife trade had gone untouched in Washington for a very long time. For decades, most of the focus had been on commercial fish and shellfish, with minimal attention to the wildlife black market. The second reason for our success was simply what we looked like and how we acted. I had shoulder-length hair (normally pulled back into a ponytail) and a beard. I could appear to be anyone from a total dirtbag to a college professor (depending on the contact). Jennifer (a former model) is almost 15 years my junior, tall, slender, and attractive.

Additionally, the two of us have worked together hundreds of hours, are close friends, and can "walk the talk." We have our stories down and are very convincing when challenged by even the most suspicious. We have been adequately trained and are experienced and confident in undercover operations. In short, we didn't look like cops, act like cops, or come across as such. We put people at ease and always tended to keep our cool.

As a team, Jennifer and I had about all the bases covered. While I have a stronger hunting and fishing background, Jennifer is sharp, observant, and possesses more common sense than almost anyone else I have worked with. What one of us didn't know or fell a bit short on, the other seemed to be able to pick up and handle with ease. Additionally, it is undoubtedly the best-case scenario in undercover work if you can trust your partner absolutely, 100%, which was definitely the case with us.

We set off on our three-day trip with a full box of business cards and a gaggle of brochures, hoping to spread the word about our new business, meet some potential suppliers, and possibly make an illegal transaction or two. We traveled from Everett to northeastern Washington, down to Tri-Cities, over to southwest Washington, then home. It seemed every business we hit up was either closed or the manager (suspect who had been referred to us) was away. A couple of suspects gave us the old "I will get back in touch with you" line, but no solid takers. While our trip wasn't a total waste, as we handed out a lot of cards and brochures, we didn't get one single offer of an illegal transaction, not at all what we had hoped for.

Jennifer and I began to worry that our days of guaranteed success were over. Neither of us was ready to throw in the towel just yet, but we both had doubts about whether Best of the Wild would succeed or not. Our fears were tempered by the fact that we had just spread business cards and our smiling faces across the state. It was now time to sit back and wait for bites.

Jennifer spent the remainder of December 2010 back in uniform, chasing deer poachers, duck hunters, and steelhead fishermen in her local area while I continued advertising and running backgrounds on potential suspects. Apparently, Christmas isn't a great time for illegal wildlife sales (no demand for a bald eagle under the tree). We both very much hoped 2011 would bring much more "business" to Best of the Wild.

CHAPTER 5- JANUARY 2011

On January 2, 2011, one of the WDFW officers from the Yakima area called and told me about a business (mini-mart) he believed might be buying bear gallbladders from local hunters. The officer said he had nothing substantial but had his suspicions and asked if we could check it out. I assured the officer we would swing into the store with a few bear gallbladders in hand on our next trip to the east side.

We received the second offer of illegal wildlife for sale on the 6th when we were sent an email offering numerous sets of deer antlers, all on the skull (as opposed to naturally shed antlers). In Washington, this sale would be legal, but the seller, in this case, said she lived in the Portland, Oregon, area and insisted we come to Oregon if we were interested. Oregon law prohibits the sale of antlers unless they are no longer attached to the skull (or skull plate). Many states have similar laws to reduce poaching, as antler values plummet dramatically if the antlers are not attached to the intact skull (as they can no longer be "scored"- a system of measuring total inches for record books). After speaking on the phone with the suspect, who identified herself as Debbie Brown, I ran a background check on her. I later called the supervisor of the Oregon State Police's Wildlife Investigations Unit.

While the sale of such antlers is illegal in Oregon, it is certainly not uncommon and doesn't raise too much excitement from their troopers. For that reason, I am pretty sure it wasn't the fact that Ms. Brown had offered to sell us deer antlers attached to the skull that got Oregon's attention, but rather the number of antlers: 57 sets. Any one person having the antlers from 57 different buck deer in a state where the sale/purchase of them is illegal will get damned near anyone's attention. Within a few short days, Oregon and Washington had worked out the details of an undercover trip for us to Oregon.

When we got the deer antler offer, I received a call from WDFW Officer Brian Fulton. Brian, who is stationed in Tri-Cities, WA, told me a citizen had given him a tip about the Duck Song Chinese Restaurant in Richland, WA. The Duck Song was reportedly buying game birds (ducks, geese, and pheasants) out of the back of the restaurant. Since we were already going on a trip, Jennifer and I decided to make the most out of the venture and hit several different targets.

Additionally, WDFW Officer Tammy Conklin had previously passed on information indicating the Happy Times Restaurant's (located in southwest WA) employees had been buying sport-caught fish out the back door. We decided to visit both restaurants on our trip, one before Portland and one the next day.

The next week, on the **12**th, we headed south with five frozen bear gallbladders in a cooler (just in case we needed them). Our first stop was at the Happy Times Chinese Restaurant. We walked into the restaurant just before they opened and launched into our introduction. It quickly became evident that we were destined for failure as none of the employees could speak English, and neither of us could speak Chinese. We left business cards and a brochure and headed towards Portland, believing we would never hear from the Happy Times clan again.

46

When Jennifer and I arrived at the OSP (Oregon State Police) office, it became instantly apparent OSP had more people interested in this one little case than WDFW had in our entire operation. We met with a myriad of troopers and supervisors, all assigned to assist in this single transaction. We discussed the plan, the backup/surveillance (something we were not at all accustomed to), and the relevant laws. We received a complete suspect workup, including photos of the suspect's home and the buy money. With cash in hand and our surveillance/backup team in tow (I have to admit they were good, as we never even saw them), we headed to the suspect's house.

With our hidden cameras recording, we arrived at the house fashionably late and were greeted by Debbie Brown. Debbie Brown was not at all what I had expected. She was in her early 50s, well-groomed, with the look of a school teacher. Brown immediately took us into the garage, where we began sorting through the multitude of antlers. While I sorted through the antlers, Jennifer and Debbie had a friendly chat, in which Debbie said the antlers had all come from deer her brother and father had killed. Jennifer and I made it crystal clear that the sale or purchase of these antlers was very much illegal, but Debbie didn't seem phased and insisted on going through with the deal. Not finding any actual trophy-quality antlers in the lot, I told Debbie I would offer her one cash amount for the whole bunch. Debbie and I quibbled back and forth on price until we finally settled on $350 for all 57 sets of antlers. Since this was half what OSP had wanted us to negotiate down to, everyone was happy.....at least for now. Jennifer and I returned to the OSP office, where we downloaded the covert videos, turned over the antlers, returned the unused cash,

47

and had a short de-briefing. Then it was off to eastern WA, where we would try out the Duck Song Chinese Restaurant the next day.

In Tri-Cities, we met with Officer Brian Fulton, who had agreed to provide us with some ducks to offer the restaurant (I already had three pheasants that I had killed while hunting off-duty). As soon as Brian pulled up to us, he began to apologize. He said his nephew had killed some ducks the day before, but the ducks were all rather undesirable (mostly scaup, with no mallards). Since beggars can't be choosy, we took the ducks and hoped the restaurant staff didn't know one duck from another.

At about 11:00 am, Jennifer and I knocked on the restaurant's back door and were met by a Chinese couple (who we immediately recognized from the driver's license photos as the restaurant owners). We introduced ourselves, provided a business card, and said we heard they might be interested in birds. The woman, Tou Liu, did all the talking and seemed to prefer negotiating with Jennifer. Liu was a fast-talking, small Asian woman who was nothing but business. Jennifer and I showed Liu the ducks, and she immediately declared our ducks to be "Shit Ducks" and said she didn't want them. Liu was much more receptive to buying the pheasant and negotiated a price with Jennifer to purchase all three birds. We quickly discovered our new "customer" was very nosy and persistent.

"What you have in that cooler?" Liu asked as she pointed at the cooler containing the frozen bear gallbladder.

I explained the cooler contained bear gallbladders for another customer. Ten more minutes of price negotiation, and we had sold all of our bear gallbladders, leaving us with nothing but some unwanted ducks to sell to our next target.

Jennifer and I followed Liu (carrying her newly purchased delicacies) into the restaurant's kitchen to get our money. As Liu counted the money, she begged Jennifer not to tell the "Police," saying she didn't want trouble. <u>Game Warden</u> Jennifer Maurstad calmly assured Liu she wouldn't tell the police, which earned Jennifer a full-fledged hug from Liu (a bear hug?).

The following day, we stopped by the Yakima area mini-mart and chatted with the store's owner. The owner was very interested in doing business with us in the future and asked explicitly about bear gallbladder. We truthfully told him we didn't have any gallbladder with us at the time, but had many at home. The suspect assured us he would be in touch with us.

On our way back to our respective homes, we downloaded the recent covert videos and placed the cash in our evidence safe. Business was looking up for Best of the Wild, and we were both excited that this might just work after all. On the downside, we had just used up 3 of the allotted "4 to 5 days per month" of Jennifer's undercover work allowance for January, and we still had two weeks to go.

On January **24th**, 2011, I received a call from a woman who identified herself as Tanya Franklin. During the call, Tanya said her boyfriend Kyle (Parker) had "found" a dead bighorn sheep. Tanya said Kyle makes numerous Indian art items using wildlife parts.

Despite the fact I warned Tanya the sale of bighorn sheep was very much illegal, she told me, "We know it's illegal, but we're ok with it anyway."

I agreed to come to their home in the Yakima, WA, area to check out the sheep and other items they might have. In the following couple of days, Tanya emailed me photos of peace pipes and dreamcatchers adorned with hawk and eagle feathers.

After talking it over with Jennifer, I decided to make the trip to Yakima alone, so on January 28[th,] I drove over to meet Tanya and Kyle. At about 10:30 am, I arrived at the Parker property and immediately heard the banjo music (from the movie Deliverance) playing in my head. The property was simply a hillbilly family compound consisting of a collection of trailers, broken-down trucks, scrubby dogs, and garbage centered around a dilapidated old house. I was greeted at the door by the poster child for meth use, aka Tanya Franklin, who was very short and thin as a rail. She was likely somewhat attractive at some point in her life before the drugs had changed her into the skeleton she had become. Tanya asked me a few questions and invited me in. As she closed the door behind us, I saw the shotgun which had been in reach behind the door during our "meet and greet." After a short conversation, Tanya fetched Kyle from one of the "luxurious" trailers in the compound.

While I found Kyle definitely fit his surroundings, he didn't appear to be as far along in his meth use as his girlfriend and still had a little bulk to his body. Both Kyle and Tanya were excited to show me their merchandise, pulling illegal hawk, owl, and eagle feathers out of every nook and cranny in their "room." The house was a virtual

50

smorgasbord of illegal wildlife, so I decided to take a few prized possessions back home. I told the two I would purchase two of the dreamcatchers, one of the peace pipes, the sheep skull, and a painted beef cow jawbone. The pipes and dreamcatchers were made using illegal feathers, leaving only the jawbone as legal to sell. Kyle and I debated prices and agreed to $200 for the sheep, $40 for the peace pipe, and $110 for the two dreamcatchers, for a total of $350.

The majority of the transaction took place in the front room of the house, where a man (whom I guessed to be in his 80s) sat motionless and silent the entire time. Kyle helped me load the items in my truck and promised to have more ready for us whenever we wanted them. I assured Kyle that on my next trip, they would get to meet my "wife." Although Kyle made Indian "art," he was clearly not a tribal member, which made things much easier for us to prosecute when the time came.

On my way home, I dropped the evidence off for Detective Clarke with clear instructions to photograph the evidence, have the wildlife items positively identified (either by DNA or by expert witnesses), and enter it into the WDFW evidence system.

About this time, I received a call from Captain Volz, who told me he was considering retiring very soon. While I considered the captain a friend, I also felt it was probably in his and the department's best interests if he did so. He was very much disconnected from our operation, had little real interest in what we were doing, and provided very little support.

CHAPTER 6- FEBRUARY 2011

On February 1st, I received a text message from Tanya Franklin. She told me Kyle had shot an enormous cougar the night before but had lost it. Franklin asked if I would want to buy the cat if they could find it. Since the cougar season was closed in that area, I told her to send me photos of the cougar if they found it without committing to the purchase.

Two days later, Franklin texted me to say they had not found the cougar, but "There's a huge bald eagle in the tree in the yard. Kyle's goin crazy wantin those feathers! So tempting," and "how much do they pay."

I later replied by telling Franklin never to ask us if we wanted them to kill eagles for us and not to put us in that position again.

During the second week of February, I decided to take a solo trip to Tri-Cities to spread the word to potential targets further and to stop by the Duck Song Chinese Restaurant. Once I arrived in Tri-Cities, I met with Officer Fulton, who provided me with three mallard ducks (much better ducks than the previous time). I arrived at the Duck Song at about 3 p.m. and met with Liu.

I showed Liu the ducks, and she agreed to buy them but said she would rather have the "big black and white ducks (geese), and colored chickens (pheasant)."

Liu explained that it took just as much time to clean a small duck as a big duck, so she wanted big ducks because they had more meat on them. Liu also said next time I came back, she wanted me to bring my "wife," as she liked dealing with my wife better than dealing with me (didn't everyone?). As with the previous sale, the ducks went straight into the restaurant's kitchen through the back door.

A day after returning home, I had a long phone conversation with Franklin. In no uncertain terms, I told her not to kill eagles on our behalf, and we wouldn't deal with them if they did so. Franklin said she understood and said they had a supply of "all the eagle and hawk feathers they want." Tanya wanted to know when we would be in the area next, and I said we would likely be over their way on the 16th, as we had some business to do in Tri-Cities anyway. We agreed we would come by their house on Wednesday, February 16th. Fortunately, neither Tanya nor Kyle were restricted by work schedules.

Jennifer and I pulled into the Parker compound, home to Kyle and Tanya, at about 5 pm on the **16th**. Jennifer took a few moments to take in the scene's ambiance (white trash theme) before I introduced her to our new friends. After introductions, Kyle and Tanya took us to the back of the house to show us their selection of Native American art items. Kyle brought out two dreamcatchers, two peace pipes, and a drum, which he said were all for sale. I noticed one of the dreamcatchers was decorated with hawk feathers, so I asked Kyle what type of feathers they were, to which he replied, "Red-tailed hawk." Jennifer and I decided we would purchase all five items, and after a little negotiation with Kyle, we settled on $200 for all of the items.

After paying Kyle, he wanted to show us his "shop." Jennifer and I followed Kyle and Tanya through the muddy yard to a very old, musty-smelling wall tent situated between the even older house and a couple of travel trailers (which evidently hadn't been capable of travel for several decades). Once in the wall tent, Kyle couldn't wait to show us his eagle and hawk feather collection. Jennifer asked Kyle how he gets so many hawk feathers, and he proudly stated he kills the hawks to protect his quail. While I had seen a lot of critters running around the compound, I had not seen any quail pens, so I asked Kyle if he raised quail, and Kyle said the quail he was protecting were the wild quail. Kyle insisted on showing Jennifer photos of the Indian art items he had created in the past and some furniture he had made.

As we walked out of the tent, Kyle blurted out, "What about deer meat? Do you want to buy some?"

It was no real surprise to either of us that these lowlifes were also into poaching deer, as obviously, they would do almost anything for money.

"We have to be careful about deer and elk meat," I answered, "We don't want anybody ever getting sick from the meat we sell, so it has to be well taken care of."

Kyle said he and Tanya "live off deer and elk meat" and get it all the time, adding he knows how to take good care of it. I told Kyle to take good care of the meat, freeze it (if he had to), and call us. Kyle, for some reason, then felt compelled to tell us about his illegal trapping and how successful he was at that as well. After telling us about what a great trapper he was, Kyle went into great detail about the cougar, he had shot (during the closed season), telling us he had shot it with a .22 rifle (an illegal firearm for cougar hunting) at night while Tanya had held the spotlight (using artificial light, such as a spotlight, to hunt big game at night is another crime). After hearing about Kyle's cougar hunting ventures, we heard the master poacher tell us he knew where three bighorn sheep lay dead and his plan to get them out using horses and a raft.

My head was swirling with all the information we had picked up in one quick contact. Jennifer feverishly wrote detailed notes as I headed the truck west. Kyle and Tanya had just shown us evidence of and detailed more wildlife crimes than we could count. We were obviously into some serious poachers and thereby had partially met the goal of our operation.

As we drove back to the west side of the state, we discussed a phenomenon we had seen many times before, as we had worked in our previous undercover assignments. While most crooks seemed to trust me and were willing to do illegal business with me, they would absolutely spill their guts to Jennifer. Whether trust or lust, men tended to openly brag to my partner about how efficient they were at poaching. After all, nothing impresses a woman like telling stories about all the animals you slaughtered illegally…right? No matter why suspects so freely opened up to Jennifer, the information gained was invaluable, and we were more than happy to reap the benefits. The male ego can be a beautiful thing.

Being an avid hunter, I was sickened by knowing people like this operated so freely and openly without apprehension, but I took solace in knowing their day was coming.

The next day, February 17th, WDFW received a tip from a concerned citizen regarding a suspect he said was selling deer and elk meat in mass quantities. I immediately called the citizen, who told me a friend had purchased illegal deer and elk meat from a man in Tacoma, Washington. The man I spoke with was clearly Asian and told me his friend had said the deer and elk meat supplier would only deal with other Asian people. The citizen had only a phone number for the suspect and no other information. I had no way of knowing it then, but this one tip would lead us to one of the most significant wildlife traffickers in Washington's history and one of the most dangerous suspects we had ever worked undercover.

Two days after receiving the citizen tip, knowing that, at best, I would have less than five minutes to make my pitch, I placed a call to the suspect's number, not knowing who I would be talking to.

An Asian man answered, and I launched into my sales pitch, "I got your phone number from a friend of mine who said you and I are in the same kind of business. I think you and I could do business together".

Before the suspect could ask any questions, I asked him if he had a computer to look up a website, which he said he did.

"Go to www.bestofthewild.com and check out our website, then I'll call you back in a few minutes," I added, "I think you will see what I am talking about after you check out our website."

The suspect agreed to look at the website, and I hung up before he could ask any questions. Five minutes later, my undercover cell phone rang from the same number I had just called.

The caller started by saying, "I see you sell elk and deer heads (antlers), but I don't bother with the heads. I only deal in meat".

56

I told the suspect that meat was what I was most interested in, as that was where the real profit was.

The caller said he sells "around 2 or 3 deer or elk a week".

After a few more minutes of conversation, the suspect gave me his email address and said he would be in touch. When I hung up, I was optimistic we would be able to do business with this mystery suspect, but only time would tell. Undoubtedly, this guy was more cautious than anyone we had dealt with before, but our website had broken the ice.

A couple more days passed before the Asian suspect called me back. The suspect said he had checked us out, and we seemed to be okay.

The suspect laid out the ground rules: "I normally sell deer for about $150-$200, and elk for $550-$600 each. I pay around $500 for each elk, and I only mark them up about $50-$100 each". He went on to say, "I sell them whole, gutted and skinned."

I warned the suspect, "You know it is illegal to sell deer and elk unless they come from an out-of-state game farm."

He replied, "I know. I am very careful."

The suspect went on to tell me, "I may do business with you, but I want to meet both of you first. I want to meet in a neutral location in Tacoma".

The suspect and I agreed that we would all meet on the 24th, and he closed the conversation by instructing me to "Call me when you are getting close to Tacoma, and I will give you directions to where we will meet."

I had tried to pry some personal information from the suspect (like his name), but he didn't budge. I still had no idea who I was dealing with, as a reverse phone number query had come up blank.

On the **24**[th,] Jennifer and I called the suspect and told him we were about 30 minutes from Tacoma. To my surprise, he gave us his home address and told us to come to his house to meet "me and my boys."

I had a sneaky feeling "his boys" wouldn't turn out to be his young children. Jennifer and I arrived at the two-story home at about 5:15 pm and were immediately invited in by the suspect, who introduced himself as Bourey. Bourey was mid-40s and in good shape, and looked very serious. Standing behind Bourey were two men in their 20s (who displayed all the signs of hardened criminals) and who Bourey referred to as a couple of his "monkeys."

Bourey and company had obviously set the stage for this little meet and greet, as he took his place in a single large chair facing us while we were told to sit on a small couch facing him (with his "monkeys" standing behind our heads). As I knew Jennifer had done, I had scanned the room for weapons when we first entered, and while I hadn't seen any firearms, I had made note of a sword and some knives positioned a few feet behind the couch we were now sitting on. While I sat facing Bourey directly, Jennifer sat with her legs pulled up underneath her and her back against the armrest sideways on the couch, as only a woman would sit. I instantly knew my partner was taking that position to keep the "monkeys" (behind our heads) in her peripheral vision. She knew nobody would realize what she was doing because it is not uncommon for women to sit that way.

Once we were seated, Bourey instructed his "monkeys" to get us a couple of beers. Immediately, one of the thugs plopped a couple of Heinekens down on the coffee table in front of us and opened them. I truthfully told Bourey that I no longer drink (I had quit about a year prior and wasn't about to start up again).

My refusal to drink definitely concerned our host, and he looked at Jennifer and said, "I suppose you don't drink either."

Jennifer said she does drink, but didn't feel like having one. Jennifer took note of Bourey's concern over our lack of alcohol consumption (a common test in undercover situations) and calmly tipped her beer back and drank it as we talked.

As we sat facing each other, with the two guards still behind our backs, Bourey began firing questions at us, one after the other. He asked about our backgrounds, family, history, and anything else he could think of to trip us up. When he began asking specific questions regarding our new business, it became apparent he had gone so far as to look up our business license online. At one point during our interview, Bourey sent me out to our truck to "get more business cards." As I walked out, I knew what he was doing, separating us to see if we would both give the same answers when questioned separately (a technique I had employed hundreds of times when I had been in uniform).

To categorize our interview as intense doesn't do it justice. I had a bad feeling that if we were to fail the interview, the consequences would be far more significant than just losing a supplier. I wondered what I had gotten us into. We had no weapons, no backup, no communication, and no real way out if things went south. This contact was all on me, and Jennifer had trusted my judgment when she had agreed to come along. Now I wondered if I had made a terrible mistake, yet this was also when all our time together as friends and partners, all of our practice, and all of our training paid off.

Bourey told us he and all of his "monkeys" were Cambodian, and he has only dealt with Asian people because he can trust them.

He repeated what he had told me on the phone about his pricing structure for deer and elk and added, "I sold 13 deer and elk, mostly elk, this week and 11 last week". Bourey went on to tell us, "I get most of them from Indians, and the seller delivers them to me. I hold them in my garage, and then I call the buyers. I have many buyers and never have trouble selling deer and elk. I have been buying and selling deer and elk for seven years and never have had any problems."

Bourey repeatedly insisted I tell him who my friend was, who had given me his phone number, but I told him that under no circumstances would I tell him. I explained to Bourey that was how we worked; what was told to us stayed with us, and we would never give up anyone. For good measure, I added that I didn't want Bourey jumping down my friend's throat for giving us the information. Bourey seemed satisfied with that particular answer.

Bourey asked how many elk and deer we wanted and could handle. We said that we would like to start with two elk. Bourey said he wouldn't deal in one at a time because it's not worth the trouble. He said he would only take cash and would never tell us who the guys were that delivered to him. I told Bourey that was fine with us as long as he promised never to tell anyone about us. We both agreed and even shook hands on it. Bourey said the elk and deer harvest would end soon, as they don't like to kill them after mid-March because they could be killing pregnant animals (a poacher with a conscience). He said they start killing again in early fall, but it's best when the snow brings the elk down in November and December. Bourey asked me if we had the money to pay him in cash for a couple of elk and some deer all in one delivery, and I said we did. Several times during our conversation, Bourey said (when referring to his deer and elk), "These aren't farm-raised."

Finally, I asked the all-important question, "Well, are we going to do business?"

Bourey replied simply, "I will call you and let you know." With that, we were done.

Jennifer and I were driving down the road, talking over the entire contact, when about 10 minutes later, Bourey called.

Bourey calmly said, "I will have two elk for you by Friday morning and possibly up to four deer. My guy is bringing them over on Friday morning, and I will call you when they get in, so you can get them on Friday afternoon or Saturday morning. Bring cash only, and only you and Tina (Jennifer), nobody else".

61

We agreed to the deal, but before we hung up, Bourey had one last thing to say, "I have never done business with <u>you people</u>, Whitie, and I hope I don't regret it."

That call relieved any tension either of us had left over. We had to admire Bourey's judgment in picking two game wardens as the first "Whities" he chose to do business with.

It wasn't until much later that evening, when I was back at my WDFW computer, that I found out who Bourey truly was. My suspicions were confirmed when I learned from his criminal history and intelligence that he was a seriously bad man. While I can't go into detail, suffice it to say he is undoubtedly dangerous. Our gut feelings had been confirmed. I shared the information regarding our newfound meat supplier with Jennifer, who was no more shocked than I was and was now even more interested in seeing this case through to the end.

The next day, on the **25**th, I received a call from Tanya Franklin. Franklin said Kyle had just shot a deer and wanted me to come over immediately to buy it. I told Franklin I was on the way, but it would take me about three hours to get there. Franklin told me to drive around to their wall tent when I arrived. I arrived at their compound at about 4 pm and was greeted by Tanya Franklin and Kyle Parker.

Kyle explained, "I killed the mule deer doe in the canyon behind our house. I shot her in the head with my .22 Hornet from over 100 yards away."

Kyle handed me a bag and said, "This was my first kill of the day."

62

I found the bag contained a whole dead red-tailed hawk. Kyle said he had killed the hawk with the .22 Hornet and that his brother-in-law had been with him. I noticed they had a new dreamcatcher hanging in the tent, which was decorated with hawk feathers. I asked about the dreamcatcher, and Tanya said she had wrapped it and they had made it for another customer, but the customer refused to pay what they wanted for it. I asked what they wanted for it, and Kyle said $125, but the woman would only pay $100. I told Kyle that I would take it. Kyle and I negotiated the price of the dead hawk, and we both agreed that the feathers alone were worth over $80, so I offered him $100, to which he agreed.

We weighed the deer meat (50 pounds), and I told him I would only pay him $150 for the deer meat, to which he agreed.

Kyle said, "I could have killed a whole bunch of elk that morning, but I didn't know if you wanted elk meat."

I told him that we deal in elk meat too, but that he better slow down and start being more careful, or he would end up in jail, as the hunting season had ended four months prior. Kyle said he only hunts on private land behind his house and would never be caught.

Tanya said, "We really like your wife. She is great. Where is she today?" I told Tanya that Tina (Jennifer) had a bad back and was in bed all day in really bad pain (which was true). Kyle and Tanya said I needed to bring her the next time I came over.

Kyle helped me load the dreamcatcher, the deer meat, and the hawk into my truck, and I paid him $375 in cash. After another couple of felony transactions with these two, I headed home to prepare for a much larger transaction I hoped would soon materialize.

It wasn't until Sunday, February 27th that Bourey called back. Bourey simply stated, "I have the two elk and three deer coming in by afternoon. I want $600 each for the elk and between $150 and $160 each for the deer, in cash. Be here Monday afternoon with the cash".

I told him we would be there and would have the cash in hand. After getting off the phone with Bourey, I called Detective Chris Clarke and asked if he would be available to hang back a few blocks from Bourey's house just in case we needed backup. Chris said he was available and was more than willing to do so. I called Jennifer and told her we were on for the next day, and for the first time in our careers, we would have backup on an undercover contact in Washington.

At about 5 pm the following day, Jennifer and I backed into Bourey's garage. As I was backing up the truck, I noticed that in addition to the three deer and two elk lying on the garage floor, Bourey had four less than friendly looking Asian men standing with him. As we walked into the garage, I looked at Jennifer and noticed her right hand shoved into her coat pocket. Knowing she had a pistol in that hand gave me a degree of comfort.

Bourey invited us to check the animals to ensure they met our approval. As I looked over the carcasses, I realized they had been cleaned and skinned within professional meat-cutting standards.....the people who had killed and processed these animals were no amateurs. Once we expressed our approval, Bourey ordered his "monkeys" to load the carcasses in our truck. The men first donned latex gloves, then proceeded to do what I thought impossible: fit two whole elk and three whole deer in the back of a short-bed pickup. Bourey told us we owed him $1,650. Jennifer counted out the amount and handed the cash to Bourey, who shoved the wad of cash in his pocket.

I asked Bourey if he was going to count it, and he said, "There is no need to."

After completing the transaction, Bourey asked if we were interested in buying sturgeon. We both said we would be happy to get a few good-quality sturgeon, but asked where he would get them. He told us he and his "monkeys" fish for sturgeon and sell them. He described where they fish and how, and said he would call us when he had some available. Bourey told us he sells meat and sturgeon to several Asian restaurants, but gets enough to sell to us, too. We thanked him and promised to stay in touch and left immediately.

After clearing Bourey's house, we called Chris to tell him we were done and he could stand down. We couldn't wait to look at the covert video of our transaction, as we were hoping to have captured video of each suspect. Jennifer drove north as I viewed the video on a tiny DVR (Digital Video Recorder) screen. The video had come out crystal clear, meaning we had high-quality video evidence of the multiple felony transaction. We were jacked, to say the least. We had just broken into a large-scale Asian organized crime group that trafficked in more wildlife than anyone the state had seen before.

While watching the video, we considered putting up a remote video surveillance camera on Bourey's house. Such a camera system is very expensive but will record whatever it is aimed at, 24 hours a day. A remote camera system would allow us to identify who delivers the elk and deer, the other buyers, and possibly any other criminal activities these guys might be involved in. These cameras can be disguised as anything, from rocks to trees to man-made objects, and are virtually undetectable. If there were ever a group that deserved the extra attention, it was these guys. I placed a few phone calls and put the wheels in motion to get a camera in place within a week or two.

Jennifer and I only had to photograph the animal carcasses and remove DNA samples before we transferred them to WDFW Officer Dave Jones to be cut and wrapped (some meat would go to charity, while the remainder would be kept for potential future sales). As Dave removed the carcasses from our truck, he stated, "Your truck smells like death." He was right, and the smell would only get worse.

Overall, February 2011 had been a pretty productive month for Best of the Wild. After just three months in business, we had over ten suspects on felony wildlife trafficking charges, and we were just beginning to roll. Maybe, just maybe, we would be allowed to run the operation for the full two years we had proposed.

CHAPTER 7- MARCH 2011

Traditionally, March is Washington's slowest month for fish and wildlife activity. The hunting seasons have long been closed, the spring trout and turkey seasons have not yet opened, and steelhead fishing has slowed down to nothing. For those reasons, we didn't have very high expectations for March. We figured the slow time would allow us to catch up on reports, ensure the evidence was being correctly handled, and maybe even take a little time off and get reacquainted with our spouses.

We learned that March 2011 would be our captain's last month before retirement during the first week of March. I had mixed emotions regarding Captain Volz's retirement, as I considered him a friend, but I also realized he was more of a detriment than an asset to Operation Cody. The captain had put in about 34 years and, without a doubt, had made some notable cases "back in the day." The big question was, now what? And who would take over the SIU?

Early in my undercover career with SIU, Captain Volz had asked me to let him know where I was going and when before I left for any undercover trip. While I always complied with that loose order, I knew that my captain had already forgotten where I was going before I had left on the majority of my undercover contacts. Nobody would know what had happened if I (or we) never came home. It appeared to me and others that our captain had the worst short-term memory on earth.

Years before, to assure investigators would at least have a starting point had I failed to return, I had a habit of giving my wife,

Judy, the names and addresses of the suspects I would be contacting. I would try my best to call her immediately after I was safely clear, putting her mind at ease and ensuring some sort of lifeline was in place. It was a very amateur way of doing business, but it was all we had. Maybe with a different supervisor, we might have some form of backup or monitoring. In short, it was past time for the captain to retire.

We enjoyed a very quiet and relaxing March all the way until March **4**th, when Bourey called. He said he was putting together an order of deer and elk and wanted to know if we were interested.

I answered, "We have been cutting and wrapping meat for days and don't want as much as last time. We could probably take two elk, or one elk and two deer, or four to five deer."

I really didn't want to buy any, as I knew the demand we were creating would mean more animals would be poached, but we had portrayed ourselves as large-scale wild game meat dealers and had to keep up the façade.

"I'll call you when I know what I have coming in," Bourey said.

Another week passed before we heard back from Bourey on Friday the **11**th.

"My people have four elk and one deer right now, and they are out trying to get more deer, but they may not get any more. The load should be at my house at about 11:00 p.m. tonight, so you can come and get yours early Saturday morning".

He asked if we wanted all four elk, and I said that the most we could handle was three, but I would talk it over with my wife and let him know. He said to call him when we are on our way down, but he is a morning person, so early is fine. Bourey told me we would get the first pick of the animals when they arrived, and he would sell whatever was left to other customers.

As luck would have it, our request for 24-hour video surveillance had been granted, and the camera was up and running on the morning of the 11th.....the day Bourey said the load was coming in.

Jennifer and I arrived at Bourey's at about 9:30 a.m. on the 12th, and as we backed into the driveway, the garage door opened for us. Bourey and two other Asian males met us.

Bourey pointed at the carcasses and announced, "This is what I've got."

I saw there were three elk carcasses and a portion of a deer carcass lying on the floor. After inspecting the carcasses, I told him we would take the elk but not the deer.

Jennifer asked Bourey how much he wanted for the three elk, to which he replied: "$600 each, so $1,800."

He and the two other men loaded the three elk in our truck while Jennifer took out 18 $100 bills and handed the cash to Bourey.

Again, he didn't count the money before shoving it in his pocket, so I had to ask, "Why don't you count the money...everyone does?"

69

Bourey's response was ice cold: "Nobody ever short-changes me and gets away with it."

I didn't doubt the truth in what he was saying. Bourey told us that if we wanted any more meat soon, he could get more, but we had to give him one week's notice. I told him that we didn't need any more. Bourey said his "monkeys" would start getting sturgeon in May, and he had told them that if they had one with eggs, to keep it for us and to keep the eggs in the fish. I told him I would be willing to pay around $30 per pound for sturgeon eggs, but we would talk when he had some. Sturgeon-bearing eggs are almost always over the legal size limit by state law, and the sale of these sport-caught fish or their eggs is highly illegal.

Again, we were entertained by our videos as we drove north to continue the ritual of photographing, taking samples, and transferring the carcasses. There were three more felony charges on Bourey and his "monkeys," .....just another day at the office.

On this most recent transaction, we were back to our norm...no backup (despite my request). However, the newly placed surveillance camera did allow for live remote surveillance. Someone sitting a hundred miles away could at least watch out for us, but we hadn't even been able to convince anyone to take the time to do that.

It wasn't until the next day, when I reviewed the video, that I found the camera had successfully captured two new suspects delivering carcasses and other customers who took their pick from the pile of animals before we were even called on the 11th. Apparently, Bourey was cheating on us (there is no honor among thieves). When I got to the video of us arriving on the 12th, I noticed something we hadn't seen while we had been there. While Jennifer and I were in the garage and driveway, buying and loading our elk, a man was standing in an upstairs window of Bourey's house, looking down on us with what appeared to be a rifle in his hands. The unidentified rifleman stood guard during the entire time we were there.

Bourey lived in a very high-crime neighborhood of Tacoma, so in all likelihood, the armed sentry was in place to protect us from being ripped off by rival thugs rather than to protect Bourey from the two of us. Still, it certainly did raise the stakes a bit. I needed to inform Captain Volz and Jennifer of the information so we could all decide if we wanted to continue doing business with Bourey.

The next morning, I called Captain Volz and briefed him about the events of our transaction and the upstairs gunman. Volz showed little concern and instead launched into stories of the dangers he had faced back when he had worked in the field (more than a decade prior).

My next call regarding the armed sentry was to my partner. She had to know, and I wanted to ensure she went into this with her eyes wide open.

After telling her about the man upstairs and emailing her a photo of him holding the rifle, I told her sincerely, "I won't think any less of you or be upset with you in any way if you want out. You've proven you have guts, but this situation is serious, and I want you to give it some thought and decide if it's worth the risk".

Jennifer's response didn't surprise me at all. "Are you going?" I told her I was. Jennifer fired back, "Then why in the hell wouldn't I go?" With that decided, we continued business as usual (as if anything about this was "usual").

In the middle of our dealings with Bourey, Tanya Franklin contacted us, saying they had more merchandise for us. In no uncertain terms, we told Tanya to stop killing things. Tanya said Kyle had quit killing deer for a while but had some native art for us to see. We agreed to look at what they had to offer within the next week or so.

On the morning of the **21st**, Jennifer and I arrived at the Parker compound. We soon learned that these two lovebirds had moved into the wall tent to live. The two "artists" showed us several Indian art wildlife items, including three dreamcatchers and three peace pipes, all of which were decorated with hawk and eagle feathers. Tanya told us she had been sorting out hawk feathers and removing them from the birds while Kyle made the artwork.

Tanya went on to say, "One day, I was working on a hawk when Kyle yelled to me to get rid of everything because he had seen an airplane flying over. Kyle gets really paranoid sometimes" (ain't meth wonderful?). Tanya said she was thrilled I had told them to stop killing because she worried about them being caught. She confided she has tried to "avoid the law" her whole life.

As with previous visits, Jennifer asked Kyle, "What kind of feathers are on these?"

Kyle quickly responded, "They are all hawk feathers, except this one (pointing to a dreamcatcher) has eagle feathers too."

Jennifer and Tanya negotiated a price of $450 for all six items, and Kyle said he would throw in a hawk talon (foot) for free. Jennifer and I loaded the items in the back of our truck, paid Kyle $450 in cash, and got out of there. We had only dealt with these folks a couple of times and were already becoming very wary of them. On the way home, we again dropped our evidence off for Detective Clarke to enter, photograph, and get identified.

After returning from the Yakima area, I received a call from WDFW Officer Dave Jones. Jones told me about a taxidermist named Randy Jackson, who ran his business in the far northwest corner of Washington. Jones said he had heard, through several citizens, that Jackson was involved in trafficking and mounting eagles. I agreed to take a trip up north and check out the business. I called Jennifer and shared Jones's information with her. Jennifer told me she was fairly certain she had been to that same taxidermy shop in uniform some years back, so bringing her along would never work.

On March 25th, I walked into Jackson's Taxidermy, ready to show Mr. Jackson I was a player in the business. Unfortunately, I picked a time when Jackson was off on a business trip, leaving only his assistant, Wyatt Wilson, to mind the shop. Wilson was in his mid-60s, heavyset, with a bush of wild, long gray hair. His hair stuck out in all directions, giving him the look of a mad scientist. Wilson was more than willing to show me around the vast taxidermy business, where I quickly noticed the head of a golden eagle in the process of being mounted atop a long walking staff.

I asked Wilson about the eagle, and he said, "We make a lot of eagle items for Indian customers. Randy (Jackson) has all the state and federal permits to work on eagles for the Indians".

That conversation led me to discuss our Yakima friends (Franklin and Parker- although I didn't name them to Wilson) and the Native American artwork they sold us.

One thing led to another, and before I knew what had happened, Wilson provided me with his name and home phone number, telling me, "I'll do any taxidermy work you want."

I told Wilson I had a cougar hide I wanted to be made into a rug, but I didn't have any paperwork for it (no license, tag, or pelt seal as required by law). Wilson said to call him anytime, and he would either have me come to his house or meet me somewhere and pick up the cougar hide to mount it. He quoted me a price of $800 to tan and mount the cat.

In a matter of minutes, Wilson had effectively undercut his boss and invited me to do my illegal business with him instead. I took Wilson's information and told him I would call. Once I returned to my WDFW computer, I did a little checking and found Wilson did not have a taxidermist license. However, he did have a very impressive wildlife criminal history, including trafficking in eagles. I guess he hadn't learned his lesson. I also found Jackson did not have the necessary permits to handle eagles.....no surprise there either. The bad news was that I would have to get someone else to take a run at Jackson now that I had formed a business deal with his helper.

I got my next call from Bourey on the **26**th. "I have a load of deer and elk coming in right now. How many do you guys want?"

Even though we portrayed ourselves as large-scale game meat dealers, this was too much, too soon. "Sorry, man, but we gotta pass this time. Our freezers are full, and we have to move some of this before taking in any more," I replied.

Bourey said that was fine and promised to start getting us some sturgeon very soon. I knew our surveillance camera would pick up this latest delivery and the subsequent sales, so we would still have evidence of the illegal transactions.

On the last day of March, with a cougar hide in hand, I called Wilson. I explained to him that the cougar was one I had purchased "over on the east side of the state" and that it had been fleshed (removing much of the meat tissue from the hide) and salted. I asked Wilson if he would be willing to drop his fee down to $700, so I could make a profit on it, and he agreed. Wilson said he would like to meet me at a truck stop parking area near Arlington, WA.

I arrived at the agreed-upon spot fashionably late and found Wilson and a woman sitting in his black KIA, just as he had described to me. I backed up to Wilson's car, opened the back of my truck, and produced the cougar hide for him to view.

"So, you don't have a tag or anything for it?" Wilson asked.

"Look, if that's going to be a problem, I'll take it to someone else," I answered as I began to put the hide back in the bag I had brought it in.

75

Wilson quickly responded with, "No, no, that's ok. I'll take it as is." Wilson asked for a $200 deposit for the work, so I wrote the unlicensed taxidermist a $200 check to have an illegal cougar mounted.

Once he had the cat hide, he asked me if I was interested in "birds."

Wilson went on to say, "It's a federal crime to even sell ducks, but do you think you would be interested in dealing in some birds?"

I calmly responded, "Look, I don't want you to be offended, but I don't know you very well. I only do that kind of business with people I know I can trust."

Wilson answered, "I am glad to hear that. I am careful too (obviously). Maybe we can do more business if you like my work on the cougar."

I told him that was possible, and time would tell. Wilson wrote his home address down for me and asked me to come up to his shop anytime to look at what he had. He said it would take him about six weeks to finish my cougar. We went our separate ways, promising each other to stay in touch.

Apparently, March wasn't always a slow month, as we had just racked up a whole bunch of new cases involving some very promising suspects.

CHAPTER 8- APRIL 2011

April 1st brought SIU a new supervisor- Sgt. Mike Hobbs. Mike was a relatively new sergeant and quite young (we later figured out he was one month old when I had been hired), but fairly intelligent and energetic. What he lacked in experience, he made up for in enthusiasm. Mike had absolutely no expertise in SIU casework and had never worked undercover, yet he seemed to be smart enough to trust the people around him who did have the experience and know-how.

One of the first things Sgt. Hobbs did was to sit down with me to review Operation Cody. I could tell instantly our new sergeant had a genuine interest in the operation and was very excited about it. After getting caught up on what we had done thus far, Hobbs asked what he could do for us to successfully run this operation through to the end. The answer was simple yet likely out of reach: "We need more bodies." I told him that as the operation continued, our business was growing exponentially.

"One thing our administration doesn't understand is the fact that I spend countless hours 24/7 answering business calls, text messages, emails, and delivering legal merchandise, just as any business owner has to do, but I also try to sort out the dummies from the serious criminals. That alone is a full-time job for one detective," I explained.

I also stated we needed someone full-time to handle evidence and case files, and could use another person to monitor/archive covert video and work intelligence. Hobbs assured me he would do what he could to ensure we had the help we so badly needed.

I expressed my concern over evidence, "Right now, Clarke is handling our evidence, but since I don't have access to the evidence, I'm not sure it's being properly photographed, entered, logged, and identified (by DNA or expert witness) as required. We need to stay on top of the evidence, so we don't have to run around at the last minute trying to get the evidence properly identified for court".

I continued, "While I'm on my wish list, how about restoring our working relationship with the US Fish and Wildlife Service and getting an MOU in place?"

An MOU is a Memorandum of Understanding, a legal document necessary to work on interagency/cross-jurisdictional cases. We hadn't had an MOU in place for many years with the USFWS (US Fish and Wildlife Service), which essentially prohibited us from shipping or receiving illegal wildlife across state or international borders.

I went on to explain, "We have already received over a dozen offers from out-of-state suspects, and one in British Columbia, who want to do business with us, but without an MOU, we have to turn them down unless we are willing to drive there and do business in person. We have missed a great many opportunities to catch some real serious traffickers in other jurisdictions because of this."

I explained that our MOUs with Oregon, Montana, and Idaho helped, but we were out of luck beyond those states. Hobbs asked several questions about the history between WDFW and USFWS and said he would do his best.

To bolster my position, I told Hobbs, "I know the Deputy Chief will want to know why we should care about what people are doing in other states. We have a golden opportunity to catch not just our poachers and traffickers but many others across the US. I would certainly like to think other states would help us out if they could. Bad guys are bad guys, no matter where they are."

Hobbs answered, "I couldn't agree more, and let me have a chance to see what I can get done."

"The last request I have," I continued, "is to see if we might be allowed to work tribal members. It makes it extremely difficult for us to do business with non-Indians and turn down offers from Indians. I am afraid that at some point, we will have an Indian suspect compare notes about us with a non-Indian we are doing business with, and they will smell a rat. We have already turned down offers from several Washington tribal members, for everything from bighorn sheep to eagles."

With all the requests I threw at Sgt. Hobbs, he only had two for me, "Please always keep me updated on what is going on with the operation, and I want you and Jennifer to always call me before and immediately after you make any undercover contacts. I think it's ridiculous you two have had no backup or anyone even monitoring where you are and if you made it clear of the contact in one piece."

Those were two requests I was more than happy to comply with.

79

I had just given Sgt. Hobbs a ton of information and some nearly impossible tasks to aid our operation. After we met, I felt more hopeful. If he could accomplish 10% of what he aimed for, we would be well ahead of where I thought we could be with our administration. Now it was time to get back to business.

Sgt. Hobbs told me he had already received his first assignment from DC Cenci. It was to "fix the G&R shellfish case." The G&R case was an oyster and clam case, which Detective Paul Buerger had led. Buerger had "completed" the case and then retired, leaving lots of loose ends and unfinished business. In short, it was a mess. While the reports had been submitted to the prosecutor's offices, they were inadequate and incomplete, leaving plenty of work to be done. Apparently, the DC had realized how much still needed to be done and assigned Hobbs to complete the case personally and ride herd over it as it went through prosecution.

Hobbs assured me he would do his best to help us out, but he had to get G&R prosecuted first.

I spent the first week of April doing some minor Best of the Wild business on the state's east side by myself. I delivered another undocumented mountain lion to another unlicensed taxidermist. I made a few transactions of illegal wildlife and continued spreading the word about our business. While my solo contacts had gone just fine, I quickly realized I had become too dependent on my partner. Jennifer's attention to detail and observation skills were badly missed on those solo contacts. I found myself having difficulty reading my chicken-scratch notes, trying to recall license plate numbers, and keeping track of who was who. Although I have always been fortunate enough to have an exceptional memory, I found I had not paid much attention to the small details crucial to case reports. In short, I had come to rely too much on my partner, and without her, I was doing a less-than-adequate job.

Fortunately, everything I had missed seeing (or at least didn't register if I saw it) was crystal clear on the covert videos I had captured during my solo contacts. This allowed me to "fill in the blanks," but I swore to myself I would get my act together and pay better attention. Getting old sucks, but it is no excuse for not doing my best, and that week I certainly was not at my best.

About a third of the way into the month, I received some interesting information from our newest detective (in Spokane). Detective Lenny Hahn informed me he had some reliable intelligence on a man named Kent Rousch. Mr. Rousch owned and operated a wildlife furniture business and was thought to be involved in commercial wildlife crimes. His business, known as Wild Ways, was run out of his $1,000,000+ home in the Spokane area and boasted customers worldwide. The information suggested Rousch might be trafficking in many different illegal wildlife items, including bighorn sheep and raptors. Lenny also provided me with the website address for the business and suggested I check it out. I promised him we would see what we could find out and perhaps visit Rousch's business the next time we were in the area.

After speaking with Lenny, I jumped on the computer and pulled up the Wild Ways website. Within 5 minutes of moving around on the website, I realized a major problem: we couldn't afford to do business with this guy. While the merchandise he offered (all made

81

from wildlife parts) appeared to be top of the line, so were his prices. Even if Jennifer and I could get an invitation to his home gallery, I had serious doubts our $4,000 monthly budget would get us very far, but we wouldn't know until we tried. If we successfully got involved with this suspect, it wouldn't be the first (or even second) million-dollar home we had been in undercover, but it would mean we would have to change our attire and persona a bit. One thing was for sure: this guy operated in a whole different world from the suspects we had been dealing with thus far.

After perusing the Wild Ways website, I called Rousch, introduced myself, and filled him in on our business, telling him, "We are always looking for new sources of unique collectible wildlife items, and you look like someone we need to meet."

After an exchange of pleasantries, we agreed on the date of May 4th to come over and view his home gallery. I picked the first week of the month as I would have the highest bank account balance at that time after WDFW had reimbursed us for our previous month's expenses.

I spent the next few weeks working alone, making more illegal wildlife transactions, and catching up on case reports while Jennifer was back in uniform, performing her regular duties.

On the **26th**, I received a citizen tip in which the caller only had a suspect's cell phone number. This time, the caller was Russian and was complaining about another Russian. The caller said he had recently visited a Russian market in Everett and had asked about caviar. Another customer at the market had overheard his request for caviar and had given him a handwritten note with nothing but a phone number on it.

The mystery man told my caller, "Call this number, and you can get all the caviar you want. The man is Russian, and you can trust him".

This was a first for me- a Russian turning in another Russian, and similar to the citizen who had turned in Bourey, this caller had no idea who the phone number belonged to.

I asked the caller the obvious question, "Why are you turning this information in?"

His answer somewhat surprised me, "I love caviar and sturgeon, but poaching is killing the entire caviar industry. People who do these things illegally ruin it for the rest of us."

I asked the caller if he was in the "caviar industry." He said he was not and even gave me his employment information to verify. Another significant lead, but one in which I was pretty sure I better have a Russian along to help me out. If I could pull this off, it would be the first long-term undercover case involving Russians in our agency's history.

White and green are the two species of Washington's sturgeon. Green sturgeon are never open to harvest and are extremely rare, while white sturgeon are open in tightly regulated seasons and are more abundant. Eggs or caviar from Washington sturgeon almost always come from illegal (oversized) sturgeon, as the regulations are set to protect sturgeon of egg-bearing size from being harvested. Caviar can legally be sold if acquired from other species, such as salmon, or if the eggs come from jurisdictions where the harvest is legal. The sale or harvest must be accompanied by documentation showing legal origin.

After getting off the phone with the Russian tipster, I ran a reverse phone lookup on the suspect's phone, and this time, I got a name and address. I worked up a background on the suspect and found he was a felon with multiple convictions. I obtained a driver's license photo of the suspect and everything else I could get my hands on. Next, I started calling every law enforcement agency in the area, looking for an officer I could borrow who was fluent in Russian. A Seattle Police Department detective steered me in the right direction by providing me with the name and number of a federal agent who might be able to help. A call to the federal agent provided me with just what I needed. Not only did they have a Russian-speaking individual working for them, but he was more than willing to help in any way we needed. What I requested was reasonably minimal; I wanted the Russian-speaking employee to meet with me, place a call to the suspect, and introduce me to the suspect (hoping the suspect spoke English so I could continue doing business with him by myself). The two of us agreed to meet in Everett on May 2nd to see what we could accomplish. There was no way I could use Jennifer in this particular case, as Everett was just too close to home for her, and she might be recognized.

Towards the end of the month, I received an email simply stating, "I have a lot of things call me. Thanks George," with an Idaho phone number to call.

On the **28th**, I placed the call and spoke with "George."

84

George was another rather direct character who started with, "Where do you get your wild game meat?"

I told him that, by law, we have to get it from game farms, and that's where we get most of it.

He asked, "Would you be willing to buy game meat? I have lived in this part of Idaho a long time and know a lot of people who can get me deer meat, and the profit is better that way if you don't have to buy it from game farms".

I asked George if he worked for "Fish and Game," and George responded, "I hate the government! I own a meat-cutting business and make sausage and pepperoni out of game meat and can sell that to you too".

Lastly, George said he had noticed we sell artificial eagle feathers on our website and that he "gets tons of eagle feathers." I took down George's address and told him that the next time my wife and I were over in the Spokane area, we might just come up to his place in Idaho for a talk. George said he was looking forward to it.

Later the same day, before I could call Idaho Fish and Game to talk to them about George, I got another offer from a different Idaho resident.

The offer started with a strange email, "I do not have a personal email account, but would you please give me a call at the following number. I have a lot of the animals you are looking for! BEFORE 8 pm, ask for Leo", with another Idaho phone number provided.

I gave Leo a call and asked what he had to offer, "I have multiple deer and elk, a moose, a bighorn sheep, and a mountain goat, all mounted and all for sale. I have a lot of other things for sale too," Leo told me.

Leo said his full name is Leo Ford, and he lives in Coeur d'Alene, Idaho. Leo said he had "tags for <u>almost</u> everything I shot." I asked Leo if he knew it was illegal to sell bighorn sheep in Idaho, but he didn't seem concerned with laws, responding simply, "I'm ok with that."

"Looks like my wife and I will be heading over your way sometime during the first week of May. Would that work for you?" I asked.

Leo was fine with our timing, so I promised to call him when we knew what time and date we would arrive.

Before I got any more offers from Idaho residents, I thought I better call Idaho Fish and Game investigators and let them know what we were up to. Fortunately, I have a few friends in Idaho who work on fish and wildlife investigations and whom I can count on to keep our conversations confidential. I placed the call, took some time to explain what we had, and within a few hours, not only had permission to work undercover in Idaho but had an assurance our agency would be reimbursed for all expenses incurred on our undercover expeditions. That's the way it should work!

CHAPTER 9- MAY 2011

The first week of May 2011 confirmed that our new boss wasn't just all talk. Sgt. Hobbs called me to say he had implemented some personnel changes to support Operation Cody. Hobbs said Detective Chris Clarke was assigned to our operation, effective immediately, on a full-time basis, to process evidence and keep up on case files. He had also arranged to have Officer Tammy Conklin monitor and archive covert video for us as much as she could fit in between her other duties. His last change was to offer Jennifer a full-time temporary appointment to the position of detective (funded at a decent pay raise).

I asked Hobbs if he had called Jennifer to offer the temporary appointment yet, and he responded, "That's my next call. Why?" I explained I wasn't sure she would take the offer, but instead would want to stay status quo (working in uniform the majority of the time and undercover 4 or 5 days a month). Jennifer and I had discussed this possible scenario before, and she had expressed reluctance to leave all of Snohomish County to two officers (at that time, there were only three game wardens, including Jennifer, in the entire county, the third most populated county in the state).

Within 24 hours, I heard back from my partner on her response to the offer of a full-time assignment as a detective: "I know you need the help, but I just can't do that to Julie (Officer Julie Cook- one of the two officers working in Snohomish County). There is way too much for two of us to handle in the county, and leaving it all to one officer isn't fair. I hope you understand".

"Not a problem at all, and I kinda thought that would be your answer. I'm sure we can offer the temporary assignment to someone else, and you can keep doing the undercover work the way we have been handling it", I answered.

I fully understood and would likely have made the same decision had the roles been reversed. It was also only a matter of offering the same position to another officer, and I had two alternatives in mind. Hobbs and I talked over the alternatives and decided on our best choice.

Hobbs called the deputy chief with our suggestion and quickly received the answer: "The DC said if Jennifer doesn't want the position, we are not going to offer it to anyone else."

Oh well, we were still better off than we were before. We now had the two of us to work undercover, Officer Conklin part-time to help with the covert videos and Clarke full-time to handle evidence and case files. That should be enough help to keep us going.

Sgt. Hobbs and I met in Everett on the 2nd with the federal agents who had agreed to help us try to get in with the Russian caviar dealer. After introductions, five of us crammed into a van to place the call to our suspect. My new Russian-speaking friend called the suspect and engaged in a long conversation about caviar. By the end of the conversation, the suspect, Liev Smirnov, agreed to sell us five pounds of black caviar at $100 per pound. Caviar is commonly referred to as "Black" or "Red." Black are sturgeon eggs, and red are salmon eggs. Liev told us he would meet us in the parking lot of a defunct Blockbuster Video store in Everett. Smirnov described the vehicle he would arrive in, and in return, my Russian-speaking friend described our vehicle.

After the call, we quickly formulated a plan. Hobbs would provide surveillance/backup in the parking lot while the two federal agents stayed back a few blocks. The Russian employee and I pulled into the parking lot at the agreed time and saw Smirnov's vehicle pull up next to us within a couple of minutes. Smirnov exited his car and got in the backseat of our car. Smirnov was a chubby-faced, large man with an expression of confusion locked on his face. At first, I thought he was scared, but as time passed, I realized his elevator didn't go all the way to the top floor, and he simply looked like what he was, a little slow. For the next four or five minutes, I sat there listening to an animated conversation in Russian, not understanding a word of it.

Finally, I broke into the conversation, asking Smirnov, "Do you speak English?"

Smirnov answered in English, "Of course."

I then demanded that the remainder of the conversation be in English, and all agreed. I explained my business to Smirnov, gave him a business card, and added that I was having trouble finding good-quality black caviar. Smirnov handed me a box containing five jars of black caviar and said the caviar was top quality. I opened one of the jars and ate a sample (one of the most challenging things I had to do undercover, as I have never developed a taste for caviar. It's awful). I expressed my satisfaction with the caviar and paid Smirnov the agreed-upon $500.

"This is white sturgeon caviar, right?" I asked.

"No, American sturgeon," Liev answered.

Great, I had just spent $500 on caviar from a fish that doesn't even exist in Washington. American sturgeon is a nickname for paddlefish, a critter that lives in the warm, muddy waters of states to the east of us, including Montana, Texas, Oklahoma, and many more.

"So, where did it come from?" I asked.

Liev explained, "This all comes from Oklahoma. I go to Oklahoma several times a year, and we catch a bunch of American sturgeon, make the caviar, and bring it back here to sell".

While I had a feeling what Liev had just described to me was illegal, I wouldn't be sure until I called the Oklahoma Department of Wildlife Conservation. If it were illegal to sell sport-caught paddlefish under Oklahoma law, then what Liev was doing would also constitute a federal offense (by crossing state lines). A little deflated, I thanked Liev and told him I would be back in touch. About 2 minutes after we pulled away from Liev, my cell phone rang, and I saw it was Liev calling me.

"Are you interested in buying steelhead? Whole fish." Liev asked.

"How many can you deliver at a time?" I asked.

Liev's answer gave me hope of making a significant Washington case out of this yet. "I get about 100 pounds at a time. I catch them myself."

Without hesitation, I replied, "Absolutely. Call me when you have some, and we will talk."

Interstate transportation (interstate commerce) of illegal caviar falls under the USFWS (US Fish and Wildlife Service) domain. Knowing they take such crimes very seriously, within an hour of purchasing the black caviar, I called USFWS Agent Chuck Richards.

I spent some time filling Chuck in on what had just transpired. I added, "We won't know for sure if it is paddlefish caviar until we get the DNA results, but my gut tells me the suspect is telling the truth since paddlefish caviar isn't worth as much as caviar from our sturgeon."

Chuck asked me to send him my case report when it was updated and asked, "What's the guy's name?"

When I told him the suspect was Liev Smirnov, the phone went silent for several seconds, followed by, "Don't screw with me! Where did you get that name?"

It was apparent I had hit a nerve, and it was equally clear Chuck was well aware of who Smirnov was.

"Sounds like you already know my new supplier," I stated.

It took about five more minutes for me to convince Chuck that I wasn't jerking him around as part of some twisted joke (which I have been known to do). Chuck finally gave in.

"We have had Smirnov and several other Russians under federal investigation for over a year and have spent a lot of time and money on the case, but could never prove the caviar they are harvesting in Oklahoma was being sold, and without sales, we have no federal crime. They seem to be legally harvesting the fish in Oklahoma, but it is illegal under Oklahoma state law to sell the meat or eggs."

So much for sharing intelligence, but obviously, this one was very hush-hush for the Feds.

"Well, it looks like the state guys just made your case for you, but if we are going to continue to buy paddlefish for USFWS, we will have to get an MOU in place pretty damned quick. I can't keep spending the state's money on fish we know are not from Washington."

Chuck said he had some calls to make and would get back to me. I would have loved to have listened in on those conversations.

While Agent Richards and Sgt. Hobbs tried their best to facilitate the creation of an MOU between the two administrations (each had shown the maturity of kindergarteners in a sandbox), Jennifer and I loaded up for a trip to Spokane and northern Idaho.

Jennifer and I called Kent Rousch on the 4th and told him we were in Spokane. Rousch invited us to visit his home to look at his merchandise and introduce ourselves. We pulled up to a gorgeous home right on the beautiful Spokane River. Rousch greeted us at the door and immediately invited us in. He had gone to great lengths to maintain good physical condition and wore clothing that displayed his toned muscles. As we introduced ourselves, I took in the intricate detail of the house. It appeared every piece of the home had been handmade, all with a wildlife theme in mind. The house was tastefully decorated with literally hundreds of wildlife items, including mounted wildlife, wildlife furniture, a sea turtle, feathered decorations, and even a huge woolly mammoth tusk. I also noted an illegal mounted owl and a cup filled with illegal eagle feathers.

Rousch, who was in his early 60s, for some reason, had to go into great detail about his ex-wife and their nasty divorce, adding he now had a young girlfriend. Rousch was one of the biggest name-droppers I had ever met and took a large chunk of our time to list off his many celebrity friends and customers. The three of us talked about wildlife and the wildlife art business, and we told Rousch we were just starting to break into the market. Rousch indicated he had contacts "all over the world" and could acquire about anything we wanted. Jennifer walked around the home, pointing out various items she liked and asking how much he wanted for each piece. Kent would answer with one digit when answering Jennifer's pricing questions, such as "5". While we both knew he didn't mean $5, I could tell Jennifer was as confused as I was, whether he meant $500 or $5,000. When asked for further clarification, we always found there were more zeros after the initial digit than we would have guessed. The prices Rousch quoted us confirmed our suspicions that we would have difficulty affording to do business with him. Since none of the items we saw were within our price range, we told him we would get back in touch with him once our business was up and running.

Jennifer and I left Kent Rousch's house with nothing in hand but knowing this man was a significant player in the illegal wildlife trafficking business. We knew we would return to see if we could begin doing business with this guy, but we would certainly have to start small.

Our next stop required us to cross into Idaho to meet with Leo Ford. We arrived at the Ford home and found it was more in line with the average American household. Mr. and Mrs. Ford met us at the door and enthusiastically invited us in. After the obligatory introductions, they asked us to follow them downstairs. Leo showed us his "trophy room," which consisted of a relatively small bedroom stuffed with wildlife mounts. He went into detail regarding where he had killed each of the various animals and told us he had decided to start selling some of them. One of the items Leo wanted to sell to us was a mounted bighorn sheep. I told Leo that while we were interested in the sheep, I was concerned about keeping the transaction confidential because buying or selling sheep was highly illegal.

Leo replied, "That's fine with me."

Jennifer and I picked out several items, including the bighorn sheep, and negotiated a price of $2,400 for the lot. As we loaded the items in our truck, Leo asked if we would come back sometime and maybe pick up some more of his items for sale. While I told him we might, I knew this was the last time we would ever see the Fords outside a courtroom. Even though Leo had over 50 sets of deer antlers (far more than he could have legally killed in his lifetime), our business was done with him. He would end up having to explain where he got all his wildlife to an Idaho Game Warden at some point in the not-too-distant future.

The next day, on May **5**th, we stopped by our favorite white trash compound at their request. We drove to the wall tent behind the main house, where Kyle Parker met us. He told us to follow him into the tent, where we found Tanya sitting. I saw that the tent now had a nasty-looking bed in it, and it appeared that Kyle and Tanya had fully moved into the tent, claiming it as their new home. Kyle showed us two peace pipes (one with hawk feathers attached) and a walking stick, saying that was all they had. We told them we hadn't sold the pipes and dreamcatchers we had already bought and didn't want any more after this. Jennifer offered them $150 for the three items, which Tanya and Kyle both agreed to. I paid Kyle $150 in cash and loaded the items into our truck.

Kyle told us there were a bunch of elk behind his place now and wanted to know if we were still buying elk and deer meat. I told Kyle that this time of year was a terrible time to kill deer and elk since they are pregnant and have babies.

Kyle said, "The bulls aren't pregnant, and I seen some bulls up there."

I told Kyle and Tanya we strongly advised them to stay away from hunting until fall, but they were adults and could make their own decisions. I warned them that hunting this time of year is very risky and could get them in a lot of trouble. Kyle asked if he got one elk, would we take it since he couldn't eat a whole elk.

I answered, "We probably would take it, but I gotta tell you, it's not a good idea. You are going to get caught."

Kyle told me he wasn't worried about it.

95

As Jennifer and I headed back over the mountains, we talked about Kyle and Tanya.

I told Jennifer, "I have no desire to keep doing business with those two because they are totally out of control, but if we turn them down and end up doing business with other suspects in the same area, how would we explain it to everyone if they compared notes about us? We also needed to keep our most serious suspects freshened until we're ready to end the operation, as no judge on earth will grant a search warrant based on old or stale information."

Jennifer agreed, "I know. I wish there were a way to get them to slow down before they kill everything in Yakima County."

Oh well, nobody said this would be easy.

On the way home, Liev called and asked if I wanted to buy another 5 to 10 pounds of caviar. Knowing my administration wouldn't be too pleased with me spending more on paddlefish eggs, I agreed to buy five more pounds, knowing this would likely lead to future Washington criminal sales. I told Liev I would meet with him sometime on the 10th.

While back at my home on the **10th**, I got a call from Wyatt Wilson telling me my cougar was done.

"Since it doesn't have any paperwork, I would like to get it out of my shop as soon as you can come up and get it," Wyatt said.

I told Wyatt I couldn't pick it up for a week, and he said that was fine.

On the **10th**, on a very dark, cloudy night, I met with Liev Smirnov in the same parking lot as our previous meeting. Liev had the five pounds of black caviar we had agreed upon and handed me some "free samples" of red caviar and canned paddlefish meat. Again, I was on my own, with no backup.

"You try this and see if you like it. If you like, I can sell you a lot more", Liev said in his heavy Russian accent.

Liev went into a little detail regarding how many steelhead and salmon he catches, but wouldn't answer my question on where he caught them, other than to say, "Right around here."

I paid Liev the $500 we had agreed on, and we went our separate ways….or at least I thought we did. As I was driving away, I looked in my rearview mirror and noticed Liev's car was a consistent three car lengths behind me. A couple of changes in my speed and lanes confirmed what I suspected; Liev was following me, but doing a pretty poor job at being discreet. Instead of driving to my real home, I turned towards the condominium complex Jennifer and I had chosen to claim as our address. As I pulled up to the condo complex gate, I noticed Liev kept going past, obviously not wanting me to see him. I was greatly relieved to see Liev's taillights fading into the distance, as I had no way of getting through the security gate into the complex. I had chosen the complex because it had a locked security gate, making it difficult for suspects to drive through the parking lot looking for our truck, but that same gate now prevented me from entering. I waited for Liev to go out of sight before making a hasty U-turn and heading to my real home. At least my Russian friend tried, and because of that, I knew I would have to be always on my toes with him. It was a good reminder of who we were dealing with in this operation.

Liev called me on the **16th** and said he had some fish he wanted me to try, "I will give you a free sample to see if this is something you would like to buy." I told Liev I was tied up until the 18th but could meet him then.

The next day, it was time to pick up my cougar rug from Wyatt Wilson. I drove up to his shop, where I was given a grand tour of what amounted to an old toolshed-turned-taxidermy shop. The shop was filled with waterfowl mounts. Ducks and geese of several species adorned the walls, along with a few big game mounts. Apparently, he preferred to work on birds and actually did a pretty admirable job on the ones I saw. Wyatt showed me my mounted cougar and explained what he had to do to complete it.

As he gave me the tour, he pointed out several ducks telling me, "I'll sell you any duck mount you want for $100 each. It's a serious federal crime to buy or sell ducks, so you have to be careful who you sell them to. It means jail time".

I told Wyatt I would take a couple of ducks and picked out the two I wanted.

After that ice-breaker, he asked, "Are you interested in a mounted bighorn sheep? I know a guy who has one for sale, and I can probably get it to you for around $600".

98

"I have a customer who has been asking me for a bighorn, and I know I can trust him to keep his mouth shut, so yeah, I'm interested," I answered.

Wyatt said he would call to check if it was still available and would let me know. I paid him for the cougar mount and the illegal ducks and said goodbye. I truthfully told Wyatt I was sure we would be doing a lot of business in the future.

After leaving Wyatt's shop, I called Agent Richards and told him what had transpired. Chuck said that between this case and Liev, we had all the ammunition we needed to try to push through an MOU and hoped to hell we could get it done.

I called Sgt. Hobbs, who gave me hope. There was a possibility we might actually get the two administrations to come to an agreement that they could live with. I certainly hoped the MOU came about sooner rather than later, as we were beginning to rack up some pretty decent federal cases.

I called Liev back on the **18**th and told him I could meet him anytime he wanted. Liev told me to meet him in the Silver Lake Costco parking lot at about 12:30. Liev pulled up next to my truck and climbed in at the agreed time, carrying a box. He handed me a vacuum-packed bag of smoked fish and a jar containing what he said was smoked fish in a Russian sauce.

Liev said, "I make both of these products. I sell the smoked fish for $12 per pound and the smoked fish in sauce for $8 per 16 oz. jar. The vacuum-packed fish is sturgeon, and the jar is paddlefish. I also make and sell smoked salmon and steelhead, but I want you to try

99

them to see if these items are something you think you could sell through your business."

I accepted the items and offered to pay him $20, but he said these were free to see if I wanted to buy much more for the business. Liev said he wanted to do a lot of business in the future. He discussed what amounted to money laundering with me, telling me he has a roofing business, which is all cash, so that he can deposit cash under that account. He went on to warn me to always deal in cash only. I thanked Liev and told him we would certainly be doing a lot of business in the future….I hoped that was true.

Two days later, I received a call from a USFWS Agent in Oklahoma. The agent and I had been talking back and forth about Smirnov. Still, this call was on a totally different subject: "Would you be willing to try to contact a suspect in Oklahoma through your business and see if he would be willing to sell you some deer antlers on the skull?"

I agreed to try it, so the agent said he would get me the suspect details and let me take it from there. He said the suspect was a target of Oklahoma Department of Conservation Game Warden Carlos Gomez, and he would certainly appreciate the help. I was told I would get the reports within a week or so.

Ironically, I knew Carlos from several years back when I had gone on an officer exchange to Oklahoma. I had more recently reconnected with Carlos at a game warden conference. I have a lot of respect for him and was more than happy to assist him.

On the last day of the month, I got the information about the Oklahoma antler dealer. His name was Steve Thomas, and I was provided with his eBay listing. I accessed his listing and sent him a message asking for his phone number so I could call him.

Most of May was taken up with relatively minor yet felony-level undercover contacts, but nothing too promising.

CHAPTER 10- JUNE 2011

Day one of June, I got an email from the Oklahoma antler dealer providing me with his phone number. I called Thomas and went through the process of introducing myself and talking about our business. Thomas said he would email me some photos of a few of the largest whitetail deer antler sets he had for sale, along with the prices, but assured me all were attached to the skull (illegal to buy or sell by Oklahoma law). The next day, I received the photos as promised and selected the two I wanted. We agreed to a price of $650, which I paid him via PayPal.

The following morning, Wyatt Wilson called and said he had picked up the bighorn sheep and asked if I could meet him. He said he was coming north from Seattle and was almost to Everett (the city where I was supposed to live). I had about a 1 1/2 hour drive south to get there, so I told him I had to wait for my wife to get home, but would meet him anywhere he wanted in about 2 hours. We agreed to meet in the Everett shopping mall parking lot (I was getting pretty used to parking lot transactions). I met Wilson in the parking lot of the Macy's store at about 2 p.m. As soon as I pulled in, Wilson began to remove the bighorn sheep mount from the back of his black Kia.

I stopped him, "Hold on, Wilson, let's do this in a more private setting. The last thing either of us needs is someone calling this in."

Wilson and I decided to take the deal to my storage unit and conduct the transaction there. Once at my storage unit, he removed the sheep from his car (a car he had just provided me with probable cause to seize for forfeiture) and put it in my storage unit. He said he wanted $550 for the sheep, which I immediately paid him in cash.

Wilson looked around my storage unit and said he was impressed with what I had to offer. He asked where several of the items had come from, and I told him I never gave anyone my suppliers' names.

He saw tremendous potential in me and said, "I'll do more business with you and will do any taxidermy work you want to be done."

I thanked Wilson and assured him we would see each other again soon.

Things were pretty quiet until the **14th,** when Bourey called and said some of his "monkeys" had a couple of sturgeon for sale. Bourey said he wanted $80 each for the fish, and they were fresh. I told him we would take them.

Bourey said his guys were "still out fishing, so they might get some more" and for us to come down the next evening.

Jennifer and I had already agreed to take another trip to Tri-Cities to make a few contacts on the 16th, then to Spokane and Idaho on the 17th, when I called Jennifer and talked over this particular Bourey transaction. We were both pretty sure I could handle buying a couple of fish from Bourey by myself so that we could save Jennifer's monthly undercover allotment.

On the **15th**, I arrived at Bourey's at about 6:30 p.m. As I walked down the driveway, I could hear voices in the backyard, so I continued into the back, where I saw a gathering of about ten Asian men and women sitting and standing around the yard, drinking beer. It was the first time I had been in the backyard, and it was also the first time I realized Bourey had about 40 rooster-fighting chickens in separate cages. Bourey saw me and ran over to greet me.

Bourey asked, "Where is Tina?" I explained she had to work. Bourey began introducing me to everyone, and when he got to one particular man, he said, "This is Dara, one of my very most trusted monkeys. Dara is the one who caught the sturgeon. You can trust him".

Following the introductions, Dara, Bourey, a couple of other Asian males, and I walked into the garage, where Bourey pulled five sturgeon from the freezer.

Bourey declared, "They are fresh. You can see two of them are still alive".

I saw one fish was still alive, one was dead but not yet frozen, and another three were wrapped in plastic and frozen solid.

Dara said he wanted "$80 each for the three smaller fish and $100 each for the two larger fish".

I told Dara and Bourey that we don't sell much sturgeon meat, and I only wanted three of the fish. I selected two of the smaller fish and one larger fish and asked Dara what I owed him.

I paid him $260 in cash, which he counted.

Dara wanted to know how to get in touch with me, and I told him that Bourey knew how. Bourey orchestrated a discussion about keeping quiet.

He warned the whole group, "Everyone knows to keep your mouths shut, and I think you know what will happen if anyone doesn't."

I was pretty sure that the lecture was solely for me, as my gut told me Bourey's "monkeys" knew full well the consequences of running their mouths.

Bourey told Dara, "At first, I was concerned about doing business with Tom because he had just called me out of the blue, but I know they are ok after meeting Tom and his wife."

Dara asked if my wife was Asian, and I told him she was not. Without directly challenging me, Dara asked Bourey why he would do business with me at all if neither my wife nor I were Asian. I told Dara that my wife hunts and fishes and showed him a photo from my wallet of Tina (Jennifer) posing with a dead black bear (a photo we had taken on a previous undercover case). Dara was pleased to see "Tina" posing with a rifle and a dead bear, and said he hunts and killed a 4-point bull elk this last season.

Bourey jumped back in, saying, "I hunt too, but only after the season."

As soon as I cleared the contact, I called my real wife, my work wife, and my Sgt. (in that order) and told everyone I was ok, and

Bourey was disappointed "Tina" wasn't there. Another purchase and an additional suspect with a felony charge. Not bad for a night's work.

The next morning (June **16**th), Jennifer and I headed east with some of the sturgeon (purchased from Dara) in a cooler in the back of our truck. As luck would have it, about an hour into our drive, we got a call from Kyle Parker telling us he had just killed two deer during the night and wanted to sell them. We told Kyle we were heading to Tri-Cities and would swing in. We pulled into the hillbilly heaven at about 11:30 a.m. and around to the wall tent. We were met by Kyle and a new female we hadn't met before (with two young children playing around her). We followed Kyle into the wall tent, where we found Tanya sitting quietly.

Kyle told us, "Me and my buddy Jim went out at 3:30 in the morning and killed two deer, both of them are bucks. That woman you met outside is Jim's wife, Crystal, and those two kids outside are theirs. I'll take you out to check out the bucks. Jim is out in the barn with them now".

I left Jennifer with Tanya and Crystal for a little girl talk while Kyle took me to a horse stall/barn behind one of the trailers. In the shed, I was met by a man who introduced himself to me as Jim Backster. What first struck me about Jim was that he apparently didn't share Kyle's affection for meth, as he had an average build and all of his teeth. Jim was about as everyday "normal" looking as any criminal I had ever dealt with. Jim and Kyle produced the heads of two freshly killed buck deer. Jim asked if I could get anything for the velvet antlers, and I said I could probably sell them.

106

Kyle stated, "We killed the deer up behind my house. We used my truck, but it was so muddy we had to take a bunch of air out of the truck's tires to get in there without getting stuck".

Kyle pointed at a GMC truck parked nearby, telling me that was the truck they had taken hunting (constituting another vehicle for us to forfeit).

I asked where the meat was, and Kyle said he had it in coolers. I followed Kyle and Jim back to a travel trailer behind the wall tent, where Kyle and Jim retrieved two coolers full of deer meat. They carried the coolers (dripping a mixture of blood and melted ice) out to our truck, where we met up with Jennifer and the other "ladies." Kyle put one cooler on the tailgate of our truck while Jim brought the second cooler to my truck. I opened the cooler and saw the meat and bones (quartered) from what appeared to be two separate deer. I took the meat out of each cooler, and Jim and I placed it in bags and weighed the bags while their two small children walked around behind us. One bag weighed just over 50 lbs, while the second weighed just over 40 lbs. Jennifer and I calculated the value of the meat and asked Kyle to come into the tent with us.

Once inside the tent, I got in Kyle's face and told him, "I'm not too damned happy that you brought someone else into this without asking us (of course, we were thrilled), and I told you to stop killing deer and elk, and it's the wrong time of year."

Kyle pleaded, "I didn't just kill them for you guys. We were going to kill them anyway and put some in our freezers."

107

"It's just stupid to kill deer and elk now because we can all get in big trouble. Rifle shots get a lot of attention this time of year", I said.

Kyle said it was no big deal and that people were always shooting. He added that he and Jim had gone out early that morning and that it had only taken two hours to get the job done. He said he was only going to shoot one, "but the second deer wouldn't move after I shot the first one."

We told Kyle and Tanya that we were only interested in feathers this time of year, and we could all get in big trouble for the deer. Kyle said he is working on getting some eagle feathers from a friend.

I told him he had to "Quit killing hawks, too."

Kyle said, "I only kill what I need for my artwork, and I only do artwork so that I can kill." Can't argue with meth logic.

Kyle, Jennifer, and I agreed to $260 for the deer meat, which we paid him in cash.

As Jennifer and I were driving away, with two iced-down deer in our cooler, we discussed the contact. While we had just added a couple of new suspects to our list of persons to be arrested, we both agreed that the group's most disappointing feature was that they had perpetuated the gene pool by breeding. We had just gotten a glimpse of the next generation of poachers.

After leaving Yakima, we headed to Tri-Cities to make our first stop at the Duck Song restaurant. We pulled up to the back door

108

of the restaurant at about 2 p.m. As we exited the vehicle, I noticed some bear gallbladders drying in the sun on a food tray situated on top of a waste container out in the open (so much for being discreet). We were immediately greeted by Liu, who asked what we had, and we said we had fish. Liu followed us to our truck and looked at the sturgeon. With a confused look on her face, Liu said she didn't know what kind of fish they were. We told her they were sturgeon. Liu said she didn't know anything about them and didn't know if they were any good. Sturgeon have to be one of the ugliest fish on earth, and appear to be just what they are, a throwback to the prehistoric ages.

Liu appeared uninterested in the fish but didn't miss a beat by pointing out the second cooler (the cooler containing the deer meat we had just purchased) and asking, "What in there?"

"It is nothing you would be interested in. It's for another customer," I answered.

That seemed only to make Liu more determined to see what was in the cooler, "I want to see," she demanded. I opened the second cooler and showed her the deer meat.

Liu was very interested in the deer meat and asked how much there was. As we looked at the deer meat, an unidentified Asian male (with one eye leaking nasty pus) appeared from the kitchen and stood by Liu. Jennifer told Liu we had two deer, both freshly killed. Liu and Jennifer began negotiations over the price of the deer meat. At one point, Liu returned to the restaurant, leaving Jennifer and me alone. We discussed the fact that the deer meat was evidence against Parker and Backster, and we absolutely had to retain at least representative samples of the meat.

Jennifer decided she would sell no more than two of the eight quarters of deer we had to ensure we kept samples from each of the two deer. Once Liu returned, she and Jennifer agreed on a price for two-quarters of the deer meat while I stood back and watched. While Jennifer and Liu were talking, a blue Ford pickup pulled into the parking lot, and we were all in plain view of the truck's occupant. Liu became very nervous and walked out to see who was in the truck. She returned and said she was very scared and didn't want someone calling the police. We told Liu we would leave and return in a while, and she agreed.

Jennifer and I drove to a parking lot a few blocks away, where we removed two-quarters of deer meat (a front shoulder and a hind quarter) and bagged them. I also cut two steaks from one of the sturgeon, which we agreed to give Liu to try as a free sample. About 20 minutes later, we returned with the deer meat and sturgeon steaks. Jennifer walked in the restaurant's back door, and I followed her a minute or two later. We met with Liu, and Jennifer handed her the bag containing the deer and fish, which Liu inspected. Liu hastily paid Jennifer in cash for the meat, said goodbye, and we were on our way.

As we drove away from this sale, we discussed a concern we both had. Were we (as an agency) creating some substantial liability risk by selling uninspected wild game meats to a restaurant when we knew that meat would likely be prepared and served to customers? Although in this case, the meat had been about as fresh as it could get, what would happen if restaurant customers were to get sick from meat they later determined had come from undercover game wardens? We talked it over, then placed a call to Sgt. Hobbs and posed the question to him, asking if he could get some advice from the Washington Attorney General's Office. Hobbs agreed we had a valid concern and assured us he would pose the question up the chain of command.

The next day, Jennifer and I traveled up to the far northern part of Idaho to meet with George Elkins (who had offered to sell me game meat and eagle feathers back in April 2011). While the scenery was beautiful, we were certainly way back in the woods.

When we arrived, we found George to be a spunky older man who appeared to be only two steps away from the grave. At the time of our visit, George had been given over a month to gather "merchandise" for us, but had not bothered to do so. George told us his main supplier of eagle feathers had failed to show up, but assured us he would come through for us if we gave him another chance. Jennifer and I heard many stories about what a serious wildlife trafficker he was, but in the end, we came out with only a red-tailed hawk and a package of elk pepperoni. We shook hands and told George we would be back in touch, but both later agreed that another trip this far north wouldn't be worth our time, and we would refer what we had to Idaho Fish and Game and let them work on George. We also remarked that George likely didn't have much time left on earth, as he told us he was suffering from some rather significant health issues. Other than seeing some new country, this side trip had been pretty much a bust.

On our way back to western Washington, we stopped by the unlicensed taxidermist in northeastern Washington, where I had

111

delivered an illegal cougar in April. Jennifer had never met the suspect- Jim Bryant, as I had made my first contact solo, so they had to go through the meet and greet. Like all suspects we worked, Bryant took a liking to my "wife" and initiated a conversation about everything from his taxidermy business to his whole life story.

Taking Jennifer along seemed to mean the contacts always lasted longer because people felt compelled to open up to her. In this case, little of what Bryant said was valuable regarding potential criminal charges, so we didn't come out with much more than we went in with, but it certainly put him more at ease.

Once back home, I checked on Jim and Crystal (the husband and wife we had met at the Parker compound). I found Jim was a multiple convicted felon, while it appeared Crystal was an animal control officer. Great, an animal control officer who was involved in commercial poaching. Strange indeed.

In the third week of June, at about 4:30 p.m., Bourey called and said he had some fresh sturgeon coming in at about 7 p.m. He said he would have two for sale, a 54" and a 42". Bourey said his "monkey" wanted $150 for the 54" and $80 for the 42". I told him I was on the way and would want both fish. Without even checking in with Jennifer, I decided to go solo on this one once again. I arrived at Bourey's house at about 7 p.m. and was immediately met, in the driveway, by Bourey and another Asian man (whom I had never met before). Bourey opened the back of a minivan, produced the fish for me (one more car to forfeit), and instructed the man to load the fish in my truck. Once the fish were loaded, he took me to the back porch, where I sat at a picnic table with Bourey, the new suspect, and Dara. I paid Dara $240 in cash for the fish and sat around solving the world's problems, at least as they saw them. Dara said that we could both get in big trouble for selling and buying the fish he caught, and that we could go to jail. I told him I knew that, and I trusted him to keep quiet.

Dara told me, "I never sell my fish to anyone but Bourey, and Bourey has always taken care of selling them for me. The last time I had fish to sell, Bourey told me to call you, but I don't trust anyone, but Bourey trusts you, so that is why I'll sell to you".

The "new" Asian male went into a long dissertation regarding the finer points of various jails and how he always likes to bunk with smaller prisoners when he is in jail, as the smaller men don't take up so much of the jail cell. During the conversation, he took out a pipe, loaded it with marijuana, and pushed it over to me with a lighter, saying, "Smoke!"

"I don't drink or do dope anymore," as I pushed the pipe back.

The man was angered by my response and instantly didn't trust me. As he became more confrontational, I noticed Bourey shake his head "no" to the man, who immediately put the pipe away.

Bourey declared, "Tom doesn't do that anymore; he's a quitter," which everyone laughed at.

I stayed and shot the breeze with my Cambodian "friends" for another 15 minutes or so, then said I better get back home. As I got up to leave, I noticed the new suspect was less than pleased with me, but was smart enough to follow Bourey's lead and shook my hand as I left.

As I drove back home, I realized just how pissed all of Bourey's "monkeys" would be with him when they found out he had foolishly invited two undercover game wardens into their inner circle. Oh well.......they will find they should have stayed with their rule, "Never trust Whitie."

Things were pretty slow for June after the 22nd, so we had a chance to catch up on case reports and return a few business calls. On the **26**th Bourey called and offered more sturgeon, which I turned down, telling him we would need to wait a week or so before we needed any more.

I received the antlers from Thomas in Oklahoma on the **28**th and emailed him to thank him and express my satisfaction with the order. I immediately called Oklahoma game warden Carlos Gomez and told him I had received the antlers, just as promised. I later emailed Carlos some photos and shipped him the antlers.

The following day, I received a call from Sgt. Hobbs, notifying me that the impossible had just happened, WDFW and USFWS had just signed a formal "case-specific" MOU. Both Chief Bjork and the Special Agent in Charge of the USFWS had agreed and put their John Hancock on the memorandum. I was simply stunned. Sgt. Hobbs and Agent Richards had done it. They had pushed past the bureaucratic infighting and had an agreement in place. I thanked them both profusely for their efforts. I can only assume Chief Bjork somehow muzzled DC Cenci or had left him chained to his desk during the meeting with the USFWS boss, but however it happened, I was thrilled.

The Feds (the USFWS) had to put their name on the operation, which I learned was "Operation Wilderness Calls." To me, "Wilderness Calls" sounded like something a game warden would say just before running into the woods with a roll of toilet paper in hand, but who cared…we had federal buy-in. I also learned Agent Steven Andrews (stationed in western WA) would be the "Case Agent" and would be assisted by Agent Richards. I had met Andrews a few times before and thought he was a decent guy with very little fish and wildlife experience. What concern I had regarding Andrews being in a lead role was balanced by Chuck being the assisting agent, and I was pretty sure things would work out just fine. After hearing the news, I called Agent Andrews to set up a meeting where Jennifer and I could bring him up to speed, provide him with our case files, and transfer the hundreds of covert camera videos we had accumulated.

At about 5 p.m. on the **30th**, Bourey called and said he had four or five fresh sturgeon. I told him we would be willing to take a couple and would be at his place at about 7:00 or 7:30 p.m. I truthfully told Bourey I had to call Tina and see if she wanted to come along. I called Jennifer and asked if she wanted to go with me, and she said she was up for it. Jennifer and I arrived at his house at about 7:30 p.m. As we exited the vehicle, we were met by Bourey just in front of the open garage door. As we approached, he reached into a small cooler, grabbed a handful of marijuana buds, and held out his hand for Jennifer to see them.

Bourey announced, "I've gotta feed my monkeys."

He called over an Asian man in his garage and handed him the loose marijuana. The Asian man grinned a semi-toothless smile, said,

115

"Medicine," took the marijuana, and scurried off. Bourey took us into his garage, opened his chest freezer, and took out four sturgeon and a catfish. As he removed the fish from his freezer, three other Asian men joined us in the garage. Bourey said one of the sturgeon was small, but he wanted $150 each for the larger fish. Bourey told us Dara had caught all the fish except for the catfish. Bourey told us if we bought the sturgeon, he would throw in the catfish for free. I told Bourey that we didn't want the catfish. Jennifer and I discussed it and decided to buy the three larger sturgeon. As we talked to Bourey, he ordered one of his men to get "Tina" a beer. The Asian man grabbed two bottles of beer from a box, opened one, and handed it to Jennifer. We agreed to $450 for the three larger sturgeon, which Jennifer paid in cash. He ordered one of his men to load the fish into our truck while we followed him into the backyard.

Once in the backyard, we found another five of Bourey's "monkeys" strewn about. Bourey showed us his fighting cock chickens and explained how they fought. He told us the chickens fight an 18-minute round and that it isn't to the death but "just like a human fight." He said he had been offered thousands of dollars for his best cocks, and stated his best fighters come from Thailand.

Bourey started talking about neighborhood problems, including a black man who had turned him in for illegal burning. Bourey said that when he has a problem like that, he just explains that a 9mm round only costs $0.39, but it will solve the problem. He said he told the black neighbor (who he said was a firefighter) that for $0.39, he would be in the ground, but Bourey might go to jail and might not, but the fireman would be dead forever.

116

Bourey also said, "I like shooting rats, and I have had them in my backyard before. When I shoot rats in my yard, I use a .22 rifle. Once, a rat came over my fence into the backyard, and I shot the rat in the hip. The good thing about a .22 is that it doesn't kill a rat, but he gets the message."

I asked, "I assume we are talking about tall, two-legged rats?" and Bourey confirmed I was correct.

I asked if the guy ever turned him in for shooting him, and Bourey said, "No way," and added that the guy who had come into his yard never said a word to anyone and never returned.

While June 2011 hadn't been too bad for us, I was anxious to take on some new suspects, yet I also realized summertime isn't exactly the best time of year for the wildlife business. I was looking forward to the fall when we could work through our first hunting season. Working with the same suspects repeatedly was necessary, but the excitement was kind of wearing off. It's not that having conversations with multiple Asian gangsters about drugs and shooting "rats" was boring, but it wasn't much of a challenge anymore.

Jennifer summed it up best, "I like working new suspects, as you never know going in whether we are going to be successful or not, or what we will come out with. With the same old suspects, we know going in what we will come out with. It's time for some new blood".

CHAPTER 11- JULY 2011

I had vacation plans with my wife in July for some much-deserved time off. Judy and I had two weeks set aside towards the end of July for a trip to Hawaii, so we knew road trips for Best of the Wild business would be on hold for a couple of weeks. Previously, Jennifer and I had agreed that she would answer the phone and emails while I was gone, but would put off any requests for sales or purchases until I returned.

Day one of the month began with a call from Liev telling me he had just received a bunch of black caviar from Oklahoma and wanted to know how much I wanted.

Liev said, "The caviar is still $100 per pound, and I also have some smoked paddlefish for $12 per pound."

I told Liev I had to make a call and would get back to him. I called Agent Andrews and told him about Liev's offer. Since we now had an MOU in place, the Feds would reimburse WDFW for any money spent on the Oklahoma caviar. He told me to go ahead and buy 20 pounds of caviar and 10 pounds of smoked fish.

Andrews told me the intelligence they had gathered indicated the head of the Russian crime business in Oklahoma was a man named Yuli Ivanov. Andrews asked if it was at all possible to see if I could find out who Liev's connection in Oklahoma was, so they could tie Ivanov into this operation. I said I would do what I could but made no guarantees (wondering how I would bring that up in conversation; So Liev, do you happen to know a guy named Yuli Ivanov?). I called

Liev back with my order and agreed to meet at our original place by the Blockbuster Video store at about 2:30 that afternoon.

I pulled into the Blockbuster parking lot a little after 2:30 and saw Liev sitting on the passenger side of an SUV with a new suspect in the driver's seat. Liev exited the car carrying boxes of caviar and smoked fish, which we placed in the cooler in the back of my truck.

Once Liev and I were sitting in my truck, I began counting out his $2,120 in cash, and I asked, "Who the hell is that in the car with you, and what is he doing here?"

"Don't worry, Tom, that is my boss Yuli. Yuli is from Oklahoma, and he wants to meet you," Liev pleaded.

For once, I was stunned. Moments after hearing Yuli's name for the first time, he was right there! I hid my excitement and asked, "Why should I trust him?"

Liev said I could completely trust Yuli, so I told Liev to get Yuli and put him in my truck. Seconds later, I sat in the front with Liev while the alleged head of Oklahoma's Russian mob sat behind my head in the back seat.

I turned to Yuli and asked, "How do I know you are not a cop?"

His answer was a question back, "How do I know you aren't a cop?"

Once we got past the "Are you a cop phase, we got down to business.

I learned Yuli was leaving on July 25th to head back to Oklahoma, but they would try to get some steelhead in the meantime. Liev asked me if I was interested in steelhead, and I said I would take a lot, and just to call me when he had some. Liev said it would be in the next week or two. Liev, Yuli, and I had a conversation about red caviar, which I told them I didn't personally like, but would be willing to sell. I asked Yuli and Liev when I could get more paddlefish caviar, and Yuli said not until April. Liev said a friend of theirs had been busted with 300 pounds, and I reminded him he had already told me about that. I told the two Russians I was heading to Hawaii at the end of the month, so anything past mid-July would have to wait until I returned. We all shook hands and parted ways. Before heading home, I put the caviar and fish into the evidence freezer, called Andrews, and filled him in. Andrews was thrilled that Yuli Ivanov was now confirmed to be involved.

About a week later, on the 7th, Jennifer and I were driving back from a minor transaction when Liev called, "Tom, I have about 100 pounds of steelhead in my freezer right now. We caught one that weighed 23 pounds. If you want them, I'll sell all of them to you for $5.00 a pound."

I told Liev I wouldn't be able to get to him until the next week, so we agreed to meet on the 13th. Liev must have finally decided to trust me completely, as he provided me with his home address in Lynnwood, WA, and told me just to come to his house. When I got off the phone and told Jennifer what Liev had just said, I could visibly see her getting mad, and I knew why. The only way to get a 100 pounds of steelhead was to snag or net them (both illegal methods of fishing),

120

where the fish gathered at a hatchery intake, and the most likely place to do so locally was in a river in or close to her patrol area.

For an officer who took such great pride in keeping her area as clean as possible, knowing these guys may have been stealing that many fish in her backyard struck a nerve. In the interest of self-preservation, I suppressed the laughter that was welling up inside me and reminded Jennifer that these guys might have gotten away with catching the fish. Still, they were now facing a much more severe penalty for selling those same fish, and "caught is caught." They were going to go down hard in the end. I am not sure my pitch did much to ease her mind, but it was the best I could come up with. Sometimes being driven is a curse, and I thought to myself how some of our less-than-motivated officers wouldn't be phased to find out the bad guys were beating them. Then again, there was always a chance these clowns were getting their fish from a river out of the area, in another officer's area.

On the **8**th, I got a call from Steve Thomas (the antler dealer from Oklahoma). During the long phone conversation, Thomas promised to deliver everything from deer steaks to eagle feathers to bear gallbladder in the coming months. I don't know what caused this sudden interest from this suspect, but at least he sounded promising. I told him to be very careful but to call me if or when he had anything to offer.

At about 11 a.m. on the **13**th, I arrived at Liev's yuppie-looking condominium. Liev met me at the front door. He took me into the garage and opened a small chest freezer, which I saw was chock-full of frozen fish. Liev said he had about 100 pounds of steelhead in the freezer, and they all appeared to be freshly frozen. He boasted he had caught about 100 total fish (which would be somewhere around 600-700 pounds) by snagging them, and the rest of the fish were at his "other place." I told him to be extremely careful not to get arrested since what he was doing was very illegal. Liev said he is careful and "can't be caught." He wanted to know how much I wanted, and I asked if he had weighed them. Liev said he had not weighed them, so I began to weigh the fish. I told him I was only willing to spend $400 total, so I weighed 80 pounds of fish (it appeared there were still about 20 pounds in the freezer). I negotiated with Liev, who said to take all 100 pounds of the fish for $400. He mentioned Yuli would be back in Washington towards the end of September. I paid Liev the $400 in cash and told him to remember I would be in Hawaii for the rest of the month.

That same afternoon, I met with WDFW Officer Worth Allen, who provided me with some valuable information. Officer Allen advised me that an informant had previously unlawfully sold salmon (and possibly other fish) to the Cascade Crest Restaurant in Marblemount, Washington. The informant had told Officer Allen that the owner of the Cascade Crest Restaurant was a man named Mike Craig and that Mike had unlawfully purchased sport-caught fish from him 20 to 30 times. The fish were sold as meals in the restaurant. To determine if the information was correct, I agreed to conduct an undercover contact with Mike when I returned from Hawaii.

For the remainder of July, I relaxed in Hawaii, leaving the Best of the Wild business in Jennifer's hands.

122

CHAPTER 12- AUGUST 2011

Once I returned from Hawaii and was still riding high from watching my wife reel in her first-ever blue marlin (I had yet to catch one despite trying on 48 fishing trips), I was ready to get back in the saddle, but I suspected August would be one of our slowest months.

Our first order of business was to sit down with Agent Andrews and get him up to speed. Jennifer and I spent a couple of hours going over the material, transferring files, and answering questions. Although Andrews was slightly behind the curve, he seemed to catch on quickly. We warned him August would be slow, but September through November should keep us all hopping.

Andrews asked if there was any portion of the operation where we had concerns, and I answered, "Yep, the evidence. Whenever we pick up new evidence, we either drop it off in our locked storage unit or lock it in a holding room for Detective Chris Clarke. His job is to photograph the evidence, tag it, log it in, and ensure any identification (either by DNA or expert witness) is initiated. He is also supposed to keep the case files up to date, so when we are ready to take this operation down, it's all good to go."

Andrews took it all in and asked, "What is your concern?"

"Pretty simple," I answered, "we have been running this operation for eight months now, yet I haven't received a single evidence photo or species identification from Chris. I know the DNA lab is slow, but we should have received some results back by now. I have called Chris several times and asked how it is going, and he says he's on track and up to speed, but my gut tells me we may be behind more than I want to know."

Andrews told us he would talk to the USFWS lab staff and see if they could help out with some of the species identification.

While I was gone, Sgt. Hobbs had run our question about selling game meats to restaurants up the chain of command to the Attorney General's Office, and the official guidance we got back was; if we had evidence the restaurant was already engaged in such activities by buying game meats from real hunters, then we were ok to sell to them as long as we took every effort to make sure the meats we sold were in good condition and safe to eat. The logic was that these restaurants would buy, sell, and serve game meat with or without us, so at least we could provide them with better quality illegal game meat than some druggie off the street. It made sense to me, but I still expected some backlash when we took these places down, and it became public.

I received an e-mail from Brandon Clark on the 3rd, stating, "Hey, man. I haven't got out (of the Army), but if you want to do business, let me know. Thanks "

I replied, "Absolutely! You still in Washington or back east?"

Brandon replied, "I'm still in Washington until January, most likely."

After a couple more e-mails, Clark called me. He asked if I still wanted to buy meat, which I said I did. He said he hadn't gone out yet, but expected to start hunting this week.

I told Brandon, "Man, it's a real bad time of year to hunt, and you better be real careful not to get caught because it would be big trouble."

Brandon said he knew, but that he was going anyway. I told Brandon I only had one other supplier who was deer hunting already, and that while they were adults, I had to warn them it was not a good idea. Brandon said he would have one (deer) within a week. He said he is trying to get out of the military on a full medical disability (for being stupid?), and he thought that would be done by January.

He added, "That would be really sweet because then the military has to pay me for the rest of my life."

Brandon ended the call by saying he would call me when he had one.

It wasn't until the 10th that Jennifer and I took our first road trip for the month. We had received information from Officer Dan Klump about a man named Carl Rogers who lived in Wenatchee, WA, and was selling sport-caught salmon eggs. The suspect was a convicted felon, but was a pretty small-time fish and wildlife trafficker. I had called Rogers and asked about buying some eggs, which he was more than willing to sell, but the quantity he was dealing in was barely worth our while.

The transaction with Rogers was about as fast and straightforward as possible. We met him at his house, talked about how illegal the sale was, took possession of the eggs, paid him, and left. Badda Bing, Badda Boom. Done and on our way home with another criminal charge under our belts.

My Russian buddy Liev called me on the **12**th and said he had more black caviar if I wanted some.

"Sure," I said, "I'll take another 5 pounds."

Liev and I agreed I would come by his house on the 15th to pick up the caviar.

After talking to Liev, I called Sgt. Hobbs, "How would you like to go on your first undercover? Liev has more caviar for me, and since I can't take Jennifer, I thought maybe you would like a chance to get out of the office."

Sgt. Hobbs jumped at the opportunity and asked if his presence might spook Liev.

"I sincerely doubt he will have any problem with it at all. I'll introduce you as my brother-in-law", I answered. With that, we were on.

Three days later, Sgt. Hobbs and I arrived at Liev's house at about 8:15 p.m. Liev produced the caviar for us and said it was the same as we had before and that he and Yuli had made it in Oklahoma. I asked when Yuli was going to be back in Washington, and Liev said that he would be at Liev's house around "9 (am) tomorrow (the 16th)", but first, he had to stop in Portland and unload some product. He said Yuli would stay for about a month. Although Yuli was now out of black caviar, he was bringing some gold for me ("Gold caviar" is just a color variation of regular caviar). I asked Liev about red caviar, and he said he didn't have any but had some steelhead caviar. He produced a jar of caviar that he identified as steelhead caviar and gave it to me for free to try.

As we were loading the caviar in my truck, I asked Liev if he had been steelhead fishing anymore. He said he hadn't, but his father had just gone over to the upper Columbia River (Rufus Woods) and had caught 80 rainbow trout in 2 days. Liev said the limit on trout is 2 per day, and his dad fishes from 6 p.m. till midnight because everybody leaves by then. He said his dad "hot" smoked his fish, and they are not good that way, and he and Yuli are going to build a smoker to cold smoke fish at Liev's father's house. Liev said his father was going back over to fish the next week. He went on to tell us that after dark, nobody stays because of all the bears.

I asked Liev where his father lives, and he said: "He lives very close."

With that, Sgt. Hobbs had completed his first undercover, and I am not sure Liev had given him a second glance.

On the **22nd,** I called Officer Worth Allen and told him it was about time for me to take a shot at the Cascade Crest Restaurant. I asked Worth if he could pick up a few salmon from one of the local fish hatcheries for me to take. Worth said that would not be a problem, and we agreed to meet on the morning of the 24th.

On the morning of the **24th**, I met with Officer Allen, who provided me with five hatchery sockeye salmon. I placed the salmon in a cooler of ice in the back of my pickup and proceeded to Marblemount. I arrived at the Cascade Crest Restaurant at about 10:30, only to find that they didn't open until noon. I left the area,

127

returned at about 11:20, and knocked on the kitchen door. I was met by a small adult woman who identified herself as "Candy," the owner's wife. I introduced myself and told Candy I had some fresh salmon for sale. Candy said that Mike makes all the purchasing decisions, and I would have to check with him. Candy hooked me up with Mike on the phone. I told Mike I was at the Cascade Crest Restaurant and had five fresh sockeye salmon to sell, and his wife had told me to call him.

Mike asked who I was and how much I wanted for the five fish (I told him I would be thrilled to get $50), and he told me to "hang tight there…I'll be right down".

At about noon, Mike arrived, and I introduced myself, provided him with my business card and flyer, and said I had some fresh sockeye salmon for sale. Mike asked to see them, so I opened the cooler and showed him the fish.

Mike asked, "Who caught the fish and where?" I told him a friend of mine had caught them, but I wouldn't tell him who or where.

I told Mike I was only interested in the eggs, as I used them to make caviar and just wanted to get rid of the fish.

Mike said, "This is totally illegal for me," and I told him that I knew it was, and it was illegal for me to sell them, too.

Mike wanted to know why I had come to him, and I said that my friend had suggested I try the Cascade Crest Restaurant, but had never actually sold to him before.

Mike said, "I have bought fish like this, but only with a few trusted locals."

128

I answered, "I know you don't know me, but you have to decide whether you want to trust me or not. I don't want to get in trouble any more than you do."

Mike said that he needed to talk to his wife. Mike took my business card and flyer into the restaurant and was gone for a few long minutes, probably checking out our website. A few minutes later, Mike returned and said he wanted to "be honest with me." Mike said he could buy marinated sockeye salmon fillets from Costco, cheaper than I was trying to get for the whole salmon. Mike said that with the fillets, he doesn't have to worry about the head and body; he can just cook them. Mike said his wife likes fish, and he should do this business at his house, and had to get the fish out of there fast. Mike offered me $30 for all five fish, which I agreed to. He reached into his pocket to get the money out, but told me he had to get change. About a minute later, Mike returned with $30 cash, which he handed me in exchange for the salmon. Mike said he would look more at what else I had to offer through my business and might get back to me. With that, I headed down the road with another restaurateur in the bag.

I spoke with Liev on the **23rd**, when he said he had some premium "Gold" caviar for sale. I told him I would swing by the next day and pick some up.

The next day, at about 2 p.m., I met with Liev at his house. He produced three different types of smoked fish, feeding me samples of smoked "rainbow trout" and two different styles of smoked "steelhead." Liev said that his father had caught the rainbow trout on Indian property on the upper Columbia and that the limit on these trout

129

is 2 per day, so his father took his grandson and several other people to cover the fish.

Liev said, "My father just finished smoking 40 pounds of trout and will soon have 40 pounds more done. The fish average about ¾ of a pound to 1 pound each. A friend of my father's has been cited, seven tickets, by the Indian police for going over the limit on trout, and they charged $200 per fish over the limit."

He said the steelhead were some that he and Yuli had caught last year and added Yuli had taken the steelhead back to Oklahoma, smoked it, packaged it, and brought it back. He stated that all the fish sell for $10 per pound, and they sell a lot of it. I tasted the smoked rainbow, told him I liked it, and would get back to him on how much we wanted. He produced two jars of "gold" caviar from his kitchen freezer and handed them to me. I asked Liev how much I owed him for the 2 pounds of gold Caviar, and he said $200. I paid him $200 in cash, which he quickly shoved in his pocket. I asked Liev how much he wanted for the three packages of smoked fish he had given me, and he said they were free samples to see if I wanted more at $10 per pound. Liev asked me if I was interested in red caviar, made from salmon eggs, as he and Yuli were going to get a bunch of salmon. I told him to call me when he had it, and we would talk.

At about 5 p.m. on the **25th**, I received a call from Mike Craig (at the Cascade Crest Restaurant). He said he was very pleased with the salmon I had sold to him and would serve it in his restaurant. Mike asked if/when I would get more salmon, and I told him it would depend on my suppliers but that it would probably be soon. Mike said I should call him first when I get more, and he would even meet me

130

somewhere to buy it. He also asked about game meat, particularly bear, deer, and elk meat. Mike said a while back, he got some bear meat, and that people even called in and reserved bear meat burgers, as it was so popular (the sale of any bear meat is illegal in Washington, no matter the source). He asked where I got my game meat.

I replied, "Legally, I need to buy it from out-of-state game farms, and it has to be boneless and individually packaged."

He said he buys about $500-$600 of game meat a year, mostly from a game farm meat supplier in Portland. I told him we buy some from Idaho, some from Michigan, and some from other sources. I told Mike we sometimes buy meat from hunters, including Indians, but we are very careful about who we buy and sell from because it is highly illegal.

I told him, "We have one Indian supplier who provides us with high-quality meat, as good as any from game farms, but it's not legal and not certified."

He proclaimed the USDA stamp just means, "Some government idiot put a stamp on it, and it doesn't mean anything."

Mike said to call him anytime I get a good deal on game meat, as he would be interested. He made it crystal clear he didn't care where the meat came from or if it was legal or not, as long as he could get it at a reasonable price. I had spoken with him for over 13 minutes, during which time he made it clear that he was not concerned with the laws and was interested in doing more business, including the sale/purchase of wild game meat.

131

I got a call from Bourey on the **28**th, and he said, "I will start to get elk and deer in mid-September and need to know how much you want?"

I told him, "We could probably use around three elk."

He asked about deer too, and I told him to call us when he gets the meat in.

Bourey said, "I never know just how many elk they are going to bring me. I have had as many as 14 elk delivered at once, and I will have a bunch of elk in mid to late September. Is there a chance you will need more than three?"

I told him we only needed three at that time, but to call us when he gets some in.

Three days after speaking with Bourey, I called Liev and told him I would like to buy 30 pounds of smoked trout and 10 pounds of warm smoked steelhead.

Liev answered, "My father had 170 pounds of rainbow trout that he had smoked up, but he only had 70 pounds left because it was selling fast. You should probably buy more, as it would all be gone soon."

I agreed to buy 40 pounds of rainbow and 10 pounds of steelhead at $10 per pound. Liev told me he would be home the next day and told me to come to his house at 9 am.

For a slow month, August had been relatively productive.

CHAPTER 13- SEPTEMBER 2011

September started with the same old thing: a trip to Liev's house. At least this time, I was going to pick up smoked fish from Washington, so we would finally have some Washington criminal charges out of this case if all went according to the plan.

On the 1st, at about 9:00 a.m., I arrived at Liev's house. Liev's young son answered the door and went to fetch him for me.

Liev came downstairs, rubbing his eyes, and announced, "I have been asleep and haven't picked up the fish yet."

While I sat patiently watching Liev make coffee, I was surprised to see Yuli coming down the stairs. As I talked to the men, I noticed Yuli's shirt riding up in the back and strongly suspected the shirt was stuck on a concealed pistol tucked in the back of his pants. I don't know why Yuli felt he needed a pistol to deal with me, but perhaps it was either habit or he had other plans for the remainder of the day.

Liev and Yuli had a private conversation, which I could not hear, then Liev told me, "Yuli will go get the fish." After Yuli was gone, Liev told me, "Yuli will be here two more weeks and will be smoking more fish."

After about a ½ hour, Yuli returned carrying a large black plastic bag, which he handed to me. I opened the bag and saw multiple vacuum-packed bags of smoked fish. I examined the fish, which appeared to be smoked steelhead and rainbow trout. I weighed the smoked fish and found they had provided me with about 54 pounds in total. I paid Liev $500 in cash, which he counted and shoved into his pocket. The three of us talked about caviar, in particular red caviar. Yuli said the commercially available red caviar is terrible, and his product is far superior.

He told me, "We can package it any way you want, in any size container, so you can put your label on it."

I told Yuli we would probably want it packaged in 16-oz jars, and he said that would be easy. Yuli said he has a lot of caviar customers, and they always come back for more (what a salesman). He said that he has contacts all the way to Florida and mentioned a friend in Florida who gets all kinds of things, including lobster. He said his Florida friend had recently harvested $170 worth of lobster while SCUBA diving in just one hour. Yuli said it's hard work, but his friend does well, and that he spears fish too. Yuli, Liev, and I agreed to stay in touch, and I left with my Washington fish evidence safely tucked away in my cooler.

At about 9 p.m. on September 6[th,] Brandon Clark called and told me he had a deer he wanted to sell. He said he had already killed it and wanted to know when I could come to get it. I told him I was on the coast, on a fishing trip, and could not pick up the deer until the next afternoon/evening. I asked Brandon if it was skinned, and he said it was not. I told him he had to skin it and get it cooling right away. I asked if he had a garage, and he said he did, so I told him to skin it, put it in the garage, and ice it down so it wouldn't spoil. After hanging up, Brandon sent me several text messages asking about caring for the meat. For a hardcore poacher, he had no idea how to handle animals once he had killed them.

Officer Julie Cook (whom I refer to as "Tres"- my third wife) and I were working together on an unrelated case on the 7th when I called Brandon and told him I was on my way. We agreed to meet near the Samurai Restaurant in Spanaway at about 5:45. Officer Cook and I arrived at the Samurai Restaurant at about 6:00. We called Brandon, and he said that he would be there in a minute or two and that when he pulled in, we should follow him. Shortly after that, Brandon pulled into the Samurai Restaurant, driving a red Ford pickup (another nice truck to forfeit).

Brandon exited the vehicle, dressed in military fatigues, told us to follow him, and said, "When I pull into a driveway, you should just back your truck up to my truck to transfer the deer." We followed Brandon to a driveway a couple of blocks behind the restaurant. As we pulled into the driveway, I saw another white male dressed in military fatigues washing blood off the driveway with a garden hose. I approached Brandon's truck and saw that he had an un-skinned buck black-tailed deer in the bed of his truck (so much for following my instructions regarding the proper care of the meat). We slid the deer from Brandon's truck to mine, and Officer Cook handed him $300 in cash without waiting for any price negotiation. We shook hands again, and Brandon said he would call.

Brandon sent me a text message as we drove away, asking me to tell him "how it turns out when you cut it."

I responded by saying, "I will. From now on, please call me before you go out to make sure we are around before you kill something."

Brandon replied, "Sounds good."

I had decided it was time to revisit the Cascade Crest Restaurant on the 9th. I picked up a dozen steelhead from a WDFW hatchery and headed towards Marblemount. On the way, I called Mike Craig on his cell phone, told him I had some fresh steelhead, and asked if he was interested. Mike asked how many I had, and I told him twelve. Mike said he was not sure he could use that many, but bring them to the restaurant, and he would see.

I arrived at the Cascade Crest Restaurant and was greeted by Mike.

I started the conversation with, "Well, I wasn't visited by any game wardens after our last transaction, so I guess we were good to do business."

Quick to his defense, Mike said, "It wouldn't make any sense for me to say anything because if you got in trouble, so would I."

I felt much better knowing he wouldn't turn me into the game wardens. Mike looked over the steelhead and asked how much I wanted for them and where they came from. I told him the fish were not Indian caught and were not caught in nets, but were caught by a guy I know and trust. I told him the guy was a drug-using "dirtbag" and poached the fish, but he takes good care of them and can keep his mouth shut. Mike and I negotiated a price of $8 per fish (they were only about 3 to 4 pounds per fish). I told Mike I didn't particularly like doing business in his restaurant parking lot because what we were doing was illegal, and he had too many customers around. Mike said the laws were "bullshit" and didn't make sense, and he wasn't worried about it. Mike said he wanted to talk to his chef and see if he (the chef) could handle all twelve steelhead.

The next thing I knew, we were joined by the chef, who inspected the fish and told Mike that he could handle all twelve easily, and they agreed the fish would be served in the restaurant as a special. They said the guys they usually buy fish from don't keep them in such good condition and are just looking for beer/drug money (nice to know). Mike told me he would take all twelve steelhead and would get me a check for the $96. Mike told the chef not to say anything to anybody about where they got the fish. As the chef bagged the steelhead, Mike returned to the restaurant to get his checkbook.

Mike paid me with a check and began to talk about elk meat, "I pay about $12 per pound for elk tenderloins and $6 per pound for burger when I buy the legal game-farmed meat."

I told him that once the weather cooled down, I would be buying elk and deer from hunters (mostly Indians). Mike said he likes the tenderloins cut into 6-8oz. pieces, but if I sold him the whole tenderloin, he could cut it up. He said he likes the burgers made into patties with a piece of wax paper between each burger. I told him that when I had elk, I would do what I could and would call him.

After leaving Mike Craig in my rearview mirror, I drove to the bank (where I had my undercover bank account), copied the check, deposited it, and took an equal amount of cash out to place into the evidence system. I would let Mike sit until I could get him some elk meat cut to his specifications.

For the next few days of September, we took care of several smaller illegal transactions, including an agreement to purchase another bighorn sheep from a WA Department of Corrections employee.

Liev called me on the **20**th and said he had plenty of red caviar ready to sell. He said he had made the caviar himself, which was made from king salmon eggs, from salmon caught in this area.

He said, "I have about fifty 16 oz jars for sale, and I only want $25 per jar. Tom, you are the first person I called, but this caviar will go quickly, and I have already had several people asking for it."

I told him to hold 15 jars for me, and I would get them on the 22nd.

I received a strange text message on September **21**st, stating, "Seen ur add I have a stuufed (LOL) follw deer."

Fallow deer are not native to the US and do not fall under Washington's definition of "Wildlife"; therefore, we have no jurisdiction over them. According to our laws, buying or selling them is not a crime.

I replied, "Email me pics and price."

The texter replied, "I can't via email my email is brokedn (I don't rember my pass) I can send via text message?"

I replied simply, "Yep."

I received the response, "I also have some other elk antlers with skulls but idk if my bf wants to sell maybe for the right price but I don't have ne pics on my phone."

I replied, "So, how much and where are you located?"

The mystery texter identified herself as Janet Rodgers and said she lives in S. Yakima, WA. After finally getting sick of texting (I am too old for that form of communication), I called the number, and a man answered. The man identified himself as Dusty and said Janet was his girlfriend. Dusty and I spoke about his elk antlers, and I told him I would be interested in looking at all of them, but I was only interested in trophy antlers. Dusty also provided me with their address, so after getting off the phone, I jumped on my WDFW computer and did some checking. After a few minutes, I found Dusty to be Dusty Hilton, and I also learned Mr. Hilton had a very impressive string of game violations (not to mention the remainder of his criminal history).

Although these two S. Yakima residents hadn't offered anything illegal, I checked a little further. The WDFW officer in that area is a very good friend of mine, who has lived there his entire life, so I placed a call to Officer Skip Caton. Without telling Skip why I was asking, I asked him to tell me what he knew about Hilton. In a nutshell, Skip's analysis was that Hilton was a major poacher who always seemed to be in the wrong place at the wrong time when it came to critters dropping. Skip was excited to hear Hilton was in our sights.

After speaking with Officer Caton, I re-contacted Hilton and his girlfriend and told them I wanted to purchase the fallow deer mount. I agreed to mail them a deposit check and said my wife and I would come over on October 3rd to pick it up. Once we met Hilton face-to-face, I hoped he might suggest we deal in more than just an exotic mounted deer, but time would tell.

It was time to pick up some red caviar from Liev once the **22nd** rolled around. I asked Sgt. Hobbs, if he wanted to tag along, and again, he was more than happy to get out of the headquarters office (affectionately called the Puzzle Palace by field officers). Sgt. Hobbs had no way of knowing it then, but this would be the last undercover contact of his career. Sgt. Hobbs and I arrived at Liev's house at about 1 p.m. and were greeted at the door by Liev, who enthusiastically invited us inside. He asked us if we would like to sample his red caviar, and I reluctantly said I would. As I choked down the raw salmon eggs, I tried not to vomit the tasty treat all over his white carpet. I found the only thing worse than eating the red caviar was trying to look pleased with it while I told Liev, "This is awesome!"

I noticed Liev was dragging a bit and asked if he was sick or just tired.

Liev explained, "I am tired and not feeling well because I have been standing in water fishing all night."

I asked Liev how much I owed him for the caviar, and he said $25 per jar, but that the jars had a little more than a pound in them. He took us into his garage, where he opened a small chest freezer and removed a box containing 12 jars of caviar and three loose jars of caviar, which he handed me, and I paid him $375 in cash. After the usual pleasantries, we departed to take the caviar to Detective Clarke for the routine evidence procedures.

The next day, at about 7 p.m., I received a phone call from Dusty Hilton. He began by asking if we were interested in elk antlers. I asked Dusty if he knew how to score antlers, and he said he didn't. I told him it would be best to wait until we could look at their antlers first-hand to see what they had. Dusty asked what else we were interested in, and I told him we don't make too much money on antlers and make most of our money on unique items (such as cougar, bear, feathers, skulls, teeth) and meat.

Dusty proceeded to ask the all-important question, "Where do you get your game meat?" I said the law only allows us to buy deer and elk meat from licensed game farms.

He responded, "I hunt with some Indian friends, and they get a lot of deer and elk. Would you be interested in buying meat that way?"

I told Dusty, "We have bought some game meat from hunters, but we don't do business like that with people we don't know."

I tried to steer Dusty back to antlers, but he kept asking about us buying elk meat.

I finally asked him, "Are you a Game Warden?"

He quickly responded, "I fucking hate Game Wardens."

Dusty said that because he hunts with Indians, the Game Wardens are always after him.

He told me, "One time, the Game Wardens even stripped my clothes off and kept them because they had some blood on them."

I asked him if Indians could sell elk meat (I knew they couldn't), and he said they couldn't and that "It's illegal for them too."

I told him we had "Bought from Yakima Indians before, but we can talk about elk meat in person. I don't want to talk more about it until we meet."

By the time I hung up, I knew we would do some serious business with this boy.

Three days later, on the **26^{th,}** I received an email from a Jane Mathews stating, "I have a full-size couger im looking to sell."

The email came with three photos of a mounted cougar attached.

I responded, "Where are you located, and how much do you want?"

I received a response, "im in milton freewater Oregon. Im looking to get 3,000 obo."

I replied, "Let me talk to my wife this afternoon, and we will get back to you."

I emailed back and asked for the phone number to contact the person, and I received a reply which included the phone number for the Mathews'. The sale of a cougar in Oregon is illegal, and even offering the cat for sale constitutes a crime.

Later that day, I called the phone number, and a man answered and identified himself as Dan Mathews and said he was Jane's husband.

I told Dan, "$3,000 is way too much for a mounted Cougar. We normally don't pay over $1,500. Would you settle for $2,000?"

Dan agreed to the $2,000 figure almost immediately (I guess I should have started with $1,000).

I asked, "Do you have any paperwork or tags for the cougar?"

Dan said they did not. Dan said he had looked at our website and thought we could do business on other things, especially whitetail deer. Dan said he has a lot of deer around his place, but that he hates Oregon's hunting regulations because he is forced to hunt archery. After moving to Oregon, Dan said that he had continued to buy WA resident hunting licenses because the seasons are better in Washington (it is a crime for a non-resident to purchase resident licenses). Dan provided me with his address in Milton-Freewater, OR, and I told him that my wife and I would be over to the Tri-Cities/Walla Walla area on October 3rd and 4th and that we would try to meet with them.

After speaking with Dan Mathews on the phone, I called the supervisor of the Oregon State Police fish and wildlife investigations unit and filled her in. She said she believed they would like us to pursue the case, but they simply didn't have the money to go through with the sale. I told her that I would check with my supervisors and USFWS to see if they could pay for it.

I received a phone call from Dusty Hilton on the **28**th at about 6 p.m.

He began by saying, "I have been talking to an Indian friend of mine, and he said it is legal for Indians to sell elk and deer meat."

I told Dusty that whether it is legal for them to sell, it is still illegal for non-Indians to buy the deer and elk, and Dusty said, "I know that."

Dusty said, "We are going hunting this Saturday, so do you want to buy an elk, and how much would you pay?"

I answered, "OK, we will try buying one from you and see how it goes. We normally pay $600 per elk, but it has to be gutted, skinned, and in good condition."

Dusty asked if my wife and I would like to have dinner at his house (with him and his girlfriend), and I said we had a lot of stops to make and probably wouldn't have the time (I had a visual image of his house and the food we would be served). We agreed to meet on Monday, October 3rd.

After getting off the phone with Hilton, I called Jennifer and Sgt. Hobbs then brought them up to speed. Both were pretty excited that we had another potential elk trafficker on the hook, but we all knew it wasn't a sure thing yet.

CHAPTER 14- OCTOBER 2011

October 2011 didn't start so well. On the **1ˢᵗ**, Sgt. Hobbs broke the news to us that Detective Clarke had been pulled off of Operation CODY and would no longer be able to assist in any fashion. The Deputy Chief had decided to reassign Clarke to geoduck investigations, leaving nobody to handle our evidence or case files. The real irony was that there were no solid geoduck cases to work on, no suspects, and no real intelligence. Still, the DC's mouth had written checks he couldn't cash when he had promised the legislature and the Department of Natural Resources (Washington's forestry agency, which owns the geoduck grounds) that WDFW would produce some major geoduck cases if we received additional funding. We got the funding, but had not yet produced a single significant case. Of course, being the suspicious type I am, I believed this was a matter of trying to ensure our operation failed rather than any valid need for additional help on geoduck. Either way, it left us high and dry.

I asked Hobbs the obvious question, "What are we supposed to do with our evidence now? The defense attorneys will crucify us if Jennifer and I seize, then process our evidence every step of the way."

Hobbs said he understood and would work on getting things fixed, but I had my doubts he would get us any help.

On the morning of the **2ⁿᵈ**, Dusty Hilton called and said, "We killed an elk yesterday. We had to cut it up to get it off the mountain, but it's all here."

I told Hilton my wife and I would be at his place the following day, but would call before we arrived.

145

The next morning, Jennifer and I took another trip east. Our first stop took us back to the Parker compound. We arrived around 1 p.m. and found Tanya in a camper behind the house. Tanya came out and told us that she and Kyle had a big fight the night before because she had learned Kyle was having an affair with another woman (trouble in paradise). Tanya said she was probably going to have to move out. After a much too-long conversation about their personal issues, Tanya showed us an Indian-style pipe and asked if we wanted to buy it. She said she also had a dreamcatcher in the house to sell.

She took us into the main house and showed us a dreamcatcher which was decorated with eagle and hawk feathers, and said, "I want to get $30 for the pipe and $175 for the dreamcatcher."

Jennifer paid Tanya $205 in cash, collected the items, and put them in our truck. We got out of there as quickly as we could.

Our next stop was Dusty Hilton's house to pick up the fallow deer mount and hopefully buy a whole elk carcass. When we were getting close, we called and told him where we were, and Hilton said he might get to his house a few minutes after we did and asked us to wait for him. Jennifer and I arrived at the Hilton "palace" at about 3:30 p.m. and were not a bit surprised by the appearance of the place. While it wasn't as bad as the Parker compound, it was an older, beat-up mobile home littered with junk and several sets of fresh and older deer and elk antlers. Rodgers met us at the door, told us that Hilton should be there soon, and invited us inside. Once inside, Rodgers showed us the fallow deer mount and told us to follow her to the bathroom, "where the elk is." At this point in my career, I had seen a lot of things, but this was the first time I had seen an entire quartered elk covered with bags of ice in a bathtub. After looking over the bathtub elk, Rodgers told us Hilton was willing to sell any of the elk antlers out front and told me to go look at them. I went back outside and began rough-scoring the antlers.

At about 3:40, Hilton raced up the driveway in a beat-to-hell Dodge pickup. Hilton erupted out of the truck and charged at me like a sow grizzly defending her cubs. Hilton was an intimidating man who had the look of a seasoned fighter. I wouldn't stand much of a chance against him if this came to blows, but I had no idea why he appeared so angry.

Hilton's charge stopped a few feet short of me, and he yelled, "Are you a fucking game warden? This is just the kinda shit a game warden would do to set someone up."

I calmly answered, "No, I'm not a game warden. Remember that you called us and offered elk, not the other way around. If anyone is trying to set someone up, it would be you setting us up."

Dusty tipped his head slightly to the side, trying to process what I had just said. I could see he was physically relaxing a little more every second while his brain mulled it over.

Hilton spoke in a much more relaxed tone, "I'm not a game warden either."

To make sure none of us were game wardens, I pointed at Jennifer and asked Hilton, "What about her? Maybe she's a game warden."

With a laugh, Hilton said, "Yeah, right, she really looks like a game warden."

With that, we were all cool.

Hilton and I looked at the antlers he had outside. He told me the fresh set was from the bull they had killed last Saturday. He asked me what I was willing to pay for the antlers, and I said that none of the bulls were what I considered to be trophy class, and I was only interested in 340" or larger bulls, and none of his bulls would score much above 300. I told him I would pay $10 per pound for antlers that size, but would still only take one set. I weighed out one set of antlers, which weighed ~24 pounds. I told him that I would consider them to be 20 pounds since they still had the skull attached, so I would give him $200 for that set.

Hilton told us they had shot the bull on Saturday, up "off the pass" from about 50 feet away. He said it was right next to the road when they first saw it, but the rifle had misfired four times, and by then, it had run a long way into the woods.

I asked if he had been shooting a muzzleloader, and he said: "No, a regular rifle" (elk hunting was only open to muzzleloader hunters at the time).

Because the elk had died so far from the road, he said they had to cut it up to get it off the mountain. Hilton said he would bring out the elk meat and began carrying out the bags of elk meat from the house. Hilton pointed out that one of the bags contained the backstraps and tenderloins. Hilton packed out five bags of elk meat, and Rodgers packed out one bag, which I loaded into our cooler in the truck.

148

Inside the house, they provided us with the fallow deer mount, and Hilton showed us a set of large mule deer antlers. He said he could get us "All the deer and elk meat you want" and asked us to call him if we wanted more, and I told him that would be fine if he could keep his mouth shut.

Hilton said, "I don't know you, and you don't know me."

He said he would try to get the elk out whole from then on. I took $1,000 in cash out and put the money into three separate piles on the coffee table. I made two $200 piles and one $600 pile. I told Hilton and Rodgers that one $200 pile was for the fallow deer, one $200 pile was for the elk antlers, and the $600 pile was for the elk meat (the only thing which was illegal for them to sell). They accepted the money, and Hilton walked us outside.

Hilton said he had seen that we sell sturgeon on our website and asked where we get the fish. I told him we don't sell a lot of sturgeon meat and that caviar is our big moneymaker, and I said we mostly get our fish from Indians.

Hilton said, "Caviar. That's only from the big ones, right?"

I told him he was right, and the sturgeon, which have eggs, are usually over the legal size limit. He said that he catches them all the time and throws out the eggs. Hilton said from now on, he would keep the eggs from all of the illegal oversized sturgeon he catches and call us.

As Jennifer and I drove away, reviewing the covert videos, we kicked around the contact with Hilton. We both theorized Hilton had told his buddies about these strangers coming over to buy an elk and had been warned to watch out for a "game warden sting." If that had been the case, it would explain the whole "Are you a game warden," as there is a widely held urban myth that says undercover cops have to tell you the truth (that they are cops) when asked, but it didn't explain the whole bluff charge he had performed on me. Perhaps he had expected us to draw our non-existent Tasers or call for our non-existent backup at that point, or maybe he was just blessed with the same charming personality traits as our deputy chief.

Our last stop of the night was at the Bush residence in the Tri-Cities area. Bush was the Department of Corrections employee who had offered to sell me a bighorn sheep head and a set of mule deer antlers. When we were about 30 minutes away, I called and was told by Bush that his wife was the only one home, but she would get us the items. This was another quick in-and-out contact, as we realized the wife had no clue about wildlife. We paid her, took the sheep and deer, and left. We both agreed that while Mrs. Bush had participated in the sale, we wouldn't charge her at all, but would undoubtedly charge her husband.

The next morning, we made a few minor transactions in the Tri-Cities area and headed into Oregon to meet with the Mathews and check out their mounted cougar. The Mathews home was a refreshing change from our last several contacts, as it was well-kept and clean. Mr. and Mrs. Mathews were pleasant people with professional jobs who both wanted to make a little extra money illegally trafficking in wildlife. After introductions, we all sat and had a friendly chat before being led upstairs to look at the mounted cougar.

150

Several times during our conversation, I threw out just how illegal it was to sell the cat, even asking if they were sure they wanted to go through with the deal. Undeterred, they both said they still wanted to sell us the cougar. Additionally, Mr. Mathews asked us if we were interested in buying whole white-tailed deer carcasses or bears. Until then, I am sure both Jennifer and I hoped we could get them to see the errors of their ways and back out of the deal. It was game on once they started talking about killing multiple deer and bears every year and offering them for sale! We didn't have to bluff them about taking the cougar with us that day (as Oregon hadn't fully blessed our transaction in their state yet), we didn't have any room left in our truck for such a large mount. We paid the Mathews a deposit for the cat and told them we would be back to pick it up on our next trip. We thanked the Mathews' and headed back to Washington while I called Oregon State Police to fill them in on our contact details (they were livid with us for going into Oregon without full authorization and backup).

On our way back home, I thought of a tip I had received from Officer Mike Johnson. Officer Johnson had told me about a Chinese restaurant in Walla Walla, Washington, which was rumored to buy deer and elk from hunters. Mike had never confirmed the intelligence but found nothing to indicate it wasn't true. Since we had to drive through Walla Walla, I thought we might swing into the Pacific Pride Restaurant and give our sales pitch. We pulled into the restaurant's parking lot at about 10:30 a.m., unsure if we'd find anyone there that early. We saw an employee in the parking lot and quickly introduced ourselves before he could scurry back inside. Jennifer asked if he was the manager, and the employee said he was not, and the manager might not be in that whole day. The employee said we could talk to the cook, but he would have to translate for us. The employee took us into the restaurant through the back door, where we met with the cook. We told both employees we sold meats and fish and asked if they would be interested. The employees took our business card and brochure and said they would pass them on to the manager.

After leaving the Pacific Pride Restaurant, Jennifer called Sgt. Hobbs to tell him our duties were done and we were on our way home.

While I was eavesdropping on their conversation, I heard Jennifer tell Sgt. Hobbs, "I guess our 100% streak on this trip is over. The restaurant we just stopped at, in Walla Walla, didn't bite."

When Jennifer got off the phone, I turned to her and said, "Our 100% streak is over? It ain't over yet. The manager wasn't in."

I knew it was still a long shot, but since the intel said the restaurant dealt in game meats, there was still a chance we might score on this one. As luck would have it, the wise old man would be right (this one time). I only wish we had placed a bet on it.

On the **6th**, I was home typing away on reports when my undercover phone rang. The caller had a heavy Asian accent and identified himself as "Jin." "Jin" said he had received our business card from a restaurant in Walla Walla (ka-ching!). I asked which restaurant, and "Jin" replied, "Pacific Pride."

"Jin" asked why we had stopped at the Pacific Pride, and I told him, "A person we do business with had told us the Pacific Pride might be interested in deer or elk."

152

Jin answered, "The owner is a friend of mine, and they have taken deer which had been given to them, but I am interested for myself."

He said he was interested in deer and elk and wanted to know how much we had and the prices. I told him it would depend on what he wanted and how much, but in bulk, we could go as low as $6-8 per pound on some steaks and $3-4 per pound on the burger.

Jin said he was most interested in elk and deer bones with meat on them, and he also wanted meat, but he was Chinese, and "Chinese people don't like steak."

I told Jin I could give him bones for free, but I wasn't going to drive all the way there for free, so next time I was in the area, I would give him the bones.

Jin responded, "I saw on your business card that you deal in bears."

He asked what bear parts we had. I told him we could get about anything, but warned him that the only legal parts to buy and sell were the hides or mounted bears. I asked what he wanted.

Jin asked me, "What do you have?"

I knew damned well what he was getting at, but I couldn't help but have a little fun with this guy, so I started listing off every body part I could think of, from head to tail, except for the gallbladder.

Whenever I listed off another body part (i.e., teeth), Jin would answer, "No. What else you have?"

153

After going over about 20 body parts, when I finally said gallbladder, Jin asked, "You have gallbladder? Gallbladder is what I really want." (Gee, what a shock, I never would have guessed it).

Why he didn't just ask about gallbladder from the start, I didn't understand. Maybe he thought he couldn't be charged with buying them if he didn't say it first.

I told him the sale of bear gallbladder was very illegal and that I had to be careful about who I was dealing with.

Jin ignored me and asked, "How many gallbladders do you have?"

To which I asked, "How many do you want?"

God, this was fun, kinda like teasing your younger brother by holding candy just out of his reach. Jin was growing impatient and asked again how many gallbladders we had, and I just said, "We have more than you can handle."

Jin proved he was serious, "I doubt that. I'll take all you have."

I asked how much he was willing to pay for a gallbladder, and he said he didn't want to talk about it over the phone. We agreed I would call him back when I knew the date(s) I would be back in Walla Walla.

After speaking with Jin, I looked up his phone number on our reverse phone directory database and found it was a cellular phone that returned to Jin Dong from Walla Walla. I looked up Dong on WDFW records and driver's licenses and found he had only a Michigan

154

driver's license, which was very strange but also very promising. I jumped on the phone and called Jennifer to rub it in, using my normal mature adult means of communication, "I was right, and you were wrong." I marked the date on my calendar, knowing this would probably be the last time that happened. I asked Jennifer what her schedule looked like for the week of the 10th and learned she didn't have time to make another trip east, so I decided to make this trip alone.

I called Jin on the **10th**, told him I was coming over to Walla Walla the next day (the 11th), and asked if he wanted to meet with me. He asked if I was bringing anything, and I told him I was bringing "What we talked about."

Jin said he would be around all day, and I should call when I knew what time I would be there. With the plans set, I went about preparing three bear gallbladders for the potential sale. This had been Detective Clarke's duty, but it fell to me now that he was on geoduck assignment. I took three gallbladders from our stockpile, turned in by permit hunters, photographed each of them, took a DNA sample, and bagged them so I could tell for sure which gall I sold (if I sold less than all three). I also gathered some elk meat and fresh elk bones from our stock.

The next afternoon at about 3:00 p.m., I called Jin and told him I was about an hour away from Walla Walla. We agreed to meet in the parking lot of the Pacific Pride in about an hour. I pulled into the Pacific Pride and noticed an Asian male waiting behind the business. The man approached me at my vehicle and introduced himself as Jin.

He asked, "Did you bring the gall?" and I asked him, "Are you a Police Officer?" He said he was not, opened his wallet, and showed me his Michigan driver's license. I asked why he was showing me his driver's license, and he said he was doing it so I would know he was not the police (I guess they don't have police in Michigan?). Jin said we should both know who we were dealing with, so I showed Jin my driver's license. Jin was in his mid-30s, unintimidating, clean-cut, with the look of a businessman. He spoke with a soft, calm voice. All in all, this man didn't seem "the type" to be engaged in such criminal activity, but then, you can't always judge a book by its cover.

Jin came and sat in my truck, where I told him, "Selling and buying gall is illegal, and you have to understand we could all go to prison."

Jin said he knew that, but "It isn't illegal to have them, just to buy or sell them."

I opened the back of the truck to show him the elk meat and gallbladder, and he went right to the gallbladder. He spread the gallbladder out on the tailgate of my truck and asked me if he could take a photo of them, which I told him was fine. Jin took a photo with his iPhone and asked me if he could send the photo to his brother in Seattle.

He asked what the price was for the gallbladder, and I produced two hand-written sheets of paper showing the weights of the gall (in grams) and the prices. One set of prices was $1.25 per gram, and the other was $1.00 per gram. I told Jin that if they bought in bulk,

I would sell them at $1.00 per gram (the gall weighed 105, 195, and 309 grams).

Jin said, "I have always bought gall by the gall and have never paid by weight."

I told him that some galls are very large, while others are small, so they should be priced by weight (It was a new policy of mine, which I was trying out for the first time on Jin). He asked where I got the gall, and I said I wouldn't tell him, but they came from hunters.

Jin asked, "Why do you have them?"

I told him, "My wife and I used to sell to a man in Seattle, but he has moved to California, and we can't find him anymore. We have been stockpiling them ever since, thinking we would find someone who wanted them someday."

Jin asked what we had charged the man in Seattle for them, and I told him we had charged him the same price we were now offering him.

He said he needed to call his brother, who would have to check with their Hong Kong people immediately and get back to us. I told him that it was fine if he didn't tell his brother too much about me. He assured me he wouldn't tell his brother who I was. He got on his phone and had a long conversation in Chinese.

When he got off the phone, he said, "When we buy the gall, we will get the gall from you, then we put the cash on a table for you to pick up, so we don't hand you the cash." (Wow, that was sure sneaky, I'm sure that trick would keep a trafficker out of jail).

He added, "Sometimes we get the gall and pay for something else so that we didn't pay for the gallbladder."

I had a bottle of Pepsi and asked, "So I give you the gall and a bottle of Pepsi, and you will pay me hundreds of dollars for this Pepsi, right?"

Jin said that was how they did it. He asked me if my wife was Asian, and I said she was not.

He asked, "Why would she be involved with bear gallbladder?"

I showed him the same photo of Jennifer posing with a dead bear. Jin said, "Oh, she hunts bear. I understand".

At one point, a vehicle drove by us, and Jin told me to put the gallbladder away "quickly, so we didn't get caught." He said he liked the Walla Walla area because there was good hunting and not-so-good game wardens.

Jin also asked if I had any dried gallbladder, and I said I did not. He explained that they usually bought dried gall and wanted to know why I didn't dry them.

I truthfully replied, "Everyone else we dealt with before wanted them either fresh or frozen, and it takes a long time to dry them."

Jin explained, "My brother is coordinating the deal with our people in Hong Kong, and they normally want them dried because they weigh less, take up less room, and stay good (not perishable). All the gall are going to Hong Kong, and Hong Kong has to approve the sale. How many gall do you have?"

I told him I wasn't sure, but I knew we had at least a dozen, and I would have to check and let him know.

Jin said he is from Michigan but moved to Washington a few years ago. He went on to say he stays and works in Walla Walla, Portland, and Seattle.

He told me, "My brother owns and operates an indoor marijuana growing equipment business in Seattle that is doing very well with the medicinal marijuana laws. My brother lives in the Beacon Hill area of Seattle."

I asked him what kind of elk meat he wanted, and he said he wasn't interested in elk meat and had only said that to get me over there. Jin said he was only interested in bear gallbladder; again, I wasn't shocked.

After several phone calls, my Chinese friend told me Hong Kong was concerned about how they would know that the gallbladder was really from a bear. I told him I had no way of proving it to him, and I showed him a gallbladder up close and found a bear hair on the gall to show him.

Jin said, "Hong Kong needs to know for sure, and I want the gall checked out first. We need to test a gall with chemicals to make sure it is good. I'll buy the small gallbladder as a sample and will get it tested, and if Hong Kong is satisfied, they will buy all of them."

Jin asked me if I had a "bear penis." I had never had anyone ask for a bear penis before and didn't have any.

He said, "They want penis too. See if you can get them too." I resisted the overwhelming urge to be a smartass at this point.

I told him I had one whole frozen bear but didn't know if it had a penis, as it might be a female.

Jin asked, "Can you sell me the whole bear?" and I told him I would.

He asked if I had a whole cougar. I said we didn't, but I could probably come up with one if he gave me enough time. Jin said he needed the whole cat and didn't want it cut up. He paid me $50 in cash for the smallest bear gallbladder and wanted a bag to put it in, as it was in a clear zip-lock bag, so people couldn't see what it was. I bagged the gall in a white plastic kitchen garbage bag, bagged up several elk bones (with some meat attached), and gave those to him as a gift. Jin kept the gallbladder on his person but put the elk bones in a utility trailer full of cardboard behind the restaurant. I shook hands with my new buddy and told him, "I look forward to doing business with you."

At 5:00 p.m., Jin called and asked me how long I would be in the area. I told him I was on the way to Tri-Cities, where I would spend the night, and I was going home the next day. He asked me to tell him how many gallbladders I had as soon as possible.

At 11:00 p.m. (while sitting in USFWS Special Agent Chuck Richards' house), Jin called and said, "The bear gallbladder was fine, and they want all you have. The people in Hong Kong said to go

160

ahead with the deal, and they agreed to your prices. They want your promise that from now on, you will only sell bear gallbladder to them and not to anyone else. It is way safer to only deal with very few people." Jin went on, "They have been buying a lot of bear gallbladder from a guy in Montana, but they want to also do business with you. They have to get the gall to Hong Kong and like to have 20 or more when they ship them."

He asked if I could dry them, and I said I could or they could. Jin said he would be in Seattle on Saturday (the 15th) and would like to meet with us to get the gallbladder. I told him, "That's the opening day of hunting season, and my wife and I were going hunting," but he insisted on Saturday. I agreed to talk to my wife and get back to him. I knew full well both my real wife, Judy, and my work wife, Jennifer, would be pissed about missing the opening day of hunting season, Jennifer because she would want to write a slew of tickets, and Judy because she wanted to go hunting; but duty called.

When Jin called back, I was staying the night at Chuck's house, discussing the case. I've got to admit, while I always have a great time with our friends (the Richards), it wasn't half as much fun since I had quit drinking; however, that one call from Jin energized us both.

"Holy shit, this guy is big-time!" Chuck exclaimed as I told him the news.

It was pretty cool to be standing next to the federal agent, who would be working the federal aspects of the case, when I received the call that we were in business with an international trafficker.

161

On my way home on the **12th**, I got a call from Tanya Franklin, "I have something for you when you are over this way next time."

I told her I was driving home from Tri-Cities and would stop by. Tanya said she and Kyle had broken up again, but she would be in the camper at the Parker property. I arrived at the camper at about 10:00 a.m. and met Tanya at the camper. She showed me another dreamcatcher made with what she said were "red-tail hawk feathers." She said she wanted $220 for the dreamcatcher. I paid her cash, took the dreamcatcher, and got the hell out of there before I had to hear more of the Kyle and Tanya saga. It's not that I didn't care, but I really didn't care!

Later that same day, I called Jin and said we had 18 bear gallbladders in our freezer with a total weight of 3,415 grams.

I said, "Since you are buying in bulk, let's round it off to $3,400 for all of them."

Jin answered, "We will take all of them."

Two days later, the day before we were supposed to meet Jin in Seattle, he sent me a text message stating there was a problem with Hong Kong. He apologized and said the deal was off, at least for now. I was pissed and told him so, but it appeared his hands were tied. We could now only sit and wait to see if the problem got ironed out while wondering what was happening. A lot of things went through my head. Did they figure out who we are? Did Jin make a deal without the final approval from the upper-level people in Hong Kong? Only time would tell. Nonetheless, I was more than a little deflated.

On the **17th,** I received an email from a Spokane area man offering us an illegal mountain goat for sale.

I called the man and went through my usual spiel, "Do you know how illegal this is?" and agreed to buy it. I told him we would pick it up from him the next time we were in Spokane.

Later that same day (the **17th**), Kyle Parker called and said, "Last night, I missed a huge buck. I shot at it from my horse a bunch of times, but missed. I do have one deer and a bird for you guys. Can you come over and pick them up tomorrow?" Kyle said, "We are camped in the Yakima River Canyon at the Big Pine Campground in space #23."

I told Kyle I would be there around noon. Well, it appeared the lovebirds were back together.

I arrived at the Parker/Franklin campsite at about 1 p.m. the next afternoon. The dynamic duo were camped in a BLM campground, surrounded by fishermen and other campers. I knocked on the camper door and was surprised to find only Tanya.

Tanya said, "Kyle is still out cleaning the deer he just shot. Come on in. I just need to change clothes."

It didn't take me 2 seconds to turn down the offer to watch Tanya change clothes, "I think I'll wait outside."

About a ½ hour later, I saw Kyle drive up in a blue Ford flatbed pickup with a deer wrapped in a plastic tarp in the truck bed. I also noticed a larger mule deer head in the back of the truck.

163

Kyle said, "That big deer was the one I had shot a couple of days ago, and it is gone. I already sold it."

He carried the small deer carcass (wrapped in a plastic tarp) to the back of my truck, where I inspected it.

The carcass was tiny, and I asked Kyle if it was a fawn, and he said, "It's a small spike."

I told Kyle I was happy to see he had at least wiped the milk off its lips when he had cleaned it. Kyle took a spike deer head out of the right-front seat of the truck and showed it to me.

He pointed across the river and said he had killed the deer "up there a few hours ago. It's still warm."

I could feel the deer was still warm to the touch and appeared to be very fresh. I asked Kyle if the area was a 3-point minimum area (deer must have at least three antler points on one side to be legal), and he said it was, but Packwood was open to spike deer hunting, and he could claim he got it there.

The deer was untagged and didn't have any paperwork with it. Kyle said his dad and the whole family were also camped in the same campground, and they had ridden their horses across the river and hunted on the opposite side. He said he had missed a huge buck in the same area.

Kyle said, "I also have a new dreamcatcher for you," and walked over to an adjacent camp and returned with the dreamcatcher (decorated with eagle feathers).

He produced a dead owl, which he said was in perfect condition. I asked Kyle how much he wanted for the three items, and he said: "Make me an offer."

I offered $50 for the deer, $100 for the owl, and $150 for the dreamcatcher, which he agreed to. I paid him $300 in cash (three $100 bills).

Once I had paid Kyle, I told him, "I don't want any more meat, feathers, birds, or artwork. From now on, I will not buy anything else from you unless I call and ask for it!"

Kyle looked hurt and confused and asked what the problem was.

"You are running around in a public campground, killing illegal deer and owls. Then you walk right through the camps carrying a dreamcatcher full of eagle feathers, and you don't know what the problem is? You are out of control, and we are not going down with you when you get caught!"

Kyle quietly answered, "OK, I will wait to hear from you guys.", and asked, "Where is Tina? I like dealing with her more."

I responded, "She's at home, but I assure you she totally agrees with me on this. Don't think you can call her and get a different answer."

With that, I left the campground and headed home, all the while wondering if anyone in the camp had turned this activity into WDFW. If not, I would be very disappointed in humanity. Within a week, I realized nobody had turned in any of the illegal activities; kind of a sad statement.

That afternoon (the **18**th), I spoke with Sgt. Hobbs, who told me the DC had significant concerns with the Jin Dong case. Hobbs had been briefing Cenci weekly on our operation. During one of those briefings, Cenci had determined we had crossed the line "into entrapment" with Jin and was leaning towards shutting down the entire operation.

I asked Hobbs, "Has he read the reports? This is as far from entrapment as we can get. Jin got our business card from a friend at the Pacific Pride Restaurant and called us. He asked about buying bear parts. It was his idea, and Jin acknowledged that he knew it was very illegal to traffic in bear parts. This whole transaction is all on Jin. This is as clean as it gets", adding, "Is Cenci really that stupid, or is this just an excuse to shut us down because he hates me and can't stand the fact we are producing a lot of great wildlife trafficking cases?"

Hobbs answered, "I explained all that to the DC and got him to at least allow me to get a legal opinion from a prosecutor."

"Great," I said, "Call Charlie Silverman in San Juan County. He is the sharpest prosecutor I have ever dealt with and can keep his mouth shut (no risk of our operation leaking)."

I provided Hobbs with Silverman's phone number, knowing what Silverman's answer would be. A few hours later, Hobbs called back and said Silverman had seen no problems at all with how we were handling the case, a fact which Hobbs passed on to the DC in the presence of Chief Bjork. That news killed Cenci's hopes of prematurely shutting us down, at least for now, but I knew more attacks would be coming.

Those few people involved in Operation Cody were often confused by the deputy chief's flagrant attacks on our operation. Why would the second-in-command of a fish and wildlife law enforcement program try to destroy an operation that was efficiently apprehending the very criminals the program was expected to catch? I, too, wondered the same thing and couldn't understand it. I knew Cenci hated me to the core, and the feelings were definitely mutual. It had also been made clear, by Cenci's own words, that he didn't feel working big game (deer, elk, and bear) cases was worthy of our time, money, and attention. All that being said, it confused us as to why he would work so hard to cut us off at the knees.

Cenci's behavior became crystal clear once a friend told me to look up Narcissistic Personality Disorder (NPD). While I am certainly not a trained psychiatrist, it did make sense once I read about NPD. It is my opinion that Cenci's behaviors and attitudes fit the symptoms of Narcissistic Personality Disorder right down the list. While reading about NPD was enlightening, it did nothing to relieve the attacks on our operation. I hoped we could keep operating through December 2012, as the chief had promised.

I received a text message from Dusty Hilton on the **23**rd, telling me he would have another whole elk for us on the 31st, asking if we wanted it. I confirmed it would work well for us, and we would be there.

167

We had taken the elk we bought from Dusty Hilton on October 3rd to a meat cutter to have it prepared the way Mike Craig had wanted, and on the 24th, I picked up the cut and wrapped elk meat. I called Mike Craig and told him what I had, and he asked me to come to his house.

Three days later, I arrived at Craig's house at about 11:30 a.m. and met Mike at his front door. I took him out to my truck, where I produced the elk meat for him to inspect. Mike said that since the elk burger was not made into patties, it wasn't as valuable to him, but he expressed interest in the steaks. He asked what the steaks weighed, and I weighed them for him (about 8 oz each).

He said, "Those are the perfect size for serving my restaurant customers, but the burger is not what I wanted since I usually sell elk in burger patties only."

As we began negotiating prices for the meat, Mike said the meat wasn't as valuable as the USDA meat he buys from legal businesses since "We are both taking a lot of risk."

I told him the elk was not killed by Indians but rather by "a white hunter, I know." After negotiation, we agreed on $225 for all of the meat. He asked me to put the meat on the ground next to his garage door, which I did, while he went inside to write me a check. He came back out and handed me a check for $225.

He said, "If this is good, I will want more. I liked the fish you sold to me and will take more fish anytime, too."

As I drove home, I wondered how many restaurants were selling illegal, uninspected game meats to their customers.

On the **26ᵗʰ,** I received an email from Mr. and Mrs. May in the Spokane area, offering "all kinds of wildlife items." The email had a phone number, which I immediately called. Steve May answered, and after a long conversation, he offered to sell us everything from eagle feathers to bear parts. I put him on the "to-do" list and told him we would call him before we headed to the Spokane area next time.

Just as October was winding to an end, Jin called, "I want to go ahead and buy four of the gallbladders. Hong Kong has still not approved the purchase, but I don't want to lose them, so I will invest my own money and buy them. When can you bring them over?"

I told Jin we were coming to Tri-Cities on the 31ˢᵗ and could meet him then. He agreed to meet us in Pasco around 5 pm.

Jennifer and I headed to Tri-Cities, on the **31ˢᵗ**, with four bear gallbladders on dry ice in a cooler. We stopped first in Yakima, bought an eagle feather fan from a new supplier, and headed to Hilton's house. We arrived at the Rodgers/Hilton house at about 1 pm, and I saw him standing by an open storage shed and noticed an elk (cut in two parts) hanging inside the shed. We met with Dusty and talked about his hunting.

Dusty told us, "Me and some friends killed the elk on Saturday. We had seven guys hunting with six guns and ran into twelve elk, but only dropped that one. It's an adult cow elk. We first saw the elk standing in the road, but after shooting it, the elk ran down into a deep draw."

169

He talked about deer hunting and said, "We filled four tags on opening day."

The elk carcass was covered with yellowjackets, and due to my severe bee allergy, I handed Jennifer my EpiPen (for bee sting allergies) in case I was stung. The three of us loaded the elk into our truck and paid him $600 cash. As we left, Jennifer and I discussed how Dusty seemed much more relaxed with us now.

Our next stop was back at the Duck Song Restaurant. We arrived at about 3:15 p.m. and walked in the back door. In a cooler, we had four whole frozen Chinese pheasants (which I had harvested by hunting recreationally).

Jennifer did all the talking with the restaurant employees, and eventually, Tou Liu came out and followed us to our truck and asked, "What do you have this time?"

Jennifer showed her the pheasant, and Liu said she wanted to purchase them. Jennifer and Liu negotiated a price for all four birds, and Liu paid Jennifer in cash while the kitchen staff took the pheasant back into the restaurant's kitchen. Once the transaction was completed, I asked Jennifer if she wanted to go in and have dinner in the Duck Song, but for some odd reason, she wasn't too keen on my suggestion. We settled for Arby's.

I called Jin and told him my wife and I were in Tri-Cities, and we had four gallbladders. Jin said that was good and we could meet in Tri-Cities, but he wouldn't be there until about 5 p.m. and asked us to wait for him. After more text messages and phone calls, it was agreed we would meet him by the Hillsboro Street truck stop (in Pasco) at about 5 p.m. Jennifer and I parked behind the Subway and Burger King restaurants amid several semis and waited. At about 5:30, I observed Jin drive up to our location in a beautiful white Lexus hatchback SUV. He met us, and I introduced him to my "wife."

Jin asked to look at the gallbladder, which I showed him in the back of our truck.

He asked, "How old are the bears the gall came from?"

I told him there was no way to know and that sometimes old big bears have small galls, and sometimes they have large galls, and that the size and age don't always correspond to the gall size. He wanted to know how much we wanted for all four gallbladders, and I told him I would add up their weight.

Jin told us, "I want to buy these and ship them to China, to get approval from China to buy more."

I added the weight of the gall and told him they added up to 815 grams, so I wanted $600. I said we usually sell them for $1.00 per gram, but I would give him a break now to assure China we have a good product.

Jin told us, "I only brought $500, and I am taking a large gamble buying these since I haven't received approval from China yet. When I buy these, I will get stuck with them if China doesn't approve the purchase."

Jennifer and I discussed it and agreed to sell all four galls for $500.

171

"Once China approves the first gall I bought from you, they will probably send me the money to buy all of them, but it takes time for me to dry them before shipping," Jin told us.

I told him we would be willing to buy a dehydrator to dry the gall in advance. Jin said the gall couldn't be dried in a dehydrator as China would reject them.

He said, "The gall must be wind-dried and can't even be dried in the sun. The sun or a dehydrator will crack the gall, and the bile will be lost or damaged. I dry the gall by hanging them in the wind under the porch of my house. That way, the gall stays moist but tough. China is very picky about the gall, and they can tell if they are not prepared properly."

Jin looked at the elk in our truck and asked how much we had paid. I told him that we had paid $600, to which he replied, "You paid too much. You can get them cheaper" (I guess he had more elk connections than we did).

I told Jin, if he knew someone who could sell them cheaper, to have that person get in touch with us.

He asked for a bag to put the gall in, and I provided him with a white plastic kitchen bag. Jin placed the bag of gall in the rear of his Lexus (which meant we could now seize the Lexus for forfeiture) and retrieved the cash.

As he came to me with the cash, he said, "Now, what can you sell me?"

I knew Jin wanted me to give him something of no value, so he could say that item was what he had paid $500 for. I retrieved a set of domestic cow jawbones from the back of our truck and handed them to him. Jin asked what they were, and I said I didn't know, but I thought they were domestic cow jawbones. He paid us $500 "for the cow jawbones."

Finally, Jin added, "I still want the whole frozen bear and will get back to you about it."

I told him we had picked up a couple of new bear gallbladders from hunters in the last week and that we may be able to get more. We all shook hands and went our separate ways.

As Jennifer and I drove to Spokane, she began writing down everything said and done during the contacts so we could complete detailed reports when we returned.

As she was writing (while I was driving), Jennifer asked me, "What was the license number on his Lexus?"

I realized I had done it again. I had not paid attention to the essential details every cop on earth observes. I hadn't even bothered to memorize the car's license number!

"Shit," I said, "I have no idea. If I even looked at the license plate, it sure didn't stick in my memory. Is this a test for me, or do you really not know it either?"

Jennifer, who had always been the detail-oriented one of the two of us, responded, "I didn't get it. Every time I looked at the car, the back of the car was open so that I couldn't see the plate number."

173

I felt like an idiot. I have trained many new officers, and I would consistently climb all over them if they had missed such an important and obvious detail as the vehicle's license number.

Finally, it dawned on me, "Since he backed his car up to the rear of our truck, we should be able to see the license number on the covert video camera mounted in the back of our truck," I announced.

We hooked the covert camera DVR to a laptop computer and slowly scanned each frame until we finally got the license number. Saved by the bell, or rather, saved by the camera.

Our last stop of this very long day was at the May residence on the outskirts of Spokane. The house was nice and tidy on the outside, but we found it cluttered with wildlife and Native American items once inside. The Mays were both heavy-set, in their late 50s, and looked like "normal folks." Mrs. May told us she has "Indian blood" (from a midwestern tribe) and identified with Indian culture. She explained that she had owned and operated a Native American store in Spokane for many years and had recently closed her store, leaving her with a vast inventory of Indian wildlife items. The Mays overwhelmed us with a steady parade of wildlife items, many of them illegal even to possess. Jennifer and I selected a few items from the vast array, including bear paws and claws (black bear and polar bear), bear skulls, an eagle feather headdress, and a cougar paw bag. All four of us discussed the illegality of the transaction and promised to keep it confidential. After an hour or so, we were ready to pay up and get out.

Mrs. May said since it is illegal to buy or sell several of the items we were getting, she suggested, "Why don't you just make it a donation to me?"

We "donated" $810 in cash to the Mays, gathered our items, and dragged our tired butts out the door.

As we had anticipated, October had been very productive. We had added around 20 new suspects to our list and had made some significant trafficking cases. We had also survived another attack from the deputy chief and were still in business. On the downside, we had evidence piling up to the ceiling and were swamped with case files. I knew November would be equally busy but hoped we would receive some badly needed help soon, thereby getting a little breathing room.

CHAPTER 15- NOVEMBER 2011

Knowing November would be another busy month for Best of the Wild, I asked Sgt. Hobbs to see if we could get a couple of paid overtime days pre-approved for the two Thanksgiving holiday days. He said he would ask; right after I told him, I was pretty sure I knew the answer.

On November 2nd, Jin Dong called me.

He said, "I found a buyer for the whole frozen bear. I need it to be quartered up with the paws left attached. I want photos of you removing the gallbladder so I can send the photos to China to prove the gall came from a bear."

I told him it would take a couple of days to thaw out the bear, but that I would do so.

Jin added, "I also want to buy a whole fresh bear."

I stated I didn't have the entire bear, only the gallbladder, as the hunters didn't want to take out the whole bear.

I told him, "Bears are very heavy, and most of the time, the hunters just remove the gall and leave the carcass behind."

He responded, "Try to come up with another whole bear because I have buyers."

I assured him I would do what I could, but couldn't promise a bear.

Sometimes I just get lucky. The **3ʳᵈ** was one of those days. On the 3ʳᵈ, Officer Julie Cook called me and said she had a live bear in a culvert trap, and the bear had to be euthanized because it was a repeat offender. I asked her to keep the bear alive so I could kill and gut it the following day. After getting off the phone with Julie, I called Jin and left him a message that I had a whole fresh bear.

At about 11:30, Jin called back and said, "I want it!"

I told him the bear only weighed about 70 pounds, and I would sell it to him for around $200 to $300.

He replied, "I want the bear gutted, photos taken of the gallbladder in the bear, and I want to buy the entire bear, especially the paws and gallbladder. I don't care about the hair (hide), but I want the remainder of the bear."

I told him I could bring over both bears on Tuesday, as I had to wait for the frozen bear to thaw, adding that "I still want $600 for the large bear."

On the **4ᵗʰ**, Jin called back and said he wanted the whole small bear and wondered if we still had it. Jennifer and I met with Officer Cook at Cook's rural home, where I shot and killed the small black bear and removed the gallbladder while Officer Cook took photos of me doing so (with my undercover cell phone). I sent the photos to Jin by text. At 8:00 pm, I called Jin and told him I would be over with the small bear the next morning. He told me he also wanted another bear gallbladder when I came over. I agreed to bring both the bear and another gallbladder and said I wanted $250 for the whole bear. He agreed to my terms without debate.

177

After speaking to Jin on the phone and arranging to meet in Walla Walla, I arrived at the Pacific Pride at about 11:00 a.m. I saw him standing in the restaurant parking lot and noticed his white Lexus parked nearby. He told me to park up against the restaurant wall, where he met me. He asked where my "wife" was, and I explained she didn't want to get out of bed that early. He followed me to the back of my truck, where he inspected both the bear and the two gallbladders (one from the whole small bear and the second from our stockpile). Jin expressed dissatisfaction with the quality of the bear gallbladder and said he would probably throw one of them away. He said he "wanted one of the galls for another person." He walked around the restaurant's corner, towards the back door, and returned with another Asian male subject wearing a white kitchen apron. The new Asian male was soon joined by an Asian female wearing a black apron (common to wait staff). The man took the gallbladder and walked back into the restaurant with it. Jin retrieved an empty cooler from his Lexus, and together we loaded the whole small bear into his cooler. As we loaded the bear into Jin's cooler, he said, "Nice fish." I assume he was referring to what I should say the bear was if anyone asked.

We both carried the bear to his Lexus and placed it in the back of the car. Jin got into the right-front seat of my truck without asking or telling me, and I joined him. In the truck, he said he was concerned about the bear not being cut up, as he had to take it to Portland to sell to several different people. He also said that the gallbladders were no good and showed me a photo on his iPhone of four gallbladders, saying they were the gall he had purchased from my wife and me.

178

"One of those galls leaked out the bile and was no good anymore, and one other still had some liver attached to it," he whined.

I told Jin that from now on, we would bring him better product and let him sort through the gallbladders to pick the ones he wanted.

I added, "I want $250 for the whole bear, but I'll discount the other gallbladder to $50."

Jin opened his wallet, showed me that he only had $250, and asked if he could owe me the other $50. I agreed to let him owe me the $50 for the other gallbladder and accepted $250 cash in payment for the whole small bear. I cleared the contact at about 11:30 a.m. Apparently, someone was pretty picky about the gallbladder, as he had never said a word before this day about the quality of our gall.

I received a text message from Jin on the 7th, stating, "The small one has 40lb meat and bone".

I responded by saying I had talked it over with Tina, and since we wanted to do long-term business and have him satisfied, we would waive the $50 he owed us and would let him pick through the gallbladders from then on, only to take the ones he wanted. I also told him we would reduce the price of the large frozen bear to $400.

Additionally, I told Jin, "We picked up four more gallbladders this week, and we were ready with them if China ever approves the purchase."

He replied, "I am drying four (gallbladders) in my garage, and in one more week, I will send two small galls to China for them to look at."

I had to have a little fun and texted Jin, stating, "My wife wants your Lexus."

Jin wrote back, "I have one for sell, 04 RX 330 74k miles. Retail stealer sold for 22000 in Seattle. How much you want to pay for?"

I responded by saying we didn't need another payment, and he should not mention it to my wife. Jin had no way of knowing that soon my "wife" would be driving his car away for good. A little while later, Jin called and asked me if I had any whole bear other than the large frozen one, as he had buyers who wanted a whole bear, and I told him I didn't have any.

He asked me, "What about the bear you just got the new gallbladder from?"

I said, "Those gallbladders had just been cut out of the bear, and the carcasses had been left in the woods."

He asked me if I could come up with another whole bear, and I told him I would put the word out for one, but there were no promises. I said I would let him know if I got one and would give him the first option on any bear we got, but it was almost the end of the season for bears. I found myself trying to explain hibernation to a guy who didn't get why we couldn't find bears year-round (still less frustrating than trying to reason with the deputy chief).

180

Kyle Parker called at 7 a.m. on the 8th, saying, "I just killed another deer. Do you want to buy it?"

I told Kyle we didn't need any more deer. Kyle asked if we needed more artwork or eagle and hawk feathers, and I gave him the same answer. So much for getting them to slow down, but I wasn't going to keep funding their poaching at this rate.

I received an email offering me a bighorn sheep for sale on the 10th. I emailed back and forth and finally called the man. We discussed the sheep, he sent me photos, and we agreed on a price. After running a check on him and finding he was a registered sex offender (child rapist), I finally committed to buying the sheep. The guy was willing to drive to Everett to bring us the sheep.

Around that same time, I got messages from several other new customers and suppliers offering to buy and sell a whole passel of illegal wildlife. Calls came from a woman who wanted some fresh illegal elk meat, another man offering an illegal mountain goat, as well as many calls from our existing customers. Business calls were stacking up, and it looked like we had a whole lot of travel to do in November.

During the second week of November, we had an SIU meeting. Sgt. Hobbs sheepishly told us Detective Golden had been approved to use up to 12 man-days of paid overtime for geoduck surveillance during the Thanksgiving holiday. Still, my request for overtime for Jennifer and me had been turned down. Hobbs apologized profusely, even though we all knew it wasn't his fault.

According to Hobbs, Cenci had said Jennifer didn't deserve overtime pay, and she should be thankful she is being allowed to work and learn from complex investigations rather than spending her time writing "chicken-shit litter tickets." I guess it went without saying I didn't deserve overtime pay, either.

The real irony was that Detective Golden hadn't asked for 12 man-days of overtime (he had asked for only four man-days) and wasn't sure he could even come up with enough officers to use it all. In essence, DC Cenci had given a pile of OT to someone who didn't have a real need for it, but turned it down for a case that had a legitimate need. Oh well, another shot, and yet we were still standing. We would schedule our undercover trips to avoid working on the two Thanksgiving holidays. If that was the best Cenci could dish out, we would be fine.

A couple of days after setting up the deal, I met with the child molester and purchased a bighorn sheep from the back of his Volvo (another car for our forfeiture pile). The convicted felon promised to get back to me with other wildlife items, but I didn't really care if he did or not, as he was still on felony probation, so this one sale would send him back to the joint, where he would no longer need his Volvo anyway.

I bought a mountain goat in Maple Valley, Washington, followed by a trip to Blaine to sell $200 worth of poached elk meat on the 15th.

On that same day, I sent Jin Dong a text message asking if he still wanted the big frozen bear, as I had another person interested in it.

At 10:00 a.m., Jin replied, "I still want the big bear. Do you know of any place in the Seattle area where you can cut it up without being seen?"

I told him that we could always cut it up in my storage unit in Everett and could close the door so that nobody could see us. Jin said that would work great. I told him to give me 3 to 4 days of advanced notice to ensure it was thawed out before cutting it up.

He said, "Yesterday, I shipped some of the gallbladders I bought from you to China. The person in China will then take them to a Chinese medicine shop for them to inspect. I have four other galls that are about dried enough to ship, and as soon as they are ready, I am going to ship them too."

Jin went on, "When you cut up the whole bear, I want Tina to take photos of you with your hands inside the bear, so I can email the photos to China to show them you were taking out the gallbladder yourself."

He said as soon as he gets the okay from China, we would do "big business." Jin said he would call me when he was ready for the whole bear or more gallbladder. With a wide grin, I couldn't possibly have suppressed, I told him, "Don't call us around Thanksgiving. We have to take those two days off."

I acquired a small dead black bear (~60 lbs) from Officer Worth Allen three days later. At about 8:00 a.m., I sent Jin a text stating: "Jin. One of our guys killed a bear last night. It is small, about 70 pounds, but fresh. I am meeting him this morning to buy it

183

from him, and I am paying $175. He left it whole. I am guessing you want it?"

I followed up the text with a photo of the bear and called him. Jin said he was in Los Angeles, conducting restaurant equipment business, and would make some calls and get back to me.

At 10:30, Jin called back and asked, "Are you willing to drive the bear down to Portland, Oregon, to deliver it to someone there?"

I asked him if the people from Portland could meet us ½-way, and he said they don't drive.

He also said, "I need the bear to be skinned, quartered, and have the paws and gallbladder removed."

I told him for $280, I would deliver the bear, as he had requested, to Portland, and I told him the bear was about 70 lbs. Through phone calls and text messages, we agreed that "Tina" and I would deliver the bear on Monday (11/21/11). He said he would not have us deliver it to "their fish business" but rather to "their" house and would give us the address on Monday when we were in the area. Jin told us the address was in the area of 82nd St and Division in Portland, so we should drive there and await further instructions.

Once I got off the phone, I called the supervisor of Oregon's wildlife investigations unit and told her it looked like we had to make another trip into her state. I briefed her, emailed my case report, and agreed to meet with her team when we got to Oregon.

Jennifer and I traveled down to Portland on the **21**st. On the way to Portland (at 10:30), Jin texted us the address we were to deliver

184

the bear. Jennifer texted Jin that the bear was much smaller than we thought, and we would reduce the price to $250. Once in the Portland area, we met with OSP and briefed them on the case. I was somewhat relieved to find they had gotten over our previous incursion into the "sovereign nation" of Oregon.

After the briefing, Jennifer and I drove to the address Jin had provided. We found it to be a decent two-story duplex. We rang the doorbell and were greeted by a Chinese woman who didn't understand a word of English. As we attempted to converse with her, I called Jin and told him we were talking to a woman who didn't understand English and asked if he could speak with her. I handed the phone to the woman and listened to a long Chinese conversation. The woman turned away from us and went into the house with our phone, closing the door behind her. I looked at Jennifer, wondering if we had just lost our phone. After a short while, the woman returned and handed the phone to me. Jin told me the man I wanted to deal with was upstairs, in that house, and would be down soon to meet with us.

Within a few minutes, a young Chinese male came to the door while speaking on his phone. The man didn't say a word to us but instead handed me his phone. Once again, I found myself speaking with Jin, "the translator." Jin said the man was the person who would take the bear from us and wanted to know if we were okay with that. I told Jin that would work fine. The young man opened the garage door and pointed inside. Jennifer and I carried the bear (in a cooler) into the garage while the man stood and watched us, not lifting a finger to help.

The young man took a minute or two to inspect the bear, and while he was looking it over, Jin called me back on my phone and said,

185

"Do not talk to the man! Just leave the bear, take the money, and get out of there!"

Not a problem since our young Chinese business associate hadn't muttered a single word to us and, as far as we could tell, didn't understand a word we had told him. Right then, without any direction on our part, the man handed me $250 in cash. We shook hands, took our cooler, and left the bear in a cardboard box in the garage.

After the contact, Jennifer and I met again with the OSP folks and provided them with copies of our covert videos.

On our way home, Jin called and asked if everything had gone well. I told him it had. He wanted to know where the rib meat was and said the buyers in Portland couldn't find any. I told him I had put the bear in four separate bags, one bag contained the four quarters, another bag had the four paws, a third bag had the gallbladder and penis, and the last bag had the carcass with the rib and back meat, but I had not skinned that. Jin said he would call his buyer back and tell him, and thanked us for delivering the bear. I told him we were sorry the bear turned out to be so small and that perhaps he could give them some meat from our 400-pound bear to make up for it.

Jin said, "I'm not worried about it."

I guess these guys were not among his top customers.

I took Thanksgiving and the day after off and went hunting with my real wife. It was great to take a little time off to have an enjoyable couple of days of hunting. When this operation was done, I might make a habit of it.

I called taxidermist Wyatt Wilson on the **28**th and told him I was in Blaine and would be coming by his place. I asked if he had anything interesting for sale. He said, "Just a bunch of ducks." He told me to stop by and take a look. I arrived at his shop at about 09:00 a.m. He showed me various mounted waterfowl and said they were all for sale.

He told me, "Remember that it is illegal to buy or sell waterfowl, so you have to be very careful who you sell them to."

He showed me several mounted ducks and a mounted snow goose and said I could have any of them I wanted for $100 each.

I told him, "I have a customer who was really into sea ducks and, in particular, wants a male harlequin."

He said he had just sold a male harlequin and got them in all the time. Wilson showed me several other sea ducks, three of which I picked to buy. I also picked out the snow goose. I noticed USFWS migratory bird tags on the mounts and asked him about them.

"I get a lot of my birds from Alaska, and they have to be tagged to be legal in case I were to be inspected. I always have the birds tagged, but I remove them before selling the birds because then the birds can't be traced back to me."

He warned me again that it is illegal to buy and sell waterfowl. I gathered the four birds on a table and paid Wilson $400 in cash. He went on to show me more sea ducks and insisted I purchase one more. I finally agreed and purchased a fifth bird for an additional $100 in cash. What a salesman!

Wilson and I had a long discussion about eagles and eagle feathers.

He said, "I just completed three different eagle head staffs for Indians. I do a lot of them."

As soon as I cleared the contact, I called USFWS Agent Andrews and told him he owed me $500 in exchange for five illegal sales of waterfowl. Agent Andrews said that was a fair trade.

November had come to a close, and we had gained another couple dozen felony cases. While I loved the activity, I hoped things would slow down a bit, so we could hopefully get caught up on evidence and case files.

CHAPTER 16- DECEMBER 2011

On December 3rd, Liev called to tell me he had been catching some fish and had 15 pounds of red caviar for sale. I committed to buying 12 pounds and told him I would pick it up on the 7th.

Three days later, I got a text message from Jin Dong, "I really want to work on the big one. I want you to cut it clean and pack frozen ship to Chicago and New York".

I responded by telling Jin I would call him the next day.

I called Jin back on the 7th and asked him what he wanted to be done with the big bear.

Jin instructed me to "Cut it into quarters, cut the paws off, and remove the gallbladder. I want you to ship one quarter, two paws, and possibly the gallbladder to New York, then ship another quarter to Chicago, and then bring the other two quarters and the paws to me in Walla Walla."

He went on, "I will pay you $400 for the bear and will also reimburse you for shipping costs to New York and Chicago."

I reminded Jin he had said earlier that he wanted us to take photos of him removing the gallbladder from the bear and asked if he still wanted to do that.

He said, "Don't worry about that."

He asked me how much "net weight" of meat I thought was on the bear, and I said I thought maybe between 200 and 225 pounds.

189

I asked him, "Have you heard back from China about the gallbladder you shipped to them? Did they approve of them?"

Jin said China approved them and wanted the rest. He asked me how many I had, and I told him I thought I had 23 or 24. Jin said he wanted to buy them and ship them over, but was worried about getting the gall past customs.

I asked him how he got the last gall past customs, and he said, "I packaged them in with a box of chocolates."

I told him I would get the bear out of the freezer to let it begin to thaw and would probably cut it up on Monday or Tuesday, and my wife and I would bring his portion over to him on the 14th or 15th.

That same day, I arrived at Liev's house at about 6 p.m. and was met at the door by Yuli. I was surprised to see Yuli and asked him what he was doing there.

"I follow the fish. Wherever the fish are, I go", Yuli said, "I came out to get some salmon with Liev and am heading back to Oklahoma the next day or the day after that."

I met with Liev in his kitchen, and he began removing 12 jars of red Caviar from his refrigerator. As Liev was boxing up the caviar, Yuli told me the eggs were from "Dog Salmon" (Chum), and they had thrown away the fish carcasses as the fish were in poor shape. I asked Yuli when I could expect to get more paddlefish caviar, and he said he would start getting it in March, so anytime in March, April, or May. He said he would have a lot of it available and would "get me all I wanted." He asked me if I had sold his caviar already and where I had sold it. I told Yuli I sold all of it, and I sold most of it in Seattle, Vancouver, and Spokane. Yuli, Liev, and I talked about the various types of caviar and how it should be served (I silently said they should be served to a garbage can). I paid $300 in cash for the red caviar and left with my treasure of nasty chum salmon eggs.

The following week, I called Kent Rousch (Wild Ways) and told him, "My wife and I are coming over to Spokane on the 14th and 15th and would like to look at your merchandise again. A client of my wife's is a very wealthy Asian man, and he wants us to pick a unique wildlife item for a Christmas gift to himself."

Rousch asked if we could meet him after lunch on the 15th, to which I agreed.

Later that day, I received a text from Jin asking if we were still coming over on Wednesday (Dec 14th). I responded by saying we were and should be in Tri-Cities around 11 am and Walla Walla around 1 or 2 pm. I told him he should consider shipping the meat by 2-day or 3-day, but Jin told me he wanted the bear meat shipped 5-day.

He said, "I send the small one last time cost $50."

I clarified that I wanted $400 for the bear, and Jin agreed and told me he wanted me to take some pictures as I cut up the bear.

Sgt. Hobbs and I spent most of the day on the **13th** cutting up a frozen bear. We had taken the bear out of the freezer four days earlier, but a frozen bear won't thaw very well when the outside temperature is 20 degrees. This task was one of the worst I have had to undertake. We used saws, knives, an ax, and even a shovel to cut the huge and

191

very greasy bear into the appropriate chunks, leaving us with four quarters, the ribcage, the ever-so-valuable penis, the four paws, and the gallbladder. When we were done, we both stunk to high heaven, and the quarters looked like they had been attacked in the chainsaw massacre, but it was done. I took an appropriate number of photos for Jin and put the quarters back in the freezer to get them good and frozen for their plane rides to their final destinations.

Later that same day, I sent Jin two photos of the bear.

He texted back, asking, "Looks good. Gallbladder?"

I responded, "Yep. Will text later."

At 9:00 p.m. that night, Jin texted me, "Did you get it all done? Bring me gallbladder from this one. Thanks."

Jennifer and I drove to the state's east side with a bear ribcage and gallbladder in the back of our truck. We intended to meet with Jin to complete the transaction in Walla Walla. At about 11:00 a.m. on the 14th, Jennifer called Jin and told him we were on our way and should be in Tri-Cities around noon to 1 p.m. He said he was working at a car lot in Milton-Freewater, Oregon, and couldn't get away. He told Jennifer he needed us to bring the bear parts to the car lot and that it was only a couple of miles further for us. No problem, as it was just about five more miles. Jennifer called Sgt. Hobbs and advised that Jin insisted we bring the bear into Oregon. Sgt. Hobbs said he would call OSP (Oregon State Police) to clear our undercover contact in Oregon.

Hobbs called back a short while later and told us OSP had denied us permission to operate in Oregon, even though we had previously done so on this same case. We asked about operating under the authority of our MOU with the US Fish and Wildlife Service. We were told that "our chain-of-command had denied us access to Oregon under federal authority as well." Hobbs told us OSP had been pissed at us for going into Oregon back on October 4th, when we met with the Mathews to buy the cougar, without getting full approval (he added we were not to continue through with that purchase either). He said one of the OSP captains is a personal friend of Cenci's and had called and complained about us violating their "sovereign state" (I guess they hadn't gotten over our incursion after all).

Hobbs didn't wait for my response and added, "This one is a direct order. You will not go into Oregon!"

I was furious. This anal policy of Oregon's had just jeopardized the whole Jin Dong case. I knew Oregon Troopers weren't allowed to breathe without backup and a detailed plan in place, but was there no room for common sense? In undercover operations, you have to go where the bad guys are and have to be flexible. The denial of access to Oregon meant not only that we had to discontinue the transaction with Jin, but I was at a total loss as to how we would explain our resistance to driving five more miles when we had already driven two hundred.

I looked at Jennifer and said, "I've got nothing for you. I have no idea what to tell Jin."

Without further discussion, Jennifer got on the phone and texted Jin, "We have other customers and can't keep driving all over. Sorry, but we aren't coming." We didn't receive a response.

Jennifer and I continued to Spokane without hearing back from Jin. We purchased another mountain goat from a gentleman I had been conversing with and then stayed the night in Spokane.

Later that night, while sitting in my motel room, I wrote Jin an email explaining I had been in a bad mood and things had not gone as planned (all true), but we would still like to do business. I implied that Tina and I had a fight. To my great relief, Jin replied that he understood and still wanted us to ship the meat to Chicago and New York. We had just dodged a bullet, no thanks to OSP.

On the morning of the **15th,** Jin texted us and said that if we gave him our bank account number, he would deposit the $400 (for the bear) into our account so that we could ship the meat. Jennifer texted Jin our bank account number, and at about 11:00 a.m. Jin called.

He never missed a beat in saying, "I want three "hands" (bear paws), the gallbladder, and the ribcage to be delivered to me, one paw and 50 pounds of bear meat delivered to Chicago, and 50 pounds of bear meat to be delivered to New York. How many deer can you get a year?"

I told him we could come up with as many as 8 to 10 deer per month. He asked how much they weighed, and I told him about 80 pounds. Jin said he was working on a deal to ship deer meat to China and label it as beef and wanted to know if we could provide it, and I told him we probably could. He ended the conversation by saying he would text us the addresses to ship the bear meat.

Within a minute, we received his text, "Get it. Need to ship 50lb and one feet to Chicago and other 50lb no feet to New York."

194

He also provided us with the names and shipping addresses in his text.

Later on the **15ᵗʰ**, Jennifer and I arrived at the Rousch home and were greeted by a grinning Kent Rousch. Jennifer explained to Rousch that a client of hers wanted a unique and high-end wildlife item for Christmas. Jennifer explained her "client" was a wealthy Asian man who fancied himself a major hunter, even though he hadn't had too much success. She told Rousch her client was especially interested in wild sheep. Rousch asked what our budget was for this purchase, and Jennifer said she would like to keep it under $2,000. Rousch pointed at his wall of mounted sheep and said he could get us a trophy sheep mount, but they were way more expensive than $2,000.

Kent suggested we look at a bighorn sheep wall sconce and took us downstairs to show us an example. He showed us what appeared to be a hollowed-out bighorn sheep horn made into a wall sconce. Jennifer enthusiastically told Rousch the sconce would be great and began discussing the wall plate and cover options. They agreed Rousch would make a bighorn sheep sconce on a wood base and ship it to us. He gave us a price of $1,200 for the sconce, which we agreed to (the sale of any bighorn sheep parts constitutes a felony). Rousch told us he used to come up with bighorn sheep horns easily, but most states had cracked down on these wildlife items.

It was finally my turn to speak, and I told Rousch, "We have three sets of bighorn sheep horns at home right now."

Rousch perked right up and asked me, "Where did you pick them up?"

195

I told him we had purchased them from several people, most of whom had found the sheep dead. Rousch said that he didn't want poached horns, but he would be interested in the horns we had.

He asked if the horns were "pinned" (drilled and plugged with a unique identifier plug by fish and wildlife agencies, required for all sheep horns), and I said, "Nope, none of them are pinned."

Rousch told us, "I have a good friend who is an Idaho game warden, and the Idaho game warden will plug any sheep horns I bring him- no questions asked."

Rousch said his Idaho game warden friend would always ask him, "You found these on the river, right?" Then he (Rousch) would say yes, and the game warden would plug them and make them appear to be legally found horns.

Rousch told us that if we brought him the horns, he would get them plugged and would make them into wildlife art items and "will split the profit with you."

I told Rousch we would bring the horns next time we came over. He asked what I had intended to do with the horns, and I said I had hoped to sell them to people, perhaps some wealthy customers in California. He said we had to be careful in dealing with sheep horns, especially in California, or we would find ourselves in federal prison. Rousch told us that the Washington game wardens had gone through his whole house looking for illegal wildlife at one point but had come up with nothing.

Rousch continued to tour us around his house, pointing out wildlife items for sale. He said he would likely not have our sheep horn sconce delivered to us before Christmas, but would try to get it to us before he left for a fishing trip in Belize on January 10th. Jennifer told Rousch we would like to take something back with us for our client, so he showed us some custom knives, including a water buffalo knife he was selling for $575. We agreed to purchase the knife and take it with us. Rousch began to write up a receipt for the sconce and knife. He asked us if there was a way for us to get around paying sales tax, and I told him we could buy the items through our business for resale and, therefore, would not have to pay sales tax. I handed him our business license (wallet card) with our business number. Rousch made out a receipt for the two items, which totaled $1,775. Jennifer paid him in cash and wrote down our address on the receipt. He provided us with some brochures for his business and a business card showing his email address. As usual, we shook hands and promised to keep in touch.

Once Jennifer and I were in our truck, we celebrated the fact that we had just made a felony-level purchase from the millionaire trafficker, but also realized we didn't want to go to trial with nothing more than a wall sconce for evidence. We needed to do more business with Rousch, and since he had shown an interest in buying sheep from us, we could now switch from buyers to suppliers, which would be much easier on our budget. We headed home excited about our success with Rousch, which pushed our frustration with OSP to the back of our minds.

First thing in the morning on the **16ᵗʰ,** Jennifer called and told me she had just killed a problem black bear. Unfortunately, this was another small (~70-pound) bear, but nonetheless, it was a fresh bear. I met with Jennifer and took the bear while commenting on what appeared to be a trend of miniature-attack bears. I took a couple of photos of the bear with my cell phone and threw it in my freezer. After putting the tiny bear to rest in my freezer, I checked our bank account to see if Jin had deposited our $400 and found that he had done so. My next stop was the UPS store, where I plopped two hefty boxes full of bear meat on the counter.

As I told the clerk, I wanted the boxes shipped by 5-day service. He warned me, "These gifts may not get to their destinations by Christmas."

I told the clerk they were not Christmas gifts, and I wanted the 5-day service; the whole while, I had a visual image of rotten-smelling bear blood dripping all over Christmas presents in a UPS warehouse somewhere. Once the packages were in the able hands of UPS, I sent the tracking numbers to Jin by text.

Jin replied, "The meat good for whole week?"

I responded, "I hope so."

I did hope so, but for a different reason than Jin might have thought, but I certainly had my doubts. I was pretty sure those two packages would be the only boxes full of bear meat, intermixed with millions of Christmas gifts, and I wanted no part of a kid getting a stuffed animal that, for some reason, smelled like rotten bear meat.

198

The next morning, I emailed Jin a photo of the bear Jennifer had killed the previous day and said, "Jin: Tina shot this one yesterday. We put it in the freezer whole. Probably only about 65-70 pounds. You want it? If so, after Christmas, we could bring all of it over at once. Let us know."

Jin replied, "Too small for me now. Because they like bigger feet and gallbladder. But keep it frozen. And see, someone in New York wants. How much?"

I replied, "Ok. Can you pay us the $100 for shipping the meat to Chicago and New York pretty soon? Tina would like to get $250 for her bear. $250 would be skinned, cut up, and brought to you".

Jin answered, "I think only get about 35lb from this".

I answered, "Probably. Make us an offer. We will deal"

Through a series of text messages, I agreed to meet Jin at the Pacific Pride Restaurant in Walla Walla on the 28th at about 5 p.m. to exchange the remainder (three paws, a gallbladder, the penis, and the carcass) of the large bear for the $100 he owed me for shipping the four bear quarters to New York and Illinois.

On Christmas Day, I received a voicemail from Bourey wishing us a "Merry Christmas" (wasn't that sweet?) and asking us to call him.

At about 11:00 a.m., I received a text message from Bourey stating, "Are you interest in buying sturgeon?"

199

At 4:00 p.m., I texted back, "Sure. But we are doing family stuff till Tuesday afternoon".

At 4:15, I called Bourey and discussed the sturgeon. Bourey said he had three large sturgeon and that the guy who caught and delivered them insisted on getting $120 each for the fish. I asked Bourey if they were worth that much, and he said they were because they were all three very large. I told Bourey I would take all three, and I would come to his place on Tuesday, the 27th, to pick them up. My wife has put up with an awful lot with my job, and I wondered how she would take my setting up illegal business deals on Christmas day, but thankfully, as I got off the phone, I turned to see her shaking her head and laughing.

The day after Christmas, I received a phone call from Jin. He told me the bear meat had arrived in excellent condition for his customers in New York and Chicago (I was genuinely shocked). Jin said the meat had still been frozen when it arrived, and his customers were pleased. He wanted to know when we would be in Walla Walla next time. I told him we would probably be back in Walla Walla on the 28th.

The next day, I arrived at Bourey's house at about 5:00 p.m. and observed six vehicles parked there (four in the driveway and two on the street). I entered Bourey's house through the front door and found Bourey's wife and two of his "monkeys" in the family room. Bourey's wife asked me where my wife was, and I told her she had to work. She asked me how many fish I wanted to buy, and I said I would buy all three. She said they had bought one for themselves and had eaten it over the weekend, and it was excellent. I asked her what

200

all the cars were there for, and she said they had a party and some of the people had left their cars there. I noticed a semi-automatic rifle leaning against the wall next to her.

A few minutes later, Bourey entered the room and declared, "It's my favorite white man." He asked, "Where is Tina, and why isn't she here?"

I told Bourey my wife had to work and couldn't make it. Bourey's wife told him that I wanted to buy all three sturgeon. He took me into the garage, opened the chest freezer, and showed me the three sturgeon. All three fish were wrapped in plastic garbage bags and appeared to be over 4 feet long. I agreed to take all three and asked Bourey if the same guy had caught these fish.

He said, "These fish came from a different guy," but wouldn't volunteer more.

I paid him $360 in cash and carried two fish out to my truck while Bourey carried the other fish. I asked him when he would have some elk, and he said his "monkeys" were having trouble getting elk because there wasn't much snow in the mountains. Bourey said without a lot of snow, the elk stay up high where they are hard to get to. He told me that as soon as we started getting a lot of snow, his "monkeys" would start getting a lot of elk, and we would be the first people he would call. I said my goodbyes to Bourey and his wife and headed home.

On December **28**th, I pulled into the Pacific Pride at about 5:00 p.m., where I observed Jin's white Lexus parked. I didn't see Jin anywhere, so I entered the restaurant through the back door. An Asian

201

male saw me and waved me back outside, where I waited for Jin. Within a couple of minutes, Jin came out and greeted me.

He led his greetings with, "Where's Tina?" (Two days in a row of "Where's Tina," I was beginning to get a complex.)

Jin told me he would pull his car around to my truck so we could load the bear in his car. Jin pulled Jennifer's future undercover Lexus alongside my truck, and I removed the bear parts from a cooler in the back of my truck. I laid out three small bags that contained three bear paws, the yummy bear penis, and a gallbladder. I also showed Jin the large bag, which contained the 75-pound bear carcass.

We loaded all the bear parts into Jin's coolers and the back of his car. We also had a little discussion about bear sales. Jin reiterated that the bear meat I had shipped for him had all arrived frozen and in good condition. He said China had approved the purchase of the rest of our bear gallbladder, but he had to wait until after the New Year. He expressed concern about getting a large quantity of bear gall to China without getting caught. He stated a friend of his had hand-carried the bear gallbladder; he had previously bought from us on the plane with him, so it did not need to be shipped. He said he was thinking about hiding the rest of the gallbladders inside toys and shipping them to China via UPS. He asked if I thought it would be better to ship all of them at once or break the load into small shipments (4 to 5 at a time). I told Jin the decision was his. He said he thought it might be best to make several small shipments, as he wouldn't lose the entire load if some were found. I asked him if he was concerned about US Customs or Customs in China. Jin said US Customs does not inspect outbound shipments, and they are only worried about what comes into the country. He confessed his concern was with Chinese Customs.

Jin said, "After the New Year, we can start making plans for me to buy the rest of your gallbladder and getting them to China."

I mentioned I had a couple of sturgeon in the truck and wanted to know if the restaurant was interested in fresh sturgeon. Jin said that Chinese people think sturgeon are slimy and gross and won't eat them (apparently, they will eat bear penis and bear paw soup but draw the line at fresh fish). I cut off a piece of sturgeon and gave it to Jin, telling him to have the people in the restaurant try it. Jin paid me the $100 he owed, and I hit the road.

The year had drawn to an end. So far, we had in the neighborhood of 65 suspects, with hundreds of criminal charges (primarily felony wildlife trafficking charges, with some drug and firearms charges thrown in for good measure). We had probable cause to forfeit ten vehicles and a multitude of firearms, and we were just getting started. If we were allowed to complete the 2-year run the chief had committed to, we would end this a year from now, and I could only imagine how far along we would be by then. As I had predicted, the business was growing exponentially every month as word got out. We were undoubtedly scooping up some significant traffickers. Even though we had minimal assistance, this operation was working!

Detective Todd Vandivert with his yellow lab pup.

Sgt. Jennifer Maurstad posing with her black bear.

Sgt. Jennifer Maurstad bonding with Kyle Parker.

Peace pipe, made with hawk feathers,

purchased from Tanya Franklin.

Undercover truck loaded with elk carcasses purchased from Bourey.

Bear gallbladder sold to Jin Dong.

Caviar purchased from Liev Smirnov and Yuli Ivanov.

Bald and Golden Eagle staffs purchased from Wyatt Wilson.

207

Officer Brian Alexander with the cougar,

sold to a Chinese Restaurant.

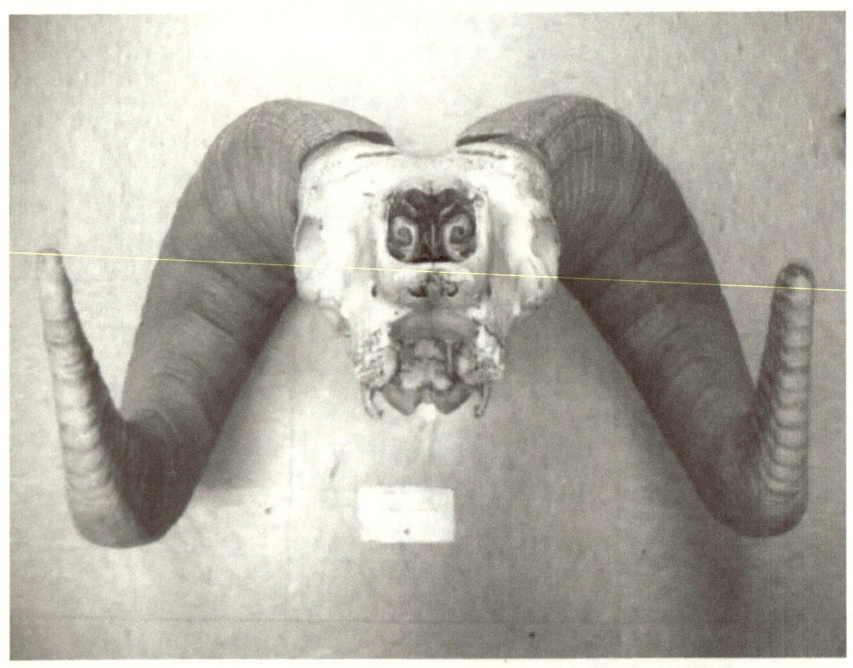

One of the bighorn sheep skulls sold to Kent Rousch.

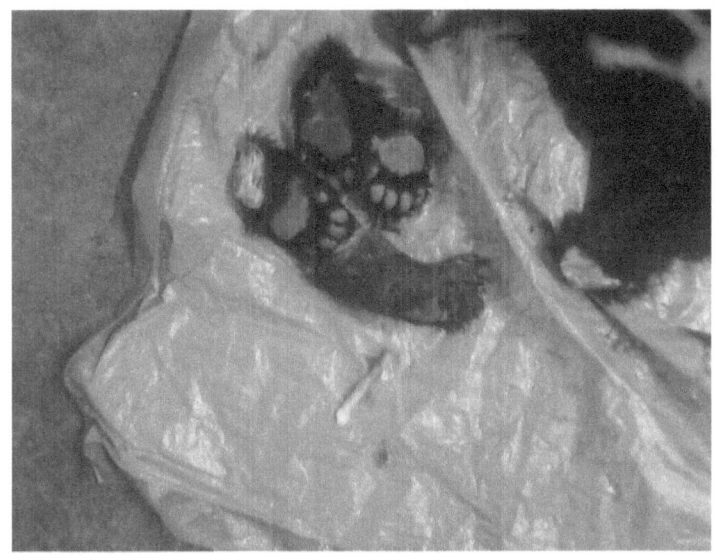

Bear paws and penis shipped to buyer out-of-state.

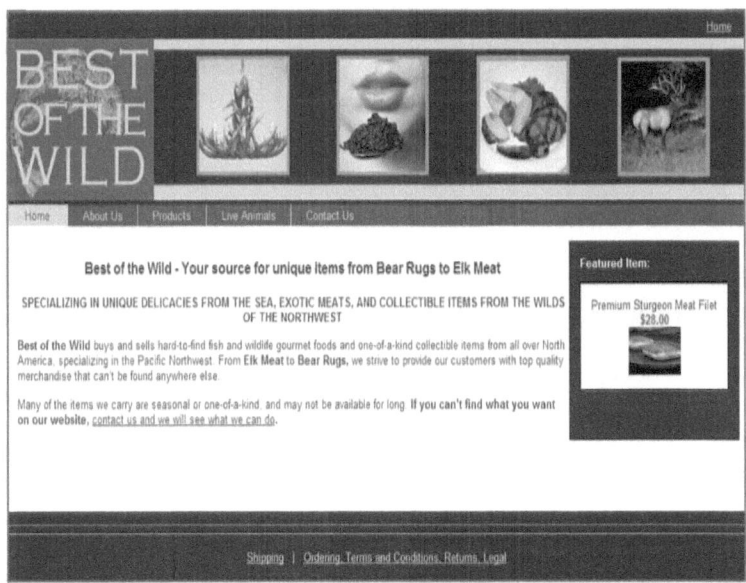

BEST OF THE WILD website.

CHAPTER 17- JANUARY 2012

January started with Sgt. Hobbs breaking the news to me that Cenci had officially pulled everyone, except Jennifer and me, off of Operation Cody. He had already pulled Detective Clarke off the operation, leaving us with Officer Conklin, who had been monitoring and archiving the covert videos (a nearly full-time job in itself). I have to say the only thing that surprised me was he continued to allow Jennifer to work the operation…..I guess she would be the next cut. It all made perfect sense. We were in the middle of the most productive undercover operation in WDFW's history, and we were gaining momentum every day, so it was a perfect time to cut us down to bare bones.

I couldn't help but ask Hobbs another question, which I suppose I already knew the answer to, "What has Conklin been assigned to do that's so important?"

"Geoduck" was the one-word answer. What could I say? At least Cenci was predictable.

The first new customer of the year came on the 4th when I received an email from a man named Brian Field. Field sent several photos of mounted animals he wanted to sell, including a mountain goat and a sheep. I called Field and discussed the illegality of selling the goat and sheep, and like most people we had dealt with, he didn't care. I made arrangements to meet him on the 10th at his house in Pierce County, WA. After I got off the phone, I did a little checking and found he was also a convicted felon and couldn't even possess a firearm. Well, maybe he killed all of these animals with a bow or before he was convicted of his felony charges.....not likely.

The very next day, on the 5th, I got an email from Steve Stuart from Tri-Cities. Mr. Stuart also attached several photos of what he wanted to sell us, bear skulls and teeth (illegal to buy or sell). I followed up with the standard phone call, getting the standard response in return. I booked Stuart for a visit on the 25th.

By the morning of the 6th, it was Bourey's turn to book us.

When I answered the phone, Bourey said, "Is my favorite white boy awake?"

He told me he was getting a shipment of fresh elk and deer the next day, which should arrive early. Bourey asked if we wanted to buy up to five of the elk. I told Bourey we would take three elk and didn't want any deer. Bourey said his suppliers wanted between $550 and $600 per elk, and he would let me know what time to come to get the elk when he heard for sure. At 2 p.m. I texted Bourey and asked if he knew what time.

He texted back, "They won't be here till about 2 p.m.".

As scheduled, on January 7th, I received a text from Bourey stating, "the animal should be here by 1:30".

At 12:30, we received another text stating, "all here." At about 1:40 p.m., Jennifer and I arrived at Bourey's house and backed up to the garage. We saw five elk and three deer carcasses spread across tarps on the floor in the garage. Bourey had a force of five of his trusty "monkeys" waiting for us in the garage.

211

Bourey stated, "I want $600 each for the larger elk and $550 for the smaller one, but I don't think anyone will want the small one, so I'll probably have to cut it up to sell it myself."

After inspecting the elk, we told Bourey we would take the first three (larger) elk. He and his "monkeys" loaded the three elk carcasses into our truck while Jennifer paid him $1,800. We were in and out of there in about 10 minutes, as Bourey wasn't in his normal chatty mood.

Soon, January 10th came around, and it was time to pick up a mountain goat from Brian Field. At about noon, Jennifer and I arrived at Field's house. Brian, a large mid-40s man in good shape, took us into his house, where he showed us his collection of wildlife mounts for sale. After looking over the extensive collection, I asked Brian why he was selling all his mounts, and he said he was mostly getting out of hunting and doing a lot more fishing.

Hoping to get an admission he had firearms in possession (a felony), I told Brian, "If you ever want to start selling off your guns, call us."

Brian answered, "I have an extensive collection of guns, and used to be on the Marine Corps Rifle team, and have been collecting guns ever since. I may start selling my guns at some point and will call you if I do."

After looking at the wildlife, we told Brian we were most interested in the mountain goat, the bear, and the pronghorn antelope. I asked Brian where he had picked up the goat, and he said he had shot it in the Snoqualmie area (of Washington). He said he hated giving the

212

goat up, as it had been tough to get. I told him that if we bought the mountain goat, it would have to stay between us, as the sale of mountain goats is illegal in Washington. He said he wanted $600 for the goat, $300 for the antelope, and $525 for the bear, for a grand total of $1,425, which we agreed to. I counted out the $1,425 in cash and handed it to Brian. He helped us carry the mounts out to our truck. Again, this was another relatively quick and smooth transaction.

On our way back from Field's house, Sgt. Hobbs called and asked if we wouldn't mind checking into a fresh lead. Hobbs said he had found an online advertisement offering sport-caught steelhead. Hobbs gave us the address, which I put in our GPS, discovering the address was only about 15 miles away. We called the seller and immediately arranged to meet the Doctor at his home. When we pulled into the driveway, it was only a matter of minutes before Doctor Trang pulled in beside us in his beautiful new Mercedes SUV. After introductions and exchanging business cards, we purchased the only steelhead he had left (he told us he had already sold a few) for $25. We, of course, explained just how illegal this was, and the good doctor told us he was aware of the laws. As we were leaving, Trang promised us "more steelhead next time," he went fishing. Jennifer and I left, scratching our heads. Why would a successful doctor risk a felony charge for $25? Oh well, it takes all kinds.

From the 10th through the 23rd, Jennifer was back in uniform while I made a few illegal transactions and caught up on paperwork. Detective Clarke had been trying to take care of as much evidence as he could fit in (around his geoduck surveillance) without drawing attention from the administration (since he was not supposed to be working on Operation Cody anymore). Still, he was falling further and further behind. I told him to let it all sit until the admin realized we were spending money and time making cases, which would all be for nothing because of the evidence situation, but he continued to try.

On the 11^{th,} I sent Kent Rousch an email stating we would be in Spokane on the 25th and 26th of January and could bring the sheep horns and possibly pick up the sconce.

At about 2:00 p.m. on the **24^{th,}** Kent Rousch called. He said he was back from Belize and was very tired, but he looked forward to seeing us.

I told him, "I am bringing over three sets of bighorn sheep horns."

Rousch was very excited to hear that and asked, "Where are you two going to stay in Spokane?"

When I told Kent we would grab a motel, he said, "Why don't you two just stay at my house? I have plenty of room and would love to have you stay here."

I thanked him for the offer, but said we would probably stay in a motel, but I would run it by my wife (which wasn't going to happen). I told Kent we would either arrive at his place on the evening of the 25th or the morning of the 26th, depending on how much business we had as we crossed the state. He said the morning of the 26th would be fine if we could make it after 10:30 a.m.

Detective Lenny Hahn had picked up four bighorn skulls from a Montana game warden buddy of mine. I had asked Lenny to grab the

214

skulls, photograph them, and take DNA samples from each, which he did immediately. Lenny had the skulls waiting for us when we came to Spokane to visit with Rousch.

At 7:00 p.m., on that same day, Bourey called, "I am getting another shipment of elk in the next couple of days. How many do you want?"

I told Bourey we were good for now and didn't need more elk.

He said, "I have many other buyers, and that's not a problem. I will call you guys in a couple of weeks to see if you want more in one of my later shipments."

Great. Now I would have to monitor and archive the covert camera at Bourey's house since Conklin had been pulled off. Oh well, at least I wouldn't be bored.

We hit the road on the morning of the **25th,** heading first to Tri-Cities to meet with Steve Stuart, who had offered to sell us bear skulls and teeth. Jennifer and I arrived at the Stuart residence at about 5 p.m. and were met at the door by Steve Stuart, a 50-year-old man with a pretty decent beer gut. Steve invited us into his house, where we met his wife, Chris. He pointed out two bear skulls and a bear tooth sitting on a table. He said he had not shot a bear this past hunting season, but these bears had come from the two prior years in the Blue Mountains of Washington. Steve took the bear hide off a chair, laid it out on the floor for us to inspect, and pointed out the mounted bear on the wall. We discussed that it is illegal to buy and or sell bear skulls.

Steve acknowledged knowing the transaction was very illegal and asked, "So what do you do with them since they are illegal to sell?"

I responded, "Look, it's legal to sell them in some states, and what we do with them or where they go is really none of your business."

Steve asked, "How do I know you're not setting me up?"

I simply didn't answer his question other than to give him a nasty look, which appeared to work.

He said they had looked at our website, had seen what we had to offer, and asked what we do the best on. I told him I anticipated we would do best on antlers, but we had not done so well on them. I said most of our money comes from unusual items, cougar paws, bears, and meat. He asked me how much I pay for elk and deer meat, to which I asked what he meant.

Steve replied, "How much would you pay me for a whole elk carcass?"

I answered that we had paid around $600 for a whole elk and $150-$300 per deer (depending on weight). Steve asked more questions about elk and deer meat, and I asked him to step outside with me.

Once outside, I told Steve that I would put a lot of trust in him. I took him to the back of our truck and opened a cooler, which contained a large quantity of wrapped and frozen elk meat. I said we were taking the meat to Spokane, where we sell it to restaurants. I

216

added that we also have several restaurants in the Seattle area that we deal with. I told him we only buy from four different hunters and trust them to keep quiet. He asked me several times if I was a game warden and if this was a sting.

I slowly answered, "Think about this. If I am a game warden, then my wife would have to be a game warden, too, right? And our business and website would all just be a fake to try to catch people. That would make it a pretty elaborate scheme for the game department to pull off, wouldn't it?"

Steve thought that over and said, "They do that kind of thing" (I don't know where he got that idea, but certainly not in Washington). I assured him we were not game wardens. He said he could get us all the deer and elk meat we wanted and stated, "That is all me and my friends do."

He told me he could make a living off selling deer and elk meat, and he also knew some Indians who "are up hunting right now," from whom he could get meat. He said he had done this (selling game meat) before, and we must be very careful. I told him I would only deal with him, didn't want our names going around, and would not take calls or business from his friends. Steve agreed, and we shook on it.

Once we went back inside the house, I asked him how much he wanted for the two skulls and the rug. Steve asked what I was willing to pay. I told him we would pay $300 for the large bear skull, $150 for the smaller bear skull, and $200 for the rug, for a grand total of $650. He said he wanted $50 more than that, which I agreed to. I paid him what turned out to be $700 in cash by laying the cash out on the table next to the bear skulls.

Steve asked, "Are the bills sequential?"

I answered, "Yep, and the black helicopter will be coming any minute."

Steve seemed to miss my sarcasm altogether but pointed at the bear rug on the floor, asked us if we were interested in "bear parts," then said, "you know......what's inside the bear."

I asked what he was talking about, and he said, "Do I have to say it?"

Steve said he knows an Asian market nearby, always trying to buy "that" (gallbladder) from him, but he would rather sell to us, and he didn't kill a bear this year anyway. I told him that whatever he gets, to call us and see if we want it first. In front of Steve, I told Jennifer I had agreed to buy deer and elk meat from him if he called. He told us he likes to let the deer and elk hang for ten days to age. He asked us who cuts our meat, to which I replied: "Our brother-in-law cuts it for us." Jennifer and I left our business cards and took the bear skulls, teeth, and rug to our truck.

We felt pretty damned good about that contact and had no doubt Stuart was a serious poacher.

Jennifer and I pulled into Kent Rousch's house a few hours later. Kent started right into a conversation about his trip to Belize, during which time I went to the truck to recover the box containing three sets of sheep horns. I entered his house with the box and set it down for him to inspect.

Kent immediately asked, "Are they pinned (as required by law)?" to which I said they were not.

In December, I reminded Kent of our earlier conversation when I told him we had three sets of unpinned bighorn sheep horns, which I had purchased. He said he remembered the conversation.

I continued, "We paid $250 each for the two larger sets and $100 for the smaller set, and I would be happy to get a 50% profit on the sale."

Kent told us we would "do way better than that."

He said the small sets were a dime a dozen, and he would probably make them into sconces and wouldn't bother to get them pinned. He said he has a "really good friend" with Idaho Fish and Game, whom he would try to get to pin the larger horns.

Kent asked where the sheep had come from, and I told him that while I wasn't certain, "the guy who sold them to me had said he had found them dead in the Yakima area."

He said he didn't think that was likely, as Washington closely monitors all of its sheep, and if three came up missing, there would be a lot of news about it. He believed the sheep had more likely come from Oregon.

Kent told us that if he could get the sheep horns pinned by his friend with Idaho Fish and Game, he would probably have the largest set mounted (for a wall mount) and try to sell them at the Safari Club International convention in Las Vegas (scheduled for February 1-4, 2012). He said he could use the horns in making furniture, which he would also try to sell at the Safari Club convention. I asked him if the sale of bighorn sheep horns was legal in Nevada and added that since it is illegal in Washington, I wondered if it was legal there. Kent said he is ok to sell bighorn sheep horns as he has a "museum license" (there is no such permit in Washington).

He asked if we wanted a receipt for the horns, and I told him, "We trust you, and that isn't necessary."

Kent dropped a bombshell on us: "I use real rhino horns to make my furniture, and at one time had paperwork to cover black rhino horns."

The sale of black rhino horns is one of the highest-priority federal and international wildlife crimes in existence. Both of us were stunned. Was Kent serious or just testing us? We both left the comment hanging without a response. About an hour after arriving, Jennifer and I said goodbye to Kent, leaving the three sets of bighorn sheep horns with him.

At 6 p.m. on the 27th, I received a phone call from Liev, who said a friend of Yuli's in Oklahoma had killed an elk and was offering the meat for sale. He said the meat was selling for $10 per pound, and he wanted to know if I wanted any. Liev also said the same hunter would try to kill a wild sheep soon, which might be available for sale. I told him I needed to know more about the elk, such as what cuts of meat were available and if it was cut and wrapped. He said the meat had been cut and wrapped by a butcher, and he thought the guy had about 200 pounds available. I told Liev I was unwilling to pay $10 for burger but would pay that much for steak. He said he would check and get back to me.

At 8 p.m., Liev sent me a text stating, "bonless."

I replied, "You mean boneless meat?"

Liev responded, "yessssss".

At about 11 p.m. on the **29**th, I received a text from Jin Dong, stating, "When do you come to Walla Walla? I have $1500. Can I buy all?"

I responded by email, "Jin: I got your text, and I have one problem. We cannot let all 24 go for $1,500. We paid around $75 each for the 24 we have (some a bit more). If we sold all 24 for $1,500, that would only be $62.50 each, so we would lose money. I told you before that we have always sold them in the past for $1.00 to $1.25 per gram, which came out to an average of about $180 each. In bulk, I'll sell them to you at $100 each, but we absolutely can't go below that price."

I said, "If you only have $1,500, then we will stand by our price and give you 15 of the 24 for that price (various sizes but an average of about 180 grams each) and will save the rest for when you get more money. We now have a guy in Vancouver, BC, interested in buying whatever you don't want, and he agreed to $1.00 per gram, but I told him that we have another buyer (you) who we promised the first choice, and we will stand by our word. Let us know if you agree to $100 each, and we will let you know when we are coming over to Tri-Cities next time, and we can do the deal. Also, one of our hunters

221

called this weekend, and he said he has four more in his freezer, so we will probably pick those up in the next week or so."

Through a series of text messages, we agreed to $2,400 for the 24 bear gallbladders, which would all be 150 grams or larger. I told Jin, my wife, and I would deliver the gallbladder on February 8th.

I sent Liev an email on the **30th**, asking about the elk meat. I asked about the price of steaks, how many pounds were available, what condition the meat was in, and how the meat was getting from Oklahoma to me. At 10 a.m. Liev called and said the seller only had about 50 pounds of "Sirloin Elk Steak" left, as he had sold the rest. Liev said the seller wanted $12 per pound for the steak and much less for the ground meat. I told him I would be interested in buying all 50 pounds of the steak at $12 per pound for a total of $600. Liev said the seller had not killed a sheep but had killed some deer and might have deer meat for sale. He told me the meat was coming to Washington in a refrigerated truck, which was hauling vegetables here anyway. I asked when the meat would arrive, and Liev said he would check and let me know. He stated the truck is driven by a Russian who makes regular trips from Tulsa, Oklahoma, to Washington. Liev said he would call me as soon as he knew when the meat was coming in.

After not hearing from Dr. Trang for a while, I called him on the **30th** and told him we wondered if he had any more steelhead for sale.

Trang said, "I was just about to call you because I have two more for sale. I probably won't get any more after these until March when the B run comes in."

I told Trang I would come down and pick them up on February 2nd.

Since I had caught up on my case reports, by the **31st,** I scanned Craigslist (a free online want ad service) for anything unusual. I found a post on Bellingham's Craigslist advertising "Smudge Fans and Native American Items." The photos of the items included what appeared to be a waterfowl wing (unlawful to sell under federal laws) and eagle parts. The seller provided the contact name "Andy" with a phone number.

At 2:30, I called the number provided. A woman answered the phone, and I asked for Andy. A man came on the phone, and I introduced myself and told him I had seen the ad on Craigslist and was interested. I told Andy, my wife, and I ran a business specializing in NW wildlife and Native American items, and we would like more information on what he had to offer. Andy said he is an unemployed construction worker who "identifies with Native Americans." He said he grew up in the Mojave Desert on the Nevada/California border and that his wife is "partially Native American." Andy said he has always been interested in Native American culture and art, and began creating Native American pieces using wildlife items.

He told me he uses "Hawk talons, hawk and eagle feathers, bear skulls" as well as other wildlife items to create his "pieces." Andy said he has a good supply of eagle feathers, and if anyone ever asks about them, they are his wife's. He told me he is always looking for supplies of feathers, skulls, claws, and talons for his artwork, but he has had trouble marketing his work (because they are illegal as hell).

223

Andy confided he was unsure how many of the items he sells are legal to sell or even own.

I told him that I have a massive stockpile of feathers, talons, skulls, teeth, and claws through my business, and perhaps I could supply him. I also said I have customers who buy Native American items if they are made with authentic materials. Andy said he would email photos of some of his pieces to me and would like to meet about doing business. A few minutes after getting off the phone with Andy, I received an email with 31 photos attached. The photos included what appeared to be items all made with raptor feathers and talons. It looks like we had hooked another genius.

For the dead of winter, January had certainly been much better than the previous January for Best of the Wild.

CHAPTER 18- FEBRUARY 2012

Sgt. Hobbs started the month by telling me he had assigned Detective Lenny Hahn to monitor and archive the covert videos for us. He said he had also told Hahn to help us out wherever possible. Even though Lenny lived on the opposite end of the state, I knew he would be very helpful to us. I believe this assignment was probably done without full approval from headquarters, and I expressed my gratitude for the assistance.

On day 1, I drove down to Dr. Trang's home to pick up the steelhead. Trang took me into his garage and produced two steelhead from his freezer (wrapped in clear plastic bags). I asked him if the price was the same ($25 each), and he said it was. I paid him a single $50 bill, and that deal was done.

He asked me if we sold deer and elk meat. I confirmed we did and that there were two choices. I told him the law only allows deer and elk meat to be sold if it comes from out-of-state game farms, and we do sell that. I told him the prices for that meat were on our website. I also said we sometimes buy deer and elk from hunters and cut and wrap the meat, but it is highly illegal, and we could all go to jail, but since it is much cheaper for us to buy, we can sell it for less. I told Trang we only sell the "hunted" meat to people we trust. Trang pointed out that since we were already involved in illegal sales (the steelhead), we should be okay. I told him he was right, and we do trust him. Trang said his wife is from France and wants deer and elk meat.

He ordered "5 lbs of the tenderloin steak and 5 pounds of the deer."

225

He said he wanted "The discount, aka not legal, meat." We agreed to meet on the 8th for that transaction.

I still couldn't fathom why Dr. Trang would take such a high risk to save a few bucks.

Two days later, at about 9 a.m. I met with Andy Miller at a storage unit in the Bellingham area. Andy was a very tall man, resembling Frankenstein, who appeared to be no smarter than I had guessed. He asked me to follow him through a maze of indoor storage units. Once we arrived at his storage unit, I met his wife, June Miller, who was seated in the hallway next to display tables holding numerous Native American items. Andy showed me all his items and gave me an introduction to how he made them and their significance. I noted the items were made of materials, including waterfowl feathers/wings, raptor claws/talons, raptor feathers, a bighorn sheep horn, and a bear skull. I told the Millers that the sale or purchase of waterfowl parts was a federal offense, and the sale/purchase of bear skulls or parts, sheep horns, and raptor parts was a state offense. June said they had never really looked into what was legal and what was illegal to sell, but knew some of it was illegal. Andy told me he had purchased bear parts from Randy Jackson at Jackson's Taxidermy in Whatcom County (what a coincidence!). Andy also said he and his wife had a stockpile of eagle feathers and talons at home, but his wife is an Alaska Native (Eskimo) and could have them. He stated the sheep horn was a bighorn sheep horn from Montana.

I told him I would be willing to deal in illegal wildlife, but it would have to stay between us, as we could all find ourselves in big trouble. I told him I had an Asian customer who buys many Native

226

American items, and I trusted him completely. I looked through the items and selected seven pieces to purchase. Andy and I agreed on the prices. All seven items were priced at $80 or less, except for the bear skull, for which he wanted $135. In total, we agreed to $445 for everything, which I paid for in cash. As I was getting ready to leave, Andy and June expressed their interest in doing more business with me, and I assured them they would see me again.

As expected, on the **5**th, we received a series of text messages from Jin wanting to know when we would be in Walla Walla. I told him we would be there between noon and 1 p.m. and did not want to go into Oregon.

Jin agreed to meet in Walla Walla and told me to be very careful and "make sure you are not followed." He said, "Big invest," indicating he was concerned about the transaction due to the amount of money involved.

Jin texted, "I sold the whole one Tina got. $? Need to ship to San Fansico."

He called and told me he had sold the small bear "Tina" had killed and wanted us to skin it, cut it up, add a large bear gallbladder to it, and ship the gall, the meat, and the paws to San Francisco. Jin wanted the bear to ship out as soon as possible. I told him I would have to thaw out the bear, cut it up, and could not ship it any earlier than Tuesday, the 7th. He said to go ahead and do so, and tell him how much he owed me for the bear and shipping. A short time later, Jin provided me with an address in Oakland, CA. I texted back, asking for the name, and Jin answered: "No name needed." During one of my

227

phone conversations with him, he asked if we could get snakes, and I told him we didn't have any snakes and didn't even know where to get them. I asked what kind of snakes he was looking for, and Jin said, "Poisonous snakes," and added he had a customer who wanted snakes to eat.

I asked if he was looking for rattlesnakes, to which Jin said: "No, the kind that lives in the mountains."

I told Jin to find out what kind of snakes his friend wanted, and I would ask around, but I don't have any contacts for snakes. He also asked me to get him a whole cougar (mountain lion). He had asked me previously if I could get him a cougar, and I told him I would ask around and try to find one for him. Lions and tigers and bears.....and now snakes- yum.

Detective Hahn and I prepared the small bear on the **6**[th] by skinning it and cutting it into parts. We gutted the bear, removed the four paws, and cut the four quarters off. I refroze the bear for shipment. I also texted Jin a photo of the bear, along with the weight of the meat and bones (~27 pounds, an absolute monster). He texted back and stated the bear was a gift for his friend in California.

The next day, I boxed the bear and a gallbladder and sent it to California via UPS. I gathered up 23 bear gallbladders (from a stock of gall that had already been photographed and DNA samples removed) and put them in a cooler full of dry ice.

Jennifer and I took off for Walla Walla the next morning (the 8th) with our bounty of bear gallbladder in a cooler in the back seat.

At 10:00 a.m., we received a text from Jin stating, "I will meet you in tri city. I will be in the mall. So you don't need to go to WW".

Later, Jin texted us that he would meet us at the Old Country Buffet (at about 11:45). We arrived at the Old Country Buffet parking lot (in the Columbia Center Mall in Kennewick, WA) at about 11:40 but saw no sign of Jin. At 11:56, I called him to see where he was, and he said he would be there in a couple of minutes.

I told him we were in the Old Country Buffet parking lot, and he responded by saying, "I see you" (which instantly told us he had counter-surveillance going), caught himself, and said he would be there in a few minutes.

At straight-up noon, Jennifer blurted out, "Here he is."

I turned to my right and saw Jin opening our truck's right rear door. We had not seen him approach us because he had walked to our truck from behind us (sneaky little shit). Jin climbed into the right rear seat, immediately opened the cooler in the backseat, and asked if he could look at the gall. He greeted "Tina" as he looked in the black plastic bag containing the gall and asked how much he owed us.

I told Jin, "We already agreed to $2,400 for the gall, so I want $2,500 total for the gall and the small bear."

He handed us a stack of $100 bills held together with a paperclip. I counted the money and found he had given us exactly $2,500.

Jin confided, "Some of the gall are going to China, and some to New York, San Francisco, and some to Chicago, but I have to find more buyers."

He told us to take him to his car (stating that he didn't want anyone to see him) and instructed me on how to get there. I drove him through the parking lot to the east. He asked me for my buyer's name and phone number in Vancouver, BC, and I told him I wouldn't give him the man's name or number. He asked if the man was Chinese, and I said I knew he was Asian, but I didn't know if he was Chinese. He asked again for his name and phone number and said he wanted to talk to the man, and I told Jin we don't do business like that.

I continued, "We won't tell anyone who you are, and I won't tell you who anyone else we deal with is."

Jin responded, "That is a good way to do business."

At one point, in the parking lot, he told me to turn left, and I noticed a fine-looking Audi SUV with Oregon plates. Jin told me to stop, and then he exited our truck, carrying the bag of gallbladder, and I saw him place the bag full of gallbladder in the back of a dark-colored Audi, which, as of that moment, was now ours.

As we left Jin behind, we discussed the fact that in all of our undercover contacts, nobody had ever snuck up on us like that. Jin had to have walked up directly behind our truck, so we couldn't see him in the side-view mirrors. The view through the rear-view mirror was obstructed because I had heavily tinted the windows on the truck's canopy. We had to admire his caution. Too bad (for him), it wouldn't work well enough to keep him out of trouble.

230

Had Jennifer and I not been in our roles when Jin had snuck up on us, we would have been done for. Fortunately, we had always stayed in character anytime we were together. On this day, it saved our case.

On the way home, we called Dr. Trang to see if he could meet us somewhere in the middle. He agreed to meet in the Burger King parking lot in Issaquah, just off I-90, at 3:15 p.m. We drove into the parking lot a few minutes late and pulled up next to Trang's black Mercedes. He exited and began talking with Jennifer while I retrieved the deer and elk meat.

I heard Jennifer tell Trang, "Please don't say anything to anyone because we could get in big trouble," to which Trang responded that he knew and would not say anything.

He told us his wife is from France and likes "weird meats." He added that his wife had asked him if buying the meat was illegal, and he told her it was just "discounted." He said he would be fishing again soon and would call us when he had more fish. Trang handed Jennifer $100 and put the illegal meat in his Mercedes. I guess we could now add a Mercedes to our list. WDFW was going to be a luxury car dealer soon.

Wyatt Wilson called me on the **14**th and said he had two mounted scaup (a drake and a hen) for sale, as well as a drake old squaw (both sea ducks). Wilson said he had just picked up the old squaw and was getting ready to mount it and asked me if I wanted it. I said I would take the old squaw, and I wanted it mounted, standing "wings in" on a wall mount. I told him I would probably pick up the scaup too. He said it would be about two weeks until he had the old squaw done and would call me. He added that he was working on getting me a drake harlequin and was sure he would come up with one soon.

On the **16**[th], Jin Dong sent me a text message stating, "I need other whole one."

I called him on the phone, and he said, "One of the gallbladders you sold me was no good and leaked all the bile."

I assured Jin we would give him a replacement the next time we saw him (the customer is always right). I also explained it was improbable that we could get him a bear right now, as they are hibernating, but we would try. I struggled to explain the whole hibernation scene to Jin, but found he couldn't understand why we could get elk in winter but not bears. I am pretty sure I could have had an easier time explaining it to a 3rd grader, but I think he finally got it.

I received an interesting call from a woman in Post Falls, Idaho, on the **20**[th], who offered anything from elephant parts to leopards. I told her we would swing in to meet with her on the 28th. We had to come over that day anyway to meet with Rousch and to buy another mountain goat from a new customer. February 27th through 29th were fully booked, which I included in my weekly report to Hobbs and Cenci.

A full week later, Officer Brian Alexander provided us with an enormous, freshly killed mountain lion. Although it smelled more than a little nasty, the cat weighed 160+ pounds and was a beautiful specimen.

232

As soon as I got the cat, I sent Jin Dong a text message telling him, "A friend just killed a very large cougar, and he will sell it to me for $250. Do you want it for $350?"

Jin replied that he did want to buy the cougar, and we agreed we would bring the cat to him in Walla Walla on the 28th.

Later in the day, on the **27^{th,}** while we were driving east, Hobbs called and informed me there would be a meeting at headquarters on the 29th regarding the progress and future of Operation Cody. Hobbs said the meeting included him, the chief, the deputy chief, several USFWS agents, and the USFWS boss from Portland. The meeting had obviously been set with the intention of tuning out the two people who knew the most about the operation. Incredible!

While I fully understood the two of us had absolutely no power over the decisions regarding the operation, it seemed very foolish not to have us at the meeting for our perspectives and opinions. It seemed equivalent to coaching a basketball game without actually watching it or talking with the players. I had a bad feeling about this meeting.

We called Jin Dong on the **28th** and told him we would be in Walla Walla at about 8:30 am. He told us to meet him "at the regular place." At about 8:20, Jennifer and I arrived at the Pacific Pride Restaurant in Walla Walla, and I saw his white Lexus parked near the restaurant's back door. We knocked on the back door, and eventually, Jin came out and met us. It appeared nobody else was at the restaurant. He came to our truck to look at the cougar and asked if we had been followed. Before showing him the cougar, I handed him a replacement gallbladder, which he placed in the back of his Lexus SUV. He looked

233

at the cougar and asked how much it weighed, and I told him it weighed more than he did, between 150 and 160 pounds.

Jin was very concerned about people seeing the cougar, and at one point, he told me to wait as a truck was moving around across the street. He said he wanted it carried into the restaurant. I rolled the cougar up in a camo tarp, and we followed Jin into the restaurant's storeroom. I placed the cougar on the floor of the storeroom. Once we were all in the storeroom, Jin told us to close the door. He asked if the price was $350, which I confirmed. In the pitch-dark room, he handed me $350 in cash. He said he would be in touch with us, and Jennifer and I left Jin in the restaurant at about 8:30. We were more than a little confused by the whole payment-in-the-dark deal. Was this ploy his way of avoiding being seen? Who was he worried about seeing us? This guy was definitely strange.

We arrived at Kent Rousch's house at about 2:30 p.m. on the **28**th. He showed us the bighorn sheep sconce he had made for us and discussed how it could be mounted on the wall. I've got to admit it was cool for a light, but certainly not worth the money. Kent went into a discussion about the three sets of bighorn sheep horns we had brought him. He said he had to wait until spring to take the horns to his Idaho Fish and Game friend to pin them and told us he would tell his friend that he (Kent) had found the sheep heads along the river while whitewater rafting. Kent told us he could not show up with the sheep before spring, as there would be no logical way to explain how he could have found them in winter. He said his friend might not want to pin the sheep, as the laws (relating to bighorn sheep) are getting strict. He went on to tell us about a friend of his who had recently been arrested for dealing in illegal bighorn sheep horns, but added, "he knew what he was doing."

Kent told us that if his friend wouldn't pin the sheep for him, he would just pay us outright for them and would make the horns into furniture and sconces. He stated he couldn't just walk into the Safari International show (in Las Vegas) with illegal or unpinned wildlife because they have federal and state game wardens checking every item coming in. If the items aren't built into furniture (or artwork), they will have to appear to be completely legal with paperwork and pins, etc.

Kent asked us what else we were doing in the Spokane area, and I told him we were going to Post Falls, Idaho, to meet with a woman who had several interesting wildlife items for sale. I explained the woman had contacted us and provided a list of items she wanted to sell. He asked if we had a lot of people offering to sell us wildlife, and I told him it happened all the time. I read him a list of African wildlife items the woman had emailed us. The list contained a zebra hide and a giraffe hide. Kent said he might be interested in the hides and told us how he judges the value of hides and what he would pay. He told us to ask the woman if she had CITES permits for the items and said it might be illegal if she didn't.

Kent went on to advise us about rhino horns and the fact that they are highly illegal. He told us it was illegal to possess them, sell them, or buy them, and it meant "prison time." Kent asked if we had seen the TV special on rhino horns, and we stated we had not. He explained that the Feds had busted a group of people for dealing in rhino horns, which was very serious trouble. He said people kill the rhino, cut off the horns, and waste the animal, in other words, poaching. He complained the laws are bullshit for rhinos, which are legally killed because you still can't sell the horns. If we ever came across rhino horns, he urged us to call him first, stating that rhino horns can be worth up to $50,000 and that he has a friend who would buy them.

After leaving Rousch's house, we drove to Post Falls, Idaho, where we met with Karen Ranken. Karen showed us numerous wildlife items, which I photographed. I told her I was very interested in the zebra and needed to call a friend to check its value. I asked if she had paperwork of any kind for the items, and she said she might have paperwork for the cheetah but not for anything else. I asked where she had obtained all the wildlife items. She said a man (I believe an ex-husband) used to guide "over there" and that he had been on the cover of Cabelas' Magazine. He had gotten some of the items. She had also bought some of the items over the years and lived in a bigger house, but no longer had room for all of it.

At 5:20, I called Agent Andrews and advised him of what we knew and that Karen was asking $500 for the zebra hide. Agent Andrews asked me to go ahead and buy the zebra, but only after making it clear to Karen that the sale was illegal. After speaking with Agent Andrews, I told Karen and her husband that my friend was interested in the zebra, but he told me it was illegal to sell, especially since we were going to take it across state lines to Washington. I asked both Karen and her husband if they still wanted to sell the zebra with that in mind. Karen said she was fine with it and didn't see why it would be illegal. I told her I didn't know the laws but that my friend did; he was certain it was illegal. I asked again about the sale, and both Karen and her husband said they wanted to sell it. I paid Karen $500 in cash and boxed up the zebra hide.

Karen mentioned she had a friend whose husband used to be a taxidermist. She said her snowy owl had come from this friend. She said her friend also had a mounted eagle, and she would talk to her friend and see if she was interested in selling the birds. We told Karen we would show some friends the photos and get back to them.

The next morning, we headed home, wondering what the supreme powers would decide to do with our operation. By the end of the day, we wondered no more. Hobbs called and told us, effective immediately, we were not to do any business with any new customers. We could only continue to do business with our "top eight" customers (which had been listed for us). The headquarters' masterminds had also decided we would take the suspects down (serve search warrants, make arrests, etc.) on September 18th, 2012. This new operational protocol was far more ridiculous than my mind could have ever imagined.

In addition to the deadline and "top eight" rule, I was also told about a new protocol. We were approved to do business with Indians (in one case) if the case was a solid off-reservation trafficking transaction of wildlife, but only with "case-by-case approval"...that would allow us to work a whopping "top-nine." That would be if/when we got an offer from a tribal member (which shouldn't be too hard, as I had already turned down many of them). Someone had decided we would take on tribal trafficking in wildlife, after all, to a small degree.

237

This decision had severe issues/flaws: 1) We were done seeking out new criminals after only 14 months of undercover work, rather than the 24 months the chief had approved. 2) If number 9 on our bad-guy list called with something very tempting and illegal, we were to turn them down, but if number 7 called, we could do business. 3) We had to keep stringing along the top eight while letting them kill more and more for no valid reason. We had been continuing to do business with people only so we could gain more suspects. However, now the only reason to keep them going was so we could keep our information fresh and could still obtain search warrants on September 18th (judges will only issue search warrants based on fresh probable cause). There has to be an expectation that the evidence listed in the search warrant will still be there. 4) Now, we knew we wouldn't be able to serve search warrants on any of the suspects not on the "top eight" list since the information would be "stale" between now and September 18th, and no judge on earth would give us a warrant based on six and a half month-old information. 5) Things would get interesting for us if we turned down anyone below the top eight and they ended up talking to one of the top eight suspects. How would we explain that?

All-in-all, this meant our operation had been brought to an end just when we were really starting to roll. Although this decision meant we still had six and a half months of undercover work to do, it would only be with the same suspects we already had in the bag. We would likely not get anything new except more charges on the suspects, which we already had. This also meant we had only been allowed to work one hunting season, thus totally missing our intended target of two full hunting seasons.

238

The only reason I was given for this new operational protocol was that DC Cenci felt we wouldn't have the manpower to handle arresting and searching more suspects. I had previously explained to the administration that we didn't have to take them all at once.....we could have taken the "top eight" or so right away and moved on to the others as time allowed. Jennifer and I also wondered where they had come up with the number eight. Was it a compromise? Did one administrator say twelve, and another say four? Or just a number they pulled out of the air?

Not only did the top desk jockeys come up with the number of eight, but they listed the "top eight" for us (mostly from a list Sgt. Hobbs and I had informally put together months back); Bourey, Wyatt Wilson, the Parker group, Jin Dong/Pacific Pride, Mike Craig/Cascade Crest, Kent Rousch, Dusty Hilton, and the Duck Song all received the honors. Smirnov was added to the list of suspects we could continue to work with, but only because of the federal case. Apparently, the restaurants were on the list not because of their level of trafficking but rather the risk they posed to the consumers.

Cenci had finally succeeded in driving a stake through the heart of our operation, and Chief Bjork had gone right along with it (even though he had promised me a two-year window of operation). While I was certainly disappointed, I wasn't shocked. The real shock would have been if we had been allowed to continue as planned. A great deal of work needed to be completed before September 18th. We still had eight (actually nine with Liev) very active cases to work, as well as getting all the case files up to speed, writing search warrant affidavits, making copies of hundreds of hours of covert video, and gathering all the evidence documentation.

It was on this date that I lost any respect I had left for Chief Bjork. The chief knew how effective our operation was and yet had allowed his deputy chief to shut us down ten months early. Was the chief that disconnected, or did he just grow tired of Cenci's insistence to terminate the operation? One should expect this when a fish and wildlife law enforcement program is run by a person who has never been a game warden.

Behind the scenes, there was a dedicated army of people helping us out already. Officer Dave Jones had taken each deer and elk we had purchased and had them cut up (either for charity or for use in undercover sales). Officer Cook had been providing us with fish and wildlife for our sales. Detective Paul Golden had been downloading and preserving our text and email messages. Detective Clarke had been photographing, logging, and submitting all of the evidence for identification and keeping up on case files (or at least we thought he had done so). Detective Hahn and Officer Conklin had been monitoring and archiving the covert video. Karen McManus (in the WDFW financial services) had kept the money flowing and the books squared away (no small task). But now that we had an actual operational deadline, it was time to focus on the take-downs and arrests. The real problem was that I was still running the operation with only one part-time officer for help. Jennifer was still only allowed to help me 4 to 5 days per month, which simply wasn't cutting it. Again, I stressed to Hobbs that I needed help. He assured me he was doing his best to get me the assistance I so desperately needed.

We had over 85 suspects (including those in other states and federal cases) at this point in our operation, with well over 1,000 criminal charges. We had nothing to be ashamed of, but I sure wished we could have kept the operation going. This new operational protocol meant we would not have an opportunity to search the homes of any suspects other than the top eight, and we would miss the opportunity of a lifetime to snap up all the major wildlife traffickers we had hoped for. This kind of idiocy was simply the cost of doing <u>wildlife</u> business in the present-day WDFW.

When this operation was completed, we were reasonably sure Cenci would create a massive media blitz out of it and expose all the intricate details of how the undercover operation was executed. Even though it was clear Cenci didn't support our operation, it was well known that he hadn't yet found a camera he didn't love. This would ensure that Jennifer and I would never safely work undercover in this state again. In our past cases, his media releases had undoubtedly jeopardized the two of us before (as well as jeopardizing all undercover fish and wildlife officers). If/when Cenci conducted his media releases on Operation Cody, all the suspects whom officers hadn't yet contacted would be dumping evidence like crazy, and the two of us would be done working undercover forever. Hopefully, Jennifer would eventually get the uniformed sergeant position she sought, but that left me wondering what I would do.......geoduck? I didn't think so.

My wife and I had been contemplating retirement for some time, and this recent Operation Cody decision made up my mind. When this operation was done, so was I. I assured both Sgt. Hobbs and Jennifer, I would stick around until all of the casework was done, the

241

case files were completed, and everything had been turned over to the various prosecutors. Several factors went into my decision, but paramount in my mind was the fact that nothing in the WDFW's "ship of fools" was ever going to change, so it was time for me to move on.

CHAPTER 19- MARCH 2012

March **3rd** was my first contact with one of the "top eight" since he had been placed on the most wanted list.

I received the following text from Bourey, "I may get some animal on Sunday if I do, it would be our last call."

I replied, "Ok. Let us know. We could take 2 big ones".

Bourey replied, "Sure will."

I came back with, "Thanks. No more after this?"

Bourey said, "If the weather getting warmer, we are not going to get any more they can only get it when the snow covers the mountain."

Wyatt Wilson called me on the **5th,** asking when I could come up and get the ducks he had for me. I told him I would be heading his way that day. Before I left for Wilson's shop, I wrote down two Native American items, commonly made with eagle and hawk parts. One of the items, the bird head staff, was something I had seen at Jackson's Taxidermy the first time I met Wilson. I got to Wilson's shop at about 10:30 a.m. and was greeted by Wilson and his entourage of dogs.

He showed me several duck mounts, including two old squaw, and said: "I need to get $300 for the old squaw, as they cost more, but all the other ducks are $100 each."

As I was talking to Wilson, I handed him my handwritten note (which I had written that morning) with the two items on it, "Shaman

Stick and Bird Head Staff." I asked him if he knew what those items were. Wilson said he was familiar with them, and he makes them all the time. He said he usually makes them with either eagle or hawk heads attached. I asked him if he or someone he knew would deal with them. Wilson warned me it was big trouble, and he didn't need to buy any. I told him I was not interested in selling. I wanted to buy them for an Asian customer of mine. He said he would make me all I wanted, for $100 each, and asked how many I wanted. I explained I only needed one of each at that time. Wilson asked if I wanted them done with eagle or hawk heads, and I chose eagle. He also asked me if I had a source for getting eagles, and I said I did.

Wilson said, "Just call me a day or two in advance to tell me you are coming, then bring the birds up, and I will make the sticks." I agreed to do so.

Wilson inquired about the Yakima man I had mentioned, who made Native American items for me. He asked if the man could make the eagle head items. I told Wilson he didn't do taxidermy, so he couldn't do the heads, but would probably do the beadwork on the sticks/staffs. He asked me what else the man makes for me, and I told him he works on bear claw necklaces for me now. I also mentioned that the man couldn't get enough bear claws. Wilson said he had plenty of bear claws and asked how much I had been paying for claws. When I told him I had paid $6 to $10 each, he said he would sell me all I wanted for $3 each (another crime committed).

I agreed to buy the two old squaw, as well as two other sea ducks, for $500. I paid him $500 in cash and followed him to the inner room of his shop. Wilson showed me some bear claws on a shelf and

244

many more in a plastic tackle box, and several bear teeth. He asked how many I wanted. I selected 20 bear claws and paid him an additional $60 in cash. I took the bear claws and ducks and said goodbye for now. Once I was heading back south, I called Agent Andrews and told him he owed me another $500 for the ducks (a federal crime).

Next, it was time for the Parker clan to step up and prove they deserved their place in the "top eight." On the **10**th, I received a phone call from Kyle Parker asking if we would be interested in elk steak.

I asked what condition the steak was in, and Kyle said, "Standing on its hooves."

I replied, "Elk was always better than deer, and we'll take one."

Before we could make it over to pick up our elk, Sgt. Hobbs called with some good news. He had somehow convinced the chief that Operation Cody really needed some full-time help. The chief authorized another offer to promote Jennifer to detective (for the duration of the operation if she chose). The chief also said he would make sure some personnel got shuffled around to cover her area while she was away from her uniformed duties.

Hobbs said, "If she wants the position, it's hers for up to six months. I'm calling her next."

When I got off the phone with Hobbs, I wondered if Jennifer would take the detective position this time. Two things had changed since she was offered the same deal the prior spring. Admin was going to make an effort to cover her work area (so it wouldn't go to hell), and she was pretty well embedded in this operation. For the first 5 or 6 months of Operation Cody, when Jennifer and I had talked about the operation, she had always referred to it as "your case." Still, in the last few months, I noticed she had changed her phrasing to "our case." I think she was hooked, but even if she took the promotion, I couldn't see her sticking to a desk when the weather and the uniformed officers' arrest activities warmed up in summer. It was simply against her nature.

On the **11th**, Tanya Franklin called to tell us Kyle had an elk ready for us, but they had moved. She gave me the address (which, from my research, I already knew was Jim Backster's residence) in Naches, WA.

The next morning, as we were on our way, Tanya called us three separate times to check on our progress. We arrived at about 11:30 and were met by Jim Backster in the driveway. I noticed the Parker camper was set up adjacent to the house. Jim took us to the back of his blue GMC pickup and showed us the carcass of a dead deer (I guess they couldn't find an elk). Soon after meeting with Jim, Kyle appeared.

Jim, the multiple convicted felon, declared, "I shot the deer using my .30-30 rifle. Kyle, my wife, and I went out spotlighting on Saturday night at about 2 a.m. I killed the deer while my wife held the spotlight, and Kyle was asleep in the truck."

Jim went on, "I shot at a different deer earlier, but the spotlight screwed up my vision in the scope. I think I hit that deer, but it never gone down, so I just shot another one."

Jim and Kyle told me they had grabbed the deer, thrown it in the truck's bed, and headed down the hill.

I asked Kyle and Jim how much they wanted for the deer, and Kyle told me to "Make us an offer."

I replied, "How about $200," which they agreed to.

I asked who I owed the money to, and they said they would split the money "50/50," so I handed each man a single $100 bill. Kyle and Jim told me they were going elk hunting next and would probably get one or two and call us. Jim said he had just purchased a five-acre piece of property, and there were elk in that area, and he planned on moving to that property within three months.

After we loaded the deer, Jennifer and I headed back west to go through the same routine of photographing, taking DNA samples, and transferring the deer to Officer Jones. By the time we were done with our top eight, the local charities would be fully stocked with poached meats.

The next day, Jennifer called and told me Hobbs had called her about the temporary appointment to detective. I was pleased to hear Jennifer announce she had accepted the offer. She said she wanted to see this operation through until the end, but may not stick in the full-time detective position for six months.

"I'll take whatever time you feel you can commit," was my honest response.

I was just glad to have her on full-time so we could wade through the pile of work that had accumulated over the last few months.

It had been quite some time since we had heard from Bourey, so on the **15**[th,] I sent him a text stating, "If there isn't enough snow now, I would be shocked. Any word on getting any big ones?"

A few minutes later, Bourey called and said there was a lot of snow in the mountains, and he had driven over Snoqualmie Pass to Moses Lake and got stuck on the pass. He said he was on his way home while he was talking to me.

Bourey stated he has been bugging his suppliers to get him elk, but the, "Fucking Indians are lazy."

He said that if or when he gets a load, he will call us, and he also wanted to get some elk for himself.

At about 8 p.m. on March **19**[th], I received a phone call from Kyle (on Jim Backster's phone) saying he and Jim had just shot an elk "behind the feed" and wanted us to come over to pick it up.

I responded, "My wife and I will head over in the morning."

At about 1 a.m. on the **20**[th], I received a text message from Jim's phone stating, "Hi Tom we ran into a little problem and jumped the gun, so we have to cancel your trip down. Talk to you soon, Jim".

At 07:20, I received another text explaining they had shot the elk, then she had gotten back up and had run away, and they were unable to find her. Jim explained that since the elk was right near a feedlot, they were concerned about being seen. He also said the elk had been shot with a .30-30 rifle at 75 yards by his "buddy" (Kyle), and was not a quick kill shot. Through a series of text messages, Jim said he had sold five firearms last year, including a Remington 12-gauge. I asked Jim about mounting a scope on his .30-30, and he texted me a photo of his scoped .30-30 rifle (nice of a convicted felon to send me photos of the firearm he couldn't legally possess). He also asked if we could take two elk if they got them later that evening, and I responded that we only wanted one.

At 9:20 that night, I received another text message from Jim stating, "Went alone on shot lol."

Through more text messages, it was agreed we would come over the following morning to get the elk.

On the morning of the **21ˢᵗ**, <u>Detective</u> Jennifer Maurstad and I were heading over the pass when I called WDFW Officer Skip Caton and told him I believed an elk had been shot the night before near one of the feed stations. Officer Caton said he would check the area and attempt to locate the kill site. At about 11:00, we arrived at Jim Backster's house and were greeted by Kyle and Jim. Jim directed me to back up to his blue GMC pickup. As I exited our vehicle, I saw a whole-skinned elk carcass in the bed of his truck. I asked Jim if he had shot the elk by himself, and he said he had gone up alone and had shot it by himself with his .30-30 rifle up by the Cowichee Feed Station (a WDFW feeding station, where our agency feeds elk to help them make

249

it through the rough winters). Jim said that after he shot the elk, he returned and got his wife and Kyle. The three of them went back up and loaded the elk in his truck. I asked if I was to pay both him and Kyle or just pay him. Jim said he and Kyle would split the money 50/50 again since Kyle helped him get the elk out and clean it. I told Jim we normally pay $600 per elk and asked if that amount was ok with him, and he said that was fine. I took $600 out of my wallet and paid Jim.

After paying for the elk, I asked Jim if I could take a look at his .30-30. He literally ran into his house and came back out with a pump-action, scoped Savage .30-30, which he handed to us. He went into detail on how he had the rifle drilled and tapped for the scope mount and had changed the stock length. After spending a little quality time with Kyle and Jim, we headed home.

When we were back on the road, I called Officer Caton. Skip said he found a fresh elk kill site near the Cowichee Feed Station and had processed the scene, including removing and retaining a DNA sample and picking up .30-30 shell casings. That evidence would tie the dynamic duo to the kill scene, thus adding another criminal charge to each of them.

Liev Smirnov popped back onto the scene on the **23rd**. He called and told me a shipment of black caviar had just arrived, but the shipping was so expensive he would have to charge $120 per pound to make up for the extra costs. I said I would still like to get 6 pounds and asked when a good time would be for pickup. Liev said he is working "on an island" in Bremerton, and it would have to be late evening next week. I told him I would call him on Monday and work out what time and day.

At about 11 p.m., on the **23rd**, I received an email from an address I hadn't seen before: "Name Glen i do fishing on the columbia river for all sorts of fish, i have many brown/white antlers/hides and do hunting for elk/deer all yr around and more etc. So what do you most interest in? you guys buy what most of all? seen you card over here yakama valley wapato Ford den store. i love everything you have i seen on ur site n the stuff i see i hunt for n fish etc."

Apparently, the email's author was either typing in the dark or wasn't much on "gramur and spelin."

After receiving the above email (which included the sender's full name), I ran driver's and criminal history checks on Glen Sullivan. I learned he was an Indian with an <u>extensive</u> criminal history.

I replied, "Thanks. You may be just the kind of supplier we are looking for. I am busy as hell right now but will get back to you in the next day or two. You have a phone number I can call you on?"

We had just been instructed to go ahead and deal with tribal members, and this had all the earmarks of trafficking in progress.

Early in the day, on the **26th**, Liev called and told me he would be home around 8 p.m., and I could come any time after that. I got to his house around 7:45 p.m. and met him in his garage. Liev opened the upright freezer, and I saw it was packed with multiple jars of black caviar. He pulled out six jars for me and loaded them into my cooler. He told me Yuli had caught and processed all of the caviar in

251

Oklahoma, and Yuli had shipped out 28 pounds. He said he had people waiting for the shipment and had no problem selling it. He told me Yuli had never found paddlefish with eggs so early, but that some other Russians in Oklahoma had told Yuli about a new place to harvest paddlefish, and these other Russians had been getting caviar from paddlefish as early as December. I asked Liev how the caviar had been shipped to him, and he told me Yuli had a Russian friend who was driving to California anyway, so Yuli paid the guy $350 extra to drive the caviar to Washington. Liev again apologized for the extra cost of the caviar. I handed over $720 in cash.

On the **29**[th], I got a call from Sullivan saying, "I looked at your website and was impressed. Are you willing to buy all the items that you offer for sale on the website?"

I told Glen it depended on what he had to offer. Glen asked if we were interested in buying elk jerky and said he sells a great deal of it to friends and "other people" around the Yakima area. I told Glen that the elk jerky we have on the website all comes from out-of-state game farms, and before we agreed to buy elk jerky from him, we would have to sample it first. I spent a great deal of time explaining the need to keep business between us confidential and that we would be breaking both state and tribal laws. I explained that my wife and I are non-Indian, so we have to abide by our laws, which are different from tribal law.

I told Glen that while we have bought elk from individual hunters before, we are very careful about who we deal with because it is illegal. He said he understood. Glen offered to sell us "about anything," including deer and elk. I told him we usually pay $600 per

252

adult elk and $200 per adult deer, but they had to be gutted, skinned, and in excellent condition. Glen said that wasn't a problem because he always takes good care of his animals. I asked him if he had decided to sell us a deer or elk, and where we would meet him. He said he could meet us in Ellensburg or even farther west. I suggested North Bend, and Glen said he would even drive it to Everett if we wanted. He confided that he would have to get someone else to drive him as he didn't have a driver's license. I told him to hold off until he heard back from me, and I would call him the next day (after I confirmed with Hobbs whether he wanted us to proceed with this one).

We conversed with Glen on the **30**[th] via a text message stating, "Glen: we are available Monday, Tuesday, and Thursday this coming week. Looks like I am having surgery on April 12th and will be down for a few weeks. So if you can get something by this coming week, let us know. Give us as much advanced notice as you can. Thanks, and I look forward to doing business with ya. Tom Davis".

Glen wrote back, "Thanks Tom for giving me a chance. I'm looking forward business with you/wife long term. You say Monday and I'm going Monday Tom. How bout that?"

I replied, "Good luck!"

Glen answered, "And what's the limit of elk can you take Monday? A deer to or just elk for now".

I replied, "Let's just go with one elk and up to two deer at first. After we get to know each other maybe more".

Glen answered, "ok tom. I can bring one elk and two deer Monday? Or just start with one of them. If you don't mind me asking- it it cash or check? 6hundred elk/deer 2hundred".

253

I answered, "One elk or up to two deer, not and two deer. Cash and you are right on price".

CHAPTER 20- APRIL 2012

I spent the first few days of April warning our "top eight" suspects that I would be down for a few weeks because of foot surgery scheduled for April 16th. I had discussed my return to duties with my surgeon, Hobbs, and my partner. The surgeon agreed to clear me back to work 3 to 4 weeks post-surgery, but I would be in a cast and on crutches for 6 to 8 weeks. The most significant hurdle was convincing Hobbs to allow me back to work.

"What a great cover this will make. Who would ever think a cop would be working on crutches?" I argued.

"Since you are already in good with all these guys, I'm not sure you need to be any more convincing, and I have to worry about your safety even if you don't," Hobbs counter-argued. "Have you talked this over with Jennifer?" he asked.

I truthfully replied, "Yep, and she is fine with it."

Crossing his t's and dotting his I's, Hobbs later called Jennifer and talked it over with her directly.

A few weeks later, I learned that when Hobbs had asked Jennifer, "What will you do if the shit hits the fan, and you guys have to get out of there quickly?"

Her thoughtful and kind response had been, "I'd just throw his scrawny ass over my shoulder and run." Apparently, my lean frame wasn't all that intimidating to my partner.

In addition to the task of informing everyone of my time away from the business, I spent a bit more time turning down some excellent offers from some outstanding prospects. I guess we would save these for seed for a time in the very distant future, when possibly a similar operation would scoop them up. We could also scare them into the straight and narrow as they watched the television reports featuring our operation on the take-down day, which I knew would be coming. More than likely, the suspects we were currently turning down would realize just how close they had come to getting busted. They would thank their lucky stars they hadn't been caught <u>when they should be thanking our chief and deputy chief</u>. Every illegal trafficker and poacher we had to turn away made me sick and furious. I had to assume Cenci was grinning from ear to ear at the same time, knowing how much it bothered me.

Glen Sullivan texted us on the **2nd**.

"Just like you say, start off with 1. Got em."

Through a series of text messages, Glen told me he had killed an elk and was going to skin it out and bring it over. Jennifer and I left to meet with Glen in North Bend, WA. At 5:00 p.m. (About when Glen told us he would meet us in North Bend), Glen sent us another text.

"Everytin be ok. This aint no trick is it?? Just thought I ask. I be leaving towards west bout 30mins."

Great. If he left in 30 minutes, he would only be 3 hours late! I sent him texts stating it was not a trick, and if he felt uncomfortable at all when he met with us, he could turn around and go back with no problems.

After many more text messages and calls, we agreed to meet Glen just off Hwy. 18 about ¼ mile west of I-90. Finally, after waiting over 4 hours, we observed a 1979 Ford Pickup pull up behind us. We met within 100 yards of Hwy. 18, and then he followed us to a point just northeast of Rattlesnake Road in King County. When we pulled over to the side of the road, I saw there were three Indian men in his truck. As the truck's occupants exited the vehicle, the far-right passenger introduced himself as Glen. I immediately recognized Glen by his driver's license photo. While he and I were talking, I overheard one of the other Indians ask Jennifer, "You want to smoke some (weed)?" I saw the trio had a skinned adult elk carcass in the back of the truck. We told the men to back their truck up to ours so we could slide the elk from truck to truck. Once Glen had backed up to the point when we heard the crunch of our trucks mashing together, they slid the elk carcass from their truck to ours. After the elk was loaded, Glen climbed into the right-rear seat of our truck while I sat in the driver's seat, and Jennifer sat in the right-front seat.

I asked him if the other two guys with him were cool, and he said: "They are my brothers."

I inquired if he meant that they literally were his brothers, which he confirmed.

Glen said, "I keep them in line" (referring to his brothers).

I asked how old they were, and he replied: "We are all 30".

I tried to explain to Glen that it was impossible to have three brothers all the same age unless they were triplets, and he said one was 29 and the other was older than him, but they were all around 30 years old, he thought. Glen told us he had killed a deer the day before, and they had left to go hunting this morning (the 4th) at about 5:30 am. He said he shot two elk, but one didn't drop (a common theme among poachers, who didn't seem to expend too much effort tracking down wounded animals). He said he was going to make a big batch of jerky out of the deer and would get us some to try. He told us he had seen our business card on the board at the Wapato store and then looked at our website. I paid Glen $600 in cash for the elk, and we finally cleared the contact at about 9:30 p.m. We had a 3-hour drive ahead of us and still had to photograph the elk,..........etc.

About 10 minutes after we left, Glen and his "brothers," Bourey, texted, "My boy want $600 each if I want the animal, and you have to pick up at least 4 of them".

Jennifer texted back, "We will get back to you tomorrow."

Bourey replied, "I need to let them know tonight," and "They may not get all that if they come they won't bring less then four and I don't have anybody who want it."

Tired of texting in the dark, we decided to call Bourey. Bourey said his supplier wanted to know if he wanted some elk very soon, but would only deliver elk in quantities of four or more. I asked him if this was the same supplier he had always used, and he said it was "the same guy." I told Bourey we had picked up an elk a week or two ago and just now had a fresh one in the back of our truck, so we didn't need four and wouldn't have room to store them. I offered to take one and possibly two, but that was the maximum we could handle. Bourey said he would ask around to see if he could find buyers for more and would let us know.

A couple of days later, on the 4th, Bourey called and told me he had a load of elk coming in that afternoon, which should arrive around 4:30 p.m. He said the load should be around seven elk and wanted to know how many we could take. I told Bourey we could handle a maximum of two. He said he had to accept the whole load; otherwise, the suppliers would never deliver to him again. Bourey said he had no other buyers lined up (which was strange) and hoped we would take the whole load. I told him we had dinner plans and wouldn't be able to get to his place until after 7 p.m. Bourey said we better hurry because otherwise, his other buyers would get first pick on the elk (even stranger since he had just told me he had no other buyers).

At 6:10 p.m., I received a text from Bourey stating, "hey animals been here."

At about 7:40 p.m., Sgt. Hobbs, who was watching the camera aimed at the Bourey residence, called and said a black SUV was backed up to Bourey's garage and appeared to have loaded an elk.

Jennifer and I arrived at Bourey's home at about 7:45 and observed a black Toyota 4-Runner (we grabbed the license number as we walked by it) backed up to his garage. I exited our vehicle, walked next to the 4-Runner twice, and noticed the carcass of an elk in the rear of the vehicle. The driver of the 4-Runner came out and moved the vehicle across the street (and returned on foot to Bourey's house) as Jennifer backed up to the garage.

I saw four elk carcasses spread across the floor of the garage. He told me to select the two we wanted. I selected two elk, and Bourey and three of his "monkeys" loaded the elk in our truck. He told us he had received six elk in this load and asked us how our deal with the Yakima Indian had gone. We told him other than being almost 5 hours late, it was fine. After loading the elk, Bourey invited us in to eat dinner with them. We told him we had just eaten dinner, but he insisted we come in anyway. Jennifer and I went into his house, where Bourey joined us and a total of five other "monkeys."

He served us some kind of sliced/cooked meat (which we didn't recognize, and realized we probably didn't want to). We dipped the mystery meat in a vegetable sauce to mask the taste. Bourey said he never goes hungry, and when he goes camping, he kills and eats everything, including deer, pheasant, rabbit, grouse, and more. He said he had just bought a .22 magnum rifle because when he shoots a .22, it doesn't make much noise. I had to suppress the urge to puke as I choked down the mystery meat, but Jennifer seemed to like it (her only problem was drinking the Heineken beer, which she had told me was her least favorite beer).

Bourey discussed fishing and told us it was almost "sturgeon time" and showed us a photo on his cell phone of a very large sturgeon (laid out on the back deck of his house). He said his monkeys would start catching sturgeon soon and asked if we were still interested, and I confirmed our interest, especially if they had eggs.

I asked him if we owed him $1,200 for the elk, and he said, "That's right." Staying in character, Jennifer demanded my wallet from me and paid him $1,200 in cash. We headed north to take care of the elk and call it a night.

By the 9th, it was time to get reacquainted with Wyatt Wilson. I called him and said I would be at his place around 11:00 to drop off the eagles. I made drawings of two Indian staffs to show him how I wanted the bird heads mounted. The bald eagle had been obtained from WDFW Officer Dave Jones, and the golden eagle was provided to me by USFWS Agent Steven Andrews. I got to Wilson's shop around 11:00 a.m. and showed him the eagles and my drawings. Once in the shop, we discussed how I wanted to have the eagle heads mounted. He said he would take the eagles to his "mother-in-law's" house just down the road, adding that the house was vacant in the winter. Wilson stated he does his eagle work there, so the birds are not in his shop. He said he should have the eagles done in a day or two.

He offered me some elk ivory teeth, and I explained they don't sell very well. I told him I could sell bear claws and teeth much easier. Wilson said he had an abundant supply of bear teeth and claws and would sell them all for $3.00 each. I selected 40 bear claws and 13 bear teeth and paid him $160 in cash. Before I left, he showed me some of his waterfowl work for sale, but I declined, saying I had all the ducks I needed.

During the first week in April, I called Mike Craig at the Cascade Crest Restaurant and told him I would have some poached elk meat all cut and wrapped the way he wanted. Mike said to bring it up when I had it ready. On the 11th, I took Jennifer to meet Mike for the first time. We arrived at Craig's house, and Mike met us at our truck. After introducing my "wife" to Mike, I showed him the elk meat. I told him we had 88 pounds of elk burger patties and about 8 pounds of elk steak, for a total of 96 pounds. I told him a friend of ours had recently killed the elk in Yakima, and all the meat was from that elk. I opened one of the burger packages to show him the patties, and he was pleased to see they were separated by paper. Mike inquired about the price, and I reminded him we had agreed on $4.00 per pound.

261

Mike said he would take it all and warned us, "Do not mention this sale to your other customers. I can't afford to have the word get out about this because this is a very small town, and it would get around quickly. Everyone in town knows if I even fart on the other side of the fence."

We agreed and asked the same of him. Mike asked us to move the elk meat to the side of his garage while he went into the house. After handing me a business check for $384.00, Mike asked Jennifer if she wanted to see his buffalo, and he then took us to the backyard and showed us his buffalo herd. While there, Mike told us he hires Russian girls to work for him in the summers. He said he brings five or so Russian girls over every summer, but the immigration laws were making it very difficult. He described the girls as beautiful, hard-working, and 18-21 years old. He went into great detail regarding the problems he has encountered getting the workers over this year because of "stupid government bureaucrats."

As Jennifer and I drove away, we both had the same opinion about why Mike was bringing young Russian girls to work at his restaurant and motel. It wasn't a pleasant thought, and he gave both of us the creeps.

Wilson called me on the 11[th,] saying he had the eagle heads done. I met with Wilson, who was accompanied by a white male who was making Indian drums. Inside his shop, I saw both the golden eagle and bald eagle heads mounted on sticks. I paid Wilson $200 in cash for the birds. After placing the eagle heads in the back seat of my truck, Wilson walked over to a black Kia and removed the two headless eagle carcasses, which we also placed in the back of my truck.

Wilson said he wanted to show me something, and after re-entering his shop, he handed me a long, thin whistle. He disclosed that the whistle was made from the wing bone of an eagle and offered it to me for $25. I accepted the deal. Outside, I handed Wilson more cash for the eagle bone whistle. He told me the Indians use the whistle in their dances, and he makes and sells many of them. I left with my eagle "popsicles" and headed home to get my work set up for a couple of weeks off to recover from the surgery I was having the next morning.

CHAPTER 21- MAY 2012

For the last two weeks of April and the first week of May, I was stuck at home, working on the computer and turning down more offers of illegal wildlife from new suspects (which pained me much more than the surgery). I was cleared to return to work in a cast and on crutches by the 10th.

While lounging around the house, I texted Jin Dong, "Jin: we haven't forgotten you. We are still trying to find you a whole one. How is everything going?"

Jin answered, "I sold ten so far. Next month, I will need more from you. How many do you have?"

I replied, "I bet we have ten already. Nobody will bring us a whole one yet, but soon".

Jin asked, "What about feet? Feet can sell also".

I said, "We will save all we can."

Jin wrote back, "How big average?"

I replied, "Haven't weighed them. Some big, some average. We turned down small ones".

Jin replied, "Good."

I finished with, "You stay in touch, my friend. Take care."

I sent Kent Rousch an email stating, "Kent: We haven't been traveling too much lately because of my foot surgery, but we plan to hit the road again, maybe next week. We still have the zebra hide to show you, plus we have a couple of other African items you might be interested in and want to see if they are what you are looking for (we don't want them). We were wondering if you would object to closing the deal on the three sets of antlers (Rousch had instructed us never to say "horns" in our emails) we brought you a few months back. We could use the cash to pick up some other items. Are you going to be around the week of the 14th (Monday is out- doctor appointment)? Thanks, and I look forward to seeing you again. Maybe we can meet your girlfriend this time?" (I had picked up a mounted leopard from the USFWS Agent Chuck Richards to offer to Kent).

I spoke with Kent Rousch by phone on the **11**th. He said he had spoken to his Idaho Game Warden buddy, and pinning the horns should not be a problem, but they were of no value to him unless they were pinned. He said his buddy is willing to pin them, but he has to wait until the rafting season is in full swing, which is "right around the corner." I mentioned we still had the zebra hide to show him, and we had also purchased a mounted leopard for $200 from a friend who had picked it up at a yard sale. Kent said he might be interested in the leopard's hide if it was in good shape and told me to bring it with us. I said another friend of ours had some kind of African animal horns, but I didn't know what they were. He offered to take a look at them, too. Kent told me he would like us to stop by on Wednesday.

Four days later, on the morning of the **15**th, Officer Dave Jones provided us with multiple black bear paws and gallbladders, which had been removed from bears killed on WDFW-authorized depredation hunts. Officer Jones also had a freshly killed black bear weighing about 150 pounds, which he had killed a few hours before on a nuisance wildlife situation. At 9:00 a.m. I called Jin, left a message for him to call me, and sent him a text stating, "Jin. A friend just pulled into my place with a fresh big one, about 150 pounds. Do you want it?"

Jin replied, "Yea."

I immediately asked, "What do you want to do with it? Bring to you or ship?"

He called and told me he wanted the whole bear skinned and cut into quarters, and the meat shipped to San Francisco. He asked how much money I wanted, and I said $400. Jin said that was too much, so we negotiated a price of $325, with Jin responsible for shipping costs.

He told me he would deposit the cash into our bank account after I knew how much the shipping would be. I told him the bear was fresh, so we had to skin it, cut it up, and freeze it, so it might be a week or so before I could ship, since I was going to Montana the coming week. Jin asked why I was going to Montana, and I said I was going fishing. He told me to keep all the fish I caught and sell them to him. He said he would take all the fish I could get him. I told Jin I would do my best. Officer Jones retained the bear and, later that day, cut it up and put it in a freezer to help out his old crippled buddy.

Jennifer and I hit the road again on the **16**th, arriving at Rousch's house in Spokane. After a brief conversation, Kent followed us out to our truck to see what we had brought. As Jennifer began pulling the items out, Kent said he would open the garage door, so we could unload the items in the garage for him to check. Kent examined the zebra hide and the mounted leopard. I also brought a bighorn

266

sheep head (we had acquired it from a Montana wildlife investigator) and showed it to Kent. He asked where we had gotten the sheep. We said our taxidermist friend had a customer who had killed the sheep in Montana, had it pinned, and brought it into our friend's taxidermy shop. I told Kent the sheep had remained in the freezer for years, and the hide was ruined, so the customer abandoned it to the taxidermist rather than pay $2,000 for a new hide. Kent and I talked about the fact that legally taken/pinned sheep were legal to sell in Montana, but Kent said: "They are still illegal to buy or sell in Washington" (good that he knew the laws he so freely violated). I told Kent I knew that, so we didn't have much of a market for them. I said we had paid $500 for the zebra hide, $200 for the leopard, and $300 for the sheep. I also told him that a friend of ours had bought the leopard at a yard sale in Seattle, and it had not come with any paperwork. Kent stated he would pay us $600 for the zebra and would "put $50 on top" of the $300 we paid for the sheep. We agreed on the prices for the sheep and the zebra.

Kent said the leopard was not much use to him, as he couldn't use the hide for furniture, but he would call his friend and discuss it. He went into a very long story about how he had sold an illegal leopard-skin coat to a very famous record producer and how he had later seen a famous singer on television wearing the same coat made from skins of "endangered species leopard."

He offered to pay us by check, which I said was fine. He issued us a check for $950.00 for the zebra and the sheep. We left the leopard mount behind to see if he could find a buyer for it. Jennifer and I left with the check, which we later cashed, and placed the money into the evidence safe.

On May **17**th, I missed a call from Jin Dong, so I texted him back, "Missed your call. I was at the doctor's office again. What address do you want this sent to? Just the four big pieces? Body, feet, and other thing saved for you?"

Jin replied, "Just save it in the freezer. The people will back from China in two weeks. But can pay you now if you need money. And I need more gall soon. Bring me lots fish. My family love all kinds fish if catch some."

I responded, "Ok. We will hold it in the freezer until we hear back from you. We are working on the fish".

Dusty Hilton reappeared on the **19**th when I received a phone call from him. Dusty bragged he had just "killed a big one," and was calling from his "Mom's place in Naches" because cell phones didn't work there. Dusty asked if we wanted the entire rib cage (intact) or if they could trim the meat off it, and I told him to trim it off and keep it all for us. He agreed to do so and would hold it in a freezer until we came over to pick it up on the 30th.

I checked back in with Liev Smirnov on the **24**th, sending him a text, "Any word on when the black will be here?"

Liev responded, "Yes, Halfway here. Toomoro evening For sure…".

At noon, I called Liev, who said Yuli was bringing 40 pounds of black caviar, and it would all go fast. I told Liev I wanted 5 pounds and asked if they would have any red caviar or fresh fish. Yuli said he had some red caviar available and didn't know if they would get any fish soon or not. He said Yuli would be in WA for 2 to 3 weeks. I asked him if his father had caught any more trout, and he said his father got caught with too many fish, and the police told him that if they caught him again, he would be in very big trouble. Liev didn't think his father was going out anymore.

After checking in with Liev, it was time to see what Parker and Backster were up to. Since we hadn't heard from them in almost two months, I sent Jim Backster (who had taken over the role of "main-man" in the group) a text, "Jim: you on here?"

He replied, "On what lol."

I replied to Jim by texting, "Whatever you can get on. Is Kyle out of jail yet? Me and Tina will be over your way next Weds. Thought we would stop by."

"Sounds good. Yes, he is," Jim answered.

I said, "Any chance of picking up some steak? The smaller one?"

To which Jim answered, "Yes."

I asked if he had moved yet, and Jim said: "Love it, yes."

"Give me an address so we can put it in the GPS. Then we will count on Weds.", I wrote back.

Jim replied, "On it.", then provided his new address.

I finished by saying, "Ok. We will talk to ya on Tuesday".

Later that day, I got an email from Andy Miller. Through a series of emails, he offered to show my "wife" and me some new Native American artwork he had for sale. He provided me with his new address (in Ferndale, WA) and asked us to come up on the 14th of June. After getting off the phone with Miller, I called Agent Andrews, who requested we go through with the Miller contact, even though he wasn't on our "top eight" list (apparently, the Feds had a different list). Andrews and Sgt. Hobbs worked it out for us to keep this contact, even though it was outside of our top eight.

Jennifer and I called Jin Dong on the **29th**, asking when he wanted the bear shipped and to where. Jin said he would probably have us take the bear and some bear "feet" to his brother in Seattle, but his brother was leaving for Mexico soon. He asked if we had any fish for him, and I said we had about 30 trout we could sell. Jin asked how many gallbladders we had, and I said we had one from the whole bear we had just cut up and ten others. Jin agreed to pay us $325 for the whole bear, including the paws and gallbladder, and $100 each for the other ten gallbladders, for a total of $1,325. We threw in the trout for an additional $25, for a total of $1,350. I said it would be a week or so before we could bring everything over. Jin ended by instructing us to get him more gallbladder and "feet."

To drive his point home, Jin Dong texted us the next day, "Don't forget tell your people save all the feet."

I replied, "Ok." Who did he think he was dealing with? We are professionals and would never forget to have our imaginary poaching buddies collect the bear "feet."

270

Jennifer and I headed over to Hilton's house on the **30ᵗʰ**, finding nobody home. A few minutes later, Dusty arrived driving a 4-wheel drive Dodge pickup (another vehicle to add to our forfeiture list). He showed us several bags of meat and asked if we also wanted two deer hindquarters, which he had in his truck, along with the entire elk (cut up and frozen). We told him we would take all of it.

After loading the meat in our truck, we agreed on a price of $700 for the meat, $600 for the elk, and $100 for the deer meat and paid him $700. As always, in cash.

Dusty began babbling about catching bass to sell to us and asked what we would pay for them. I said we hadn't agreed to a price with our customers, but guessed we could pay him about $1.00 per pound. He said he had a friend with a private pond, and it was full of large bass, so he would get us all we wanted. He asked us if it was worth our time to drive over just for some bass. We explained we always group several customers/suppliers together on our trips, and we were meeting another supplier in Yakima when we were done with him. Dusty asked what we were getting from the next guy, and I exclaimed, "Really expensive birds." Dusty questioned if I was talking about live birds, and I said no, I meant the kind of birds used for Indian artwork. Dusty admitted to knowing what we were talking about, as he had just shot two red-tailed hawks and had given the hawks to a friend of his. He also asked what kind of trouble we would get in if we got caught with those birds. I said, "Jail time. Big trouble". Dusty offered to get us about anything and wanted to know what else we needed. I told him mostly birds, meats, and fish. He said he could get all the elk and deer we wanted now that they were starting to grow their horns.

271

After leaving Hilton, we headed over to Jim Backster's new address and were met by Kyle, Jim, and his wife, Crystal. Jim told us he had a deer for us in a horse trailer down the hill on his property. Jennifer backed our truck down to a silver horse trailer (another addition to our list of vehicles for forfeiture). Jim and Kyle showed us a skinned-out buck deer (the hide and head were lying beneath the carcass) hanging in the trailer.

While we were talking, Kyle opened his hand, showing me two bone fragments, and stated, "This is all I got out of the elk I shot last night. I shot a huge cow elk at about 30 yards, with Jim's .30-30, but then we couldn't find it."

Jim confirmed he had shot and killed the deer, and Kyle had wounded an elk and shot a red-tailed hawk. They loaded the deer carcass into our truck, and we paid them $300 in cash.

Kyle confided that he and Tanya were no longer together because Tanya was heavily into meth (what a shock). He said Tanya got him into using meth too, but he had "mostly" stopped using, and she had moved in with her drug friends. Jim told us that he and his wife had purchased the property they were living on for $55,000 from a Craigslist advertisement. He said the property included the main stone-covered house, a second house (a very old wooden structure), and the surrounding acreage.

Before we left, Jim reminded us that they could "get all the deer and elk we wanted, and we are even going to put in a walk-in cooler to hang animals in."

272

We promised we would be back in touch when we needed more.

Our last contact in May was to pick up some caviar from Liev. On the evening of the **30**th, Jennifer and I arrived at Liev's house. Jennifer remained in the truck (as we were concerned they might recognize her as a game warden) while I contacted Liev. When we pulled up, I noticed Liev's Mercedes was parked outside the garage, and the garage door was open. Liev told me his neighbors had been watching him, which was "not so good." He was very concerned his neighbors might see him conducting transactions and said he would pull his Mercedes into the garage so my wife could back into his driveway to block the view of his neighbors. Liev's wife came into the garage, followed by Yuli. While we talked, I saw Yuli taking the jars of caviar out of a small chest freezer and placing them into a paper bag. Yuli told me the season had not been very good, and they didn't get much caviar. He said it had all sold quickly. I confirmed with Yuli that the price was still $100 per jar. I paid Yuli $500 in cash and asked him how long he was going to stay in Washington. He said another week or so.

During our conversation about caviar, I asked Liev and Yuli how long they had been making and selling the caviar.

Liev said, "7 years for me, but longer for Yuli".

Yuli said, "No, not so long."

Yuli apologized for not getting the deer and elk meat to me, which I said was fine. I told Liev and Yuli to come with me to my truck. I showed them a whole deer (the one we had just purchased

273

from Backster) and cut up portions of another deer and an elk. Yuli asked if it was killed by a car, and I told him it was shot and that it was top-quality meat.

"I will get you deer and elk," Yuli said.

Yuli and Liev said they had heard there would be no fishing season for salmon in Washington this year (I have no idea where they got that information) and wanted to know if I knew about that. I told them I had not heard anything. Yuli said they had a place to get "huge king salmon" and wanted to know if I would be interested in buying them. I told Yuli to call me when he got some.

Jennifer and I headed out to start processing the edibles we had purchased over the long and tiresome day.

CHAPTER 22- JUNE 2012

By the first week of June, I was finally off crutches and gimping along pretty well. On the 1st, I received a text from Jin Dong, "The $1350 is ready. Make all the gall are good. Last time, some were bracken."

I responded, "We will do our best. If there are problems, we will make it right".

"I m staring sell good to China. More people know about it. But I m doing low key. Be safe.", Jin texted back.

I replied, "We will count on meeting with you in the next two weeks for the stuff. Take care,".

Jin wrote back, "I m still wanting other people. You can bring other stuff and day. See you my friend."

The next morning, I received an email from Tanya Franklin with photos of Native American items she had made and was offering for sale. Tanya said she and Kyle had broken up, and she was living on her own and wanted to sell native art merchandise. The photos had several feathers, which appeared to be from raptors (possibly hawks), so I responded by asking her what kind of feathers were in the photos. Tanya said the feathers were "baby hawk feathers." I told Tanya we were coming to the east side the next week and could meet with her then. Tanya called later and gave me her new address in Cowiche, WA.

275

I texted Jin Dong on the **11**th, telling him we could be in Walla Walla the next day or could meet him in Tri-Cities earlier, and we had a total of 12 gall and the fish.

He responded, "Come to Walla Walla, please. And only c bring merge gall and fish only. Kept all others in your freezer. Thanks."

"Will do. Around 6 pm tomorrow, ok?" I responded.

Jin wrote back: "Let me know in 30min. Before you arrive. $1300. Total. Chinese asked me what kind the bear".

I responded, "We agreed on $1,350. $325 for the whole one (including that gall and four feet), $1000 for the 10 more gall and $25 for the fish. We also have one more gall for a total of 12 (one from the whole bear). So if you want all 12 how about $1,450? If you don't need the 12th one now, we will save it. We should get a lot of them in August, when the season opens."

"Do you what kind bear? Now I only have $1350", Jin replied.

I provided the final answers, "Ok we will bring the 11 gall and fish." and "All American black bear."

Later the same day, after texting back and forth with Bourey (about seeing if he was ok since we hadn't heard from him in a while), he called at about 10:00 a.m. He said he thought his guys on the east side were selling the animals (deer and elk) to someone in Portland because they (his suppliers) wanted more money than he was willing to pay. Bourey said he didn't know the Portland buyer, but the Indians

276

had told him the Portland people would pay more. He said he hadn't gotten any fish lately and had only been offered one sturgeon, but the seller wanted too much money for it. He asked if we wanted ocean fish, and I said we would consider anything, including crab. Bourey told me he had an Indian source for lingcod and other ocean fish in Neah Bay, and he paid the guy in weed (marijuana). Bourey said he would keep us in mind, and we would be the first he called when he had some fish.

Jennifer and I drove to Walla Walla on the 12th at 4:10 p.m. I texted Jin, "We should be in Walla Walla about 530".

At 4:30, after not hearing back from Jin, I called him. Jin told us he was inside the restaurant (Pacific Pride) and to meet him there. He said for me to call him when we were about 30 minutes away. We arrived at the Pacific Pride Restaurant at 5:30, where I saw Jin standing next to his white Lexus. As we backed up towards his vehicle, he opened a cooler in the rear of his car.

I removed a small cooler containing the 11 bear gallbladders from the back of our truck and asked him to follow me to the truck's cab to inspect the gall.

As Jin picked up the cooler, he said, "I don't need to look at them. I trust you."

He said if we screwed him, we would not do business together, so we had to trust each other. I placed the black plastic bag full of 11 gallbladders in the cooler in the rear of his Lexus. Jin walked to the back of our truck and asked to see the fish. I produced a bag we had obtained from a WDFW hatchery containing 30 trout. Jin said it didn't feel very heavy, and I said that was a lot of trout. He took the bag of trout and placed it in the same cooler in the back of his car.

He returned to our truck and wanted to know what we had in the other large cooler. We told him we had some pheasant and some fish, but they were for another customer. Jin asked why we had never offered him pheasant, and I said because he had never asked for them. He stated he wanted pheasant, ducks, or geese. He repeated that sales to China were going very well, so he wanted all the bear gallbladder and "feet" we could get him. Jin explained that Chinese people eat only fish and vegetables in summer, but ducks, pheasant, geese, deer, and elk the rest of the year. I told him we would keep that in mind and try to get him birds. Jin handed me a wad of cash and told me to count it. I counted out $1,350, and we were done.

Before leaving for the west side, Jennifer and I decided to stop at Duck Song again. We gathered a handful of rockfish and some rooster pheasant. Jennifer and I walked in the back door of the Duck Song restaurant at about 8:00 p.m. on the 12th and were met by a young Asian male who accompanied us back out to our truck. The young man asked me for our phone number, stating he wanted to call us later. He said he didn't speak English well, but wanted to talk to us and would find someone to call us for him. I provided the man with our business card and showed him the pheasant and fish we had in a cooler in the truck's bed.

The Asian male went back into the restaurant and returned with Tou Liu, followed by two other Asian males. A minute or so later, a fourth Asian male came out to look over what we had. Jennifer and Tou Liu began negotiating prices for both the fish and

278

pheasant. Tou Liu asked if the fish and pheasant were all fresh, and I told her they had been frozen but were all very fresh and in good condition. She told Jennifer she was not familiar with that kind of fish and wanted to try only one to see if they were good. Jennifer stated that we were going home after we were done with them, wanted to get rid of all the fish, and wouldn't bring them back. Jennifer and Tou Liu agreed on a price for all the birds and fish. Liu carried the pheasant into the restaurant when the deal was done, while another Asian male followed with the fish.

Jennifer and I drove to Yakima and spent the night. We arrived at Tanya's new address the next morning (the 13th). The gate to the property was closed, and we didn't see Tanya, so I called her. Tanya said she was about 2 minutes away and asked us to wait there for her. At about 9:35, a pickup truck drove up next to us, and I could see Tanya sitting on the passenger side. She got out and escorted us onto the property, where she introduced us to Mr. Sterns (an older white male who said the property was his). Tanya took us to the back of the property, where I saw the camper she and Kyle had previously lived in. Inside the camper, she showed us a small dreamcatcher she had made. Tanya told us the feathers on the dreamcatcher were "baby hawk feathers" and had been very hard to work with. She showed us her hand-made animal hide pouches and a collection of different adult hawk feathers, which were also for sale. Tanya told us Kyle had stolen many of her personal effects, claiming the value of what he stole was $2,500 (oh, so sad).

We told her we wanted to buy the dreamcatcher, some adult hawk feathers, and one of the pouches. We negotiated prices for the

279

items and paid Tanya $100 in cash, which we were pretty sure would be converted to meth in a matter of hours. Tanya said her supply of hawk feathers had slowed down with Kyle gone, but she would start contacting some people she knew to try to get more. With our treasures in hand, Jennifer and I headed home.

We met with Andy Miller in his garage on the **14**th. I noticed many of the items on display had wildlife parts attached, including waterfowl feathers, raptor feathers, skulls, and a sheep horn. As we were looking at the items, June Miller joined us. I told June and Andy, in no uncertain terms, that the sale/purchase of waterfowl parts was a federal crime, the sale of native sheep (bighorn) was illegal by state law, and the sale of any eagle, hawk, or owl parts (including feathers) was also illegal. They both acknowledged this and said they remembered me telling them on previous visits. Andy said he had been trying to come up with enough eagle feathers to make us an eagle feather smudge fan but hadn't yet gotten enough. He said he sold many Native American items to "New Age" people in the Bellingham area and planned to sell more at an event on the Lummi Indian Reservation.

After looking through the merchandise, Jennifer agreed to buy a "Shamans Ceremonial Stick" (Andy told us the feather on it was an eagle feather) priced at $95, a two-part "talking stick" (two sticks) priced at $75, a "Smudge Fan" priced at $45, a "Ceremonial Rattle" made from "Montana bighorn ram horn and tooth, with mallard duck feathers" priced at $65, and a carved "Abalone Shell" priced at $35. I offered Andy $300 for all the items, and he accepted. We said our (final) goodbyes, loaded the merchandise, and headed south.

I knew as we left, like many of our other suspects, Andy would never see us outside of a courtroom again.

On the morning of the **19**th, I sent Jin another text asking him when he wanted us to deliver the bear to his brother.

I immediately received a response from Jin, "I m sorry. Wad very busy all day. Let me call him later today. Thanks"

"Ok. We could meet him anytime Wednesday or Thursday….day or night", I replied.

He responded, "Ok. Call Jimmy. You can take to Seattle tomorrow but put in black plastic bag. Thanks." The text message included Jimmy's phone number.

At 10:53, I called Jimmy, identified myself as Tom Davis, and said Jin told me to call him. Jimmy asked if he could call me back as he could not talk.

At 12:06, I sent Jimmy the following text message, "Jimmy: don't need to talk to you right now, just need to know what time we can meet tomorrow. I have to drive north to get meat out of the freezer. So we need to know about what time you can meet with us. We can talk later about where you want to meet. Thanks, Tom Davis".

I received a response from Jimmy, "Hi Tom, meet me tomorrow at 10 a.m. Thx" (with the address where we were to meet him).

I replied, "Will do. Thanks and see ya tomorrow."

Later, I texted Jin, "I got in touch with Jimmy, and we will meet him tomorrow and give him the whole one. Does he get the four feet from that one? Or save them for you?"

Jin texted back, "Just save for me! I m going to sell them together. I m still wait for the people from Chicago."

Early on the morning of the **20**th, Officer Dave Jones delivered the cut-up and frozen bear, which he had killed on 05/05/12. Officer Jones had the meat portions of the bear wrapped in plastic bags, the four paws in a separate bag, and the gallbladder in a small zip-lock bag.

At about 10:00 a.m., Jennifer and I arrived at Jimmy's business in Seattle, where we saw Jimmy outside waiting for us in front of his indoor growing supply business. He approached the back of our truck and opened the canopy as I approached him. I recognized "Jimmy" from a Michigan driver's license photo provided to us by USFWS Agent Andrews. We showed Jimmy the two large coolers full of bear meat, and he said he needed to get a cart. I followed Jimmy into his business (which I admit was impressive), where he retrieved a hand cart. Two young, gangster-looking Asian males accompanied him as he returned to our truck. As I was loading the frozen bear meat from our truck onto his hand cart, Jimmy asked how big it was, and I told him it was a medium-sized bear and weighed about 150 pounds. He asked about the contents of each bag, and I explained the large bag was the carcass and rib cage, while the other bags were the quarters. After he had the bear on his hand cart, he and one of the other Asian males pushed the cart back into the store, and Jennifer and I pulled away.

After we left, I texted Jin, "Jin: got that dropped off to Jimmy. Nice guy and one hell of a business! Are you going to want any more whole ones soon? I just got a call from a friend, and he has one spotted. He wanted to know if we needed a whole one or just the parts. Let us know as soon as you can."

Jin replied, "No. I only want the feet and galls. Meat hard to sell and to big to sell".

"Ok. That is fine. Take care", I responded.

Jin wrote back, "The base idea. I want to save all the meat and sell to China but very hard to export to China. I m thinking buy some beef and ship them together".

I replied, "Ok. So do you want me to save some meat for you then?"

"No. Just the galls and feet," Jin replied.

Jin texted me, "What do you think indoor green business"

"Awesome! Makes me want to get back into that. I used to do some growing years ago. I think I already told you, but two years ago I went through drug/alcohol treatment. Haven't touched anything since. But I still like making money", I replied.

After receiving no response, I texted, "What's wrong? You thought I was pure as the driven snow or something?"

Jin texted back, "Tom. Make some idea from green business. We have all the equipment ready. Just need somebody work good and knew how to grow indoor plant!"

I replied, "I don't have the space, but if you are serious, we can talk in person next time we meet. I know we could sell a lot of green, but we gotta talk in person, not here".

283

"We are always look want to move this project going. But we need profession person", Jin replied.

I replied, "We will talk later."

"K. Don't forget to clear all the conversation," Jin answered.

After the last text, Jennifer and I discussed the fact that we were going to be offered new jobs as marijuana growers.

I joked, "Who knows, this might work into a good retirement plan for me."

After kicking it around quite thoroughly, we called Hobbs and updated him, telling him we were both up to the task but assumed we would need to bring DEA or at least Seattle Police Department on board before we started exercising our green thumbs (it turned out to be DEA)

On the morning of the 24th, I got a call from Wyatt Wilson. He said he had a pair of hooded merganser ducks and some other things for me to see. I told him I was in Idaho and would return the next week. I also mentioned I had a cougar that had been partially mounted for a rug, but the taxidermist had gone out of business. Wilson said he would look it over.

CHAPTER 23- JULY 2012

As July rolled around, so did the realization that we only had 2 ½ months of the undercover left (before the Sept. 18th take-down), and we still had massive amounts of paperwork to complete. I had picked up the case files from Detective Clarke, only to find that while they were in properly labeled, nice, neat binders, the binders were almost entirely empty. The only documentation in most of them was my case reports (which I had emailed to Clarke). They didn't contain any evidence, photos or evidence, identification documents, or much of anything else. We instantly realized we had way more work to do than I thought.

Apparently, Clarke had not kept up with what I was told he would do. In his defense, he had been on, off, and on the operation so many times that none of us knew who was supposed to be doing what when it came to evidence and files. Now it was crystal clear that Jennifer and I had our work cut out for us. In addition to getting the evidence and case files up to speed, we also had plenty of work to prepare all the search warrants we would apply for.

Additionally, as I had predicted, Jennifer was getting more than a little antsy to get back in uniform and out into the field. She decided she wanted to end her temporary appointment as a detective, return to uniform, and participate in any undercover work we had to accomplish through the end of the operation. I wasn't opposed to her decision, even though it meant I would lose a valuable resource in managing all the paperwork. I also knew that WDFW was testing soon for both sergeant (which Jennifer wanted badly) and detective promotions (which Officer Julie Cook wanted). Jennifer agreed to stay in place through mid-July, and hopefully, by then, I would have a permanent detective assigned to assist me.

I called Wilson and scheduled a visit with him the next day at about 10 a.m. On the 2nd, I walked into his shop carrying the cougar hide. The cougar had no seal or any of the required paperwork, and Wilson didn't ask for any. I told him I had purchased the cougar hide for $100 from a Colville taxidermist who was going out of business. He examined it and offered to finish it for $500, and I agreed. He showed me three different bear hides he was mounting and explained to me how they had been tanned. He said he would have to soak the cougar hide to make it soft, enabling him to stretch it to its full size, as he had done with the bear.

We discussed my business, and I told him our best sellers had been the bear claw/teeth necklaces. I also stated we had a guy in Yakima make up the necklaces, which we shipped to Idaho to be sold, as selling bear claws and teeth was illegal in Washington but legal in Idaho. Wilson said he had about 20 bear claws and a lot more drying, and wanted me to buy them. I told him to wait until he had 30 or more, and I would buy them all at once.

He said, "Basically everything in my shop is for sale," and showed me several duck mounts, stating, "$100 per bird".

I chose two hooded mergansers (mounted on the same woodblock) for $200. Wilson and I discussed how strange it was that we could buy and sell pheasant, turkey, and other birds but not ducks and geese.

Wilson said, "Because they are federal."

286

He said his girlfriend had copied the law for him and posted it on his door (which he pointed out to me). He said selling ducks could get you a $10,000 fine and jail time for each bird. Wilson told me the sale of mounted ducks is even illegal if the ducks came from a game farm. He showed me his taxidermy ledger and pointed out where he had entered birds he had purchased from a game farm. He also said he sells a lot of ducks but tells people to say they bought them at a yard sale and never to mention his name. He assured me that if he ever gets questioned about it, he will deny ever having sold any ducks (that should be entertaining when he sees himself selling ducks on my covert videos).

Wilson told me a customer had brought in 3 or 4 dead hummingbirds, and Wilson mounted them for him. He had also mounted a goldfinch and a bat for the same customer.

He told me he would have my cougar done in early August. I paid him $200 in cash for the two mounted ducks and hit the road. I updated Agent Andrews and told him I needed another $200 from the Feds.

I received a phone call on the 10th from a man with a heavy Asian accent. He identified himself as "Wang" and asked if we sold deer, elk, and bears. I asked him how he had gotten our names and phone number. Wang said he had our business card, and we had come into his restaurant a long time ago, and he had kept the card. I asked what restaurant, and he said it is now called the Happy Times Chinese Restaurant (a business Jennifer and I had stopped at back in January 2011). I told Wang I remembered coming to the restaurant a long time ago and asked what he was looking for. He said he wanted to buy "fresh" deer and elk meat and also wanted some bear. He asked me how much we charged, and I told him it depended on what he wanted. I asked Wang to send me an email and explained I would respond to his questions after receiving his email (as I was having difficulty understanding him on the phone).

At 12:30, I received an email from "Wang" stating, "Hi Tom My name is Wang. Very nice talk to you today. Can you send me your pricing? Thank you for your time. Thanks Wang."

A few minutes later, I received a second email from the same email address: "Hi Tom I am looking for some fresh bear, elk, deer meets."

I replied, "Wang: We sell deer and elk meat, but here is what we face. The law says that we can only sell deer and elk meats if it comes from a licensed game farm, is individually packaged, boneless, and has a receipt. It is very expensive for us to buy, but we do buy and sell it. As for bear meat, it is against the law to buy and sell it, but we do get a lot of bear from hunters we trust. We have been doing business for a couple of years and have many people supplying us with bear, cougar, deer, and elk. We must be very careful with who we do business with to stay out of trouble. If we do business, you have to give us your word that what we do stays between us.....you can't talk to anyone! If you want the legal game-farmed meat, that's easy; just let us know how much you want (how many pounds) and what cuts of meat (steaks, burgers, tenderloin, etc.,) and we will send you a quote. If you want other kinds of deer and elk meat or any parts of bear, we have to have a trust going to make sure you are not working for the police. Then we would like to talk to you in person. Let us know

288

exactly what you are looking for, and we will talk. Please delete this email once you have read it. Thanks. Tom"

"Hi Tom Thank you for yor email. I totally understand what you talking about. I'm Chinese guy. I just looking for bear hands, elks, and deer meets for myself and my family. I love those thing. I am not dealing with anyone or police. I will have a word with you, not talking to anyone. I would like meet with you in person" Wang provided his phone number and business address.

I replied, "Ok. Just so we understand each other. I will talk to my wife, and I am sure we will come down and meet with you. Maybe this week? What days and hours will you be there?"

"I can be here every day, 1 am to 9 pm. Just let me know the a day before you come. Thanks", Wang replied.

I answered, "Will do thanks. Are you interested in anything other than the hands?"

Wang came back with, "Not Wednesday ,we close on Wednesday. I am the owner of the chinese restaurant".

"Ok. Not weds", I replied.

Wang asked, "Any seafood? I love seafood."

I answered, "What kind? We should be getting some salmon soon, and we can always get a lot of crab......all you want."

"I love crab. Geoduck"

I ended the conversation string with, "We will see what we can do." Great, he had just spoken the word I never wanted to hear again in my whole life, geoduck!

After my conversations with Wang, I called Hobbs, "I just got a new customer who wants to make some illegal purchases, including bear. I know we are only allowed to deal with our "top eight," but here

289

is my concern regarding passing this one up. Of all the Asian buyers we have sold bear parts to, this guy is only the second person to ask for bear paws; I guess you know Jin Dong is the first. Also, both this guy and Jin Dong own Chinese restaurants. I think they may be connected, and Jin may have told Wang to deal with us. If we don't deal with this guy, we may jeopardize the case on Dong," I added the one thing I knew would sell this case to the DC, "And he asked about buying Cenci's favorite thing, geoduck."

Hobbs agreed with my analysis and said he would run it up the chain to see if we could proceed. A few hours later, Hobbs called back and said we were cleared to work Wang.

On Tuesday, the **10**[th], I received a call from Wyatt Wilson saying our cougar was done and to come and get it as soon as possible. Since the cougar didn't have a seal or tag, or any other paperwork, he didn't want to get caught with it. I told him I would move some things around and would be at his shop around 11:15. When I arrived at his shop, I noticed Wilson was outside working on two bear hides. We went into his shop, and he showed me the cougar he had mounted. He described how he worked on it and stated I got one hell of a deal since I had paid only $100 for the cat and $500 to him. After paying him, Wilson complained that the game wardens could walk in and inspect his shop whenever they wanted, but they hadn't done so in a long time (because I had asked Officer Jones to stay away from Wilson's shop). He said he recently had a guy who didn't have much money who wanted a mounted pheasant, so they worked out a deal where the guy paid Wilson with five sockeye salmon for the pheasant.

Wilson said, "It was illegal as hell, but I wanted the fish."

Wilson talked about a friend who had a dall sheep for sale. I mentioned I had a bighorn sheep, which was un-pinned, and had a customer who wanted it but wouldn't buy it un-pinned. Wilson suggested we could change the paperwork from the dall sheep to the bighorn sheep to cover it but said he didn't think that would work since my sheep was a bighorn (glad he worked that one out in his brain). He offered to get me pictures of the Dall sheep, and I told him I'd look at them and let him know if I wanted it.

After leaving Wilson's shop, I emailed Wang, "Wang: My wife and I will be there on Tuesday the 17th. Will that work for you?"

"Yes. Thanks", Wang replied.

I added, "We will bring a little of everything—a couple of bear feet some deer and elk meat and hopefully some crab. We can get to know each other, talk prices, then hopefully do a lot of business in the future. Do you want a gallbladder or do you know anyone who does want a few? Please delete this email after you read it."

Wang replied, "Ok, thanks you so much", and "Yes, I need gallbladder. Hopefully your price is good for me. If too expensive, I can't afford it. You have a great day."

"We normally sell them for $1.00 per gram, but if you are going to be regular customer then we can sell for 75 cents per gram. Most weigh 80 to 150 grams each. Sometimes we get them much bigger, but we have a large buyer who buys our big ones. If you have asked around, you will know our prices are fair. We have to pay hunters for them, so we don't make a lot of money", I wrote back.

Through subsequent e-mails, Wang advised me he would not be available to meet us on Tuesday, July 17th, but his brother and sister

291

would meet us at the Happy Times Restaurant and would negotiate the purchase of the wildlife and crab.

I needed to keep Mike Craig freshened up, so I picked up four chinook salmon and one steelhead from one of our hatcheries. On the 12th, at about noon, I called Mike's home and told him I was in Darrington and had five fresh fish. He asked what they were and the price. I told him about the fish and that I had paid $20 for all five and wanted some gas money on top of that, but I had already removed the eggs from the fish, which was what I really wanted. Mike said he didn't want them right then, as he was too busy to deal with them, but to call him next time I had some.

About 2 minutes after hanging up, Mike called me back and asked how much money I wanted on top of the $20. I said I would take $8 to $10. Mike said he wanted them after all and would pay me $28. When I arrived at Mike's house, he asked me to look at the fish. He said he would take them and went into his house for his checkbook. When Mike returned with his checkbook, I told him the fish were not Indian caught but instead were caught by a regular fisherman from the bank, with hook and line, and were good quality.

Mike said, "I don't give a shit where they came from as long as they are good."

He handed me a check for $28.00 and put the fish directly in the bed of his pickup. I knew we would be seizing that truck as well.

Later the same day, I phoned Liev asking if he had anything to offer. He said he had been very busy doing remodel construction and hadn't had time for much else. Liev informed me Yuli was there now and would be on a short trip until Sunday. He said Yuli had brought out more black caviar but only had 3 or 4 jars left. I told him I would take the remaining jars and asked him to hold them for me. Liev complained that the steelhead fishing was no good right now, but as soon as it picked up, they would start getting more steelhead, and he would call me.

Jennifer and I met with a WDFW Marine Officer early on the morning of the **17**th, and he provided us with 28 live Dungeness crabs. The crabs were a mixture of legal (6 ¼" males) and illegal (undersized males and females). I photographed the crab and put them in a cooler with the frozen meats and gallbladder, and we headed down to the Happy Times Restaurant.

We walked inside and were met by an Asian female who took us to a back room. We were then joined by an Asian male who told us he was Wang's brother and said we should talk to the female (Wang's sister) because she spoke English better. After introductions, we took them to our truck and showed them the live crab. We said we wanted $1.50 per pound for the crab and that the sale was not legal. We showed them the four bear paws. Again, we warned them that the sale or purchase of bear parts was illegal and said we had to be very careful not to be seen. Both of them said they understood.

We showed them the package of four bear gallbladders and produced a list of weights and prices for each gall. The Asian male said they were not interested in the gallbladder as they didn't know how to eat it. Lastly, we showed them the deer and elk meat. I took out a package of the legal game-farmed meat and explained that, legally, deer and elk meat had to be packaged in this manner from an out-of-state game farm. I pointed at the remainder of the deer and elk meat and told them it was illegal to buy and sell because hunters in Washington had killed them. Both of them said they understood. I returned the legal meat to the cooler.

Jennifer and the two Asian subjects began negotiating prices for the bear paws and the illegal meat. They agreed to $50 for all the meat (excluding the legal meat) and another $50 for the four bear paws. The Asian male used my cell phone to talk to Wang (I dialed it for him). I got on the phone with Wang, who asked me the price for the crab, and I told him $1.50 per pound. We were then joined by an older Asian woman who picked the crab they wanted.

The Asian male asked if we sold antlers, and I said we did, but we didn't have any with us. The older Asian woman and the Asian male picked out 17 crabs, including several undersized males and at least two females. The 17 crabs weighed ~22 pounds. Jennifer told the three subjects they owed us $50 for the meat, $50 for the bear paws, and $33 for the crab, totaling $133. We followed them back into the restaurant as they carried the meat, crab, and bear paws into the kitchen. I saw the meat and paws sitting on a stainless steel counter in the kitchen. The younger woman handed us a check for $132.00 (shorting us $1.00). After I took the check, I told all three people that what we had just done was illegal, and they had to promise not to say anything to anyone. The two younger customers said they would not say anything.

I called Liev back on the **17th** and told him I would be at his place at about 2 p.m. Liev said he was not there, as he had a job to do, but he would call and see if Yuli could meet me. A few minutes later, Liev called back and said Yuli would be there to sell me the caviar. Liev told me to go to the front door this time because his neighbors were watching him. When I arrived at Liev's front door, Yuli greeted me. In the garage, Yuli opened the largest of the freezers and took out six jars of black caviar. As he loaded the jars in my cooler, he said that because a couple of the jars were different sizes (other than 16 oz.), the amount actually came out to more than 4 pounds, so he wanted $420 for the six jars. I agreed and paid him $420 in cash. I asked Yuli how much he had brought out this trip, and he said: "Not very much." I asked when he was returning to Oklahoma, and he said he would be leaving the next day but would return in September and might have some more (black) caviar, but very little. I thanked Yuli and left to turn the caviar over to the Feds.

CHAPTER 24- AUGUST 2012

With only about six weeks to go, we were kicking it into high gear. Jennifer went back to the field but was still available for undercover, and Julie Cook had taken the detective test, so at least for a few weeks, I was riding the desk solo. Fortunately, the paperwork Jennifer had completed had put us back on our desired timeline to be ready for the September 18th takedown.

On the **6th**, I texted Jin, "Jin: A friend of ours got a large whole one recently. He gutted it and put it in the freezer. Do you want the whole one or just the feet and gall?"

Jin replied, "Just feet and gall. Meat hard to sell."

"Ok. We will have plenty of them. Thanks", I responded.

Jin asked, "How about the greenhouse?"

"We are up for that. What do you propose? We are busy as hell this week, but we have late next week open. We are planning a trip east on the 16th. Would we deal with you or your brother on that?" I asked.

Jin answered, "Only you and me. But I need to know all number investment and return plan."

"You want to meet in person next week and talk about it?" I asked.

"What day are you planning to come?" Jin asked.

I told Jin, "16th and 17th".

Jin asked, "Are you coming to WW?"

I came back with, "We have to go to Tri-Cities, so we can come to WW if you want."

Jin wrote back, "Ok. I want to meet you and talk about the plan."

I wrote back, "Let us know if you want us to bring anything. See ya next week".

"Bring me some fish if you have some," Jin replied.

I replied, "I will try."

I received a text message from Tanya Franklin on the **8**[th], asking, "Did you get the pictures I sent"

I answered, "Yep, thanks."

Through a series of text messages and emails, we agreed to meet Tanya at her place on Thursday, August 17th.

Jimmy Backster was next, and on the **11**[th,] he sent me a series of text messages indicating Kyle had been "beat up, and they busted his jaw with a jack handle." Jim told me Kyle was now living at his parents' house and gave me the phone number (in case I wanted to talk to him and wish him well).

Two days later, I called Kent Rousch's and left a message stating we were coming to the state's east side on the 16th and 17th and would like to pick up the horns if he had no use for them. Kent called back and said he had no luck getting the horns plugged but would buy them from us anyway. Kent and I agreed to meet on Friday, the 17[th,] at his house at about 10:30 a.m.

Through multiple emails with Wang, he asked us for velvet antlers (soft antlers) and fish (lingcod and rockfish). I advised Wang, in the emails, that the sale of velvet antlers is illegal, as would be the sale of lingcod and rockfish. He indicated he wanted to go through with the sale. I quoted $25 per pound for velvet antlers, $1.25 per pound for whole gutted rockfish, and $2.00 per pound for whole gutted lingcod. He told me he wanted all the velvet antlers we could get and 40 pounds each of lingcod and rockfish. We agreed to the prices, and I told him I would have some friends out trying to catch his fish and find him some velvet antlers. We told Wang we would arrive on the 16th.

Officer Dave Jones provided me with two small sets of antlers. One set was still covered in velvet, while the second set had the velvet stripped off. I called WDFW Sgt. Dan Chadwick and asked if he could provide me with 40 pounds each of lingcod and rockfish. Sgt. Chadwick thought he could buy the fish from a local wholesale dealer.

On the **16th**, Jennifer and I met with Sgt. Chadwick in Longview and received 80 pounds of fresh fish on ice. We headed south to the Happy Times Chinese Restaurant with our merchandise in hand. Wang walked us into the restaurant and asked what we had. I told Wang we had the fish and two sets of antlers. I explained that one set of antlers had velvet, but the other set had been stripped. Wang and another Asian male accompanied us to our truck, where they inspected the fish and antlers. Wang said he wanted the antlers to be soft and was concerned these were hard. I tried to explain to him that antlers are only soft in the spring and early summer, and they had missed their opportunity to get soft antlers. He said he would take all of it and helped me carry the cooler full of fish into the restaurant's kitchen. Wang and the other Asian male re-inspected the antlers and the fish. Wang asked if the fish were fresh, and I told him they had been caught the day before. The other Asian man and the older Asian woman began removing the fish and placing them in the kitchen sink. He agreed to our price of $20 for both sets of antlers. I showed him a list of prices: $50 for the rockfish, $80 for the lingcod, and $20 for the antlers, for a total of $150. Wang paid us $150 in cash. We shook hands, said our goodbyes, and headed to the state's east side, knowing we had visited this restaurant for the last time.

Our next stop was meeting with Jin in Walla Walla at the Pacific Pride restaurant. We entered the restaurant through the back door and were led to Jin in the front of the restaurant. He took us into a small dining room, laid out menus, and asked if we wanted dinner. Even though we were both starving, for some reason, we declined the meal, saying we had to get going. Jin said to come to his office. We followed him to a small stockroom (filled with paper products, disposable plates, and a set of golf clubs). Three chairs were set up in the room, and I sat next to Jennifer while Jin sat directly across from us, within reach.

He began the conversation by saying, "We got the business in Seattle" (which I understood to be the indoor growing business) and explained they needed people to grow marijuana for them.

Jin asked about our experience growing "weed" and whether we grow hydroponic (without soil). I told him it had been a very long time since I had grown weed, and I had never grown hydroponic, but had used dirt. I explained that I knew very little about growing, but that we could certainly read and learn about it, and that we were trustworthy. He explained we could find information regarding indoor growing on the internet and that he was looking for someone who would grow for a living, not for fun. He went on to say he wanted a long-term grower. Jin mentioned he was happy with our business thus far and wanted us to commit to long-term growth. I told him we also wanted to grow long-term, not just once. He asked what we would need to get started, and I said we would need the equipment and starter plants, and I had no idea where to get the starter plants.

Jin said he would provide the equipment, and the starter plants, adding that the plants he would deliver would be all-female (he said he takes cuts off of other female plants and clones them) and would be at least 10" tall. He wanted to start us with 200 plants. We talked about getting power, and he suggested we "steal the power" by cutting into the power line before the power went into the circuit box. He confided that his people (Chinese) stole the power and used newer houses in their growing business.

Jin stated he had no problem growing in soil, as it is safer and less complicated. He also said hydroponic growing produces much better yields (I believe he said 3 pounds per plant), but we should get 60-70 pounds from our "soil" plants in each grow house per harvest. He recommended we consider the risk and asked how much risk we could carry. I asked him if we found a house, got the power, and started growing for them, would he want to inspect the grow, or could we keep the location just between Tina and myself? Jin said he did not need to see the grow and knew what we should yield. He explained he would like us to work up to three grow houses, but that if we didn't produce what he thought we should, there would not be an opportunity for a second house after that first grow house.

Jennifer asked if we would harvest the weed and sell it to him. He said that was correct. He said he gets about "2 grand per pound" and would pay us "$1,000 per pound". With his system, we should only take 65 days from start to harvest. Jin said that whenever we were ready, he would immediately get us the equipment and starter plants.

300

He suggested we start small, and I said I would like to start with 100 plants. Jin agreed that would be good.

He asked if we would grow in the Seattle area, and we said Everett. He agreed that Everett was a good place to grow. We talked more about the power situation, and Jin said that from his experience, he had some grow houses where the power lines heated up way too much because the wiring wasn't done correctly. We mentioned we had a friend (retired officer Shane Brazier is an electrician) who we were sure could do the wiring for us.

Jin launched into a lecture on money laundering, telling us people get caught because they don't have a way to explain all the money they suddenly have, and we needed to come up with a cash business that would explain the extra cash flow. He also warned us about spending too much money too fast and attracting unwanted attention.

At the end of the conversation, he asked if we had any questions, and we both said we did not, but we might as we went along. We told him we would start looking for a grow house immediately. In a sheepish voice, Jennifer announced she was nervous about this. He assured her it would all be fine, and she responded with a smile. For a minute, I thought she was serious, but I realized she was playing her role to the max.

Outside, we gave him the bear parts and the fish. Jin asked where we got the fish. We said we had caught some of it and the rest from a friend who ran a charter boat. The fish weighed 29 pounds, and we asked for $2.00 per pound. He paid us $60 in cash and placed the fish and bear parts in the back of "our future Audi."

301

Our last stop was back at the Duck Song Restaurant, where we offered a few black rockfish and a small steelhead. Several men from the kitchen came out to look at the fish and were joined later by Tou Liu. They did not seem to know what the steelhead was until I explained it was like a salmon. They agreed on a price for the fish, and Tou Liu paid Jennifer in cash while the men carried the fish cooler into the restaurant kitchen. We were finally done for the day.

The next morning, the 17th, we headed to Spokane to meet with Rousch. When we arrived, we were met at the door by Kent's 30-year-old girlfriend, Jan, who walked us to the kitchen, where Rousch was waiting. After Kent told us about his exercise and nutritional regimens, we discussed the bighorn sheep horns we had brought him (on 01/26/12). He told us he still couldn't get them plugged because the states use helicopters and GPS to track every ram, so it's tough to explain how he came up with three dead rams all at once. Kent said his buddy in Idaho told him he couldn't plug them this year, but maybe next year. He told us Idaho is the only state that will allow people to bring in sheep horns they "found" and get them plugged. He said that Montana will allow the sale of sheep horns, but only if they are plugged and have the paperwork. Montana will not plug horns that have been "found."

Kent also showed us the mounted leopard we had brought him, and said we could either take it back with us or he would keep trying to sell it. I asked what he wanted to do, and he said he didn't mind keeping it there to sell. We agreed to leave the leopard with him. He opened his checkbook and asked what price we had agreed on for the sheep horns. I reminded him we had $600 total into the three sets. I stressed we weren't out to make a fortune, but did want something extra. He wrote out a check for $700 and handed it to me. Kent had written "Antler- For stock" in the corner of the check. He asked me for a receipt, and I told him I would have to mail it to him. As we left, I made mental notes of everything illegal I could see in the house to include in our search warrant affidavit. We said goodbye to Kent for the last time and headed towards Ellensburg.

Jennifer called Tanya Franklin and told her to meet us at the truck stop on Canyon Road in Ellensburg at 1:30 pm. We arrived at the truck stop and saw Tanya Franklin sitting in the passenger seat of a grey Ford Escort. Franklin got out and introduced us to her friend (the driver), Tanya Larson (great, two Tanyas). The two Tanyas took various Native American items from their vehicle's trunk. Larson also produced two tanned bobcat hides and a bear hide and asked us if we were interested in buying them as well. We reviewed the items and noted that most were decorated with raptor (hawk and owl) feathers. I asked the women to separate the items by whose item was whose. Once Larson sorted her items, I asked if she knew what the feathers were on the items. Larson identified the feathers as being from a red-tailed hawk and an owl. I told her it was illegal to possess or sell those feathers, and she said she knew. She also pointed out a bird talon decorating one of the items and said, "That's from a falcon." Jennifer and I selected nine items from Larson's collection (including smudge fans and peace pipes) and paid her $400 in cash.

Franklin had very few items and told us her eagle feather items were still back in Cowiche. She said she hadn't been able to get home to get her eagle feather items, but had them ready whenever we could come over to get them. I selected three items from her limited collection, including a small dreamcatcher decorated with hawk feathers. I told Tanya we could talk about prices when I got the other items. Franklin said she understood and asked when we could come to get the remaining items. I stated I would probably come over by myself next week. We took the nine items from Larson and the three items from Franklin and put them in the backseat of our truck (separated, so we could identify which items came from each individual). Larson gave Jennifer her phone number "in case you change your mind on some of the other items."

Done with another trip, we headed west to log in all the evidence.

While driving home, we sent Jin Dong a follow-up text, "Jin: we called our electrician friend about electrical work, and he said he will do the work for us in less than one day, no problem. We will work on finding a place this week as long as you are sure we're good to go. We have to put out some serious $ upfront. I want to make sure we have your approval. And Tina told me I have to cut my hair."

I absolutely couldn't wait to cut my hair, as I hated it long and had decided that even if we were allowed to continue to work undercover longer, this would be a good excuse to cut this crap off my head.....for good.

Jin replied, "Before you make your final decision. Make all $ plan first and how much you can make each time."

Jennifer replied, "Ok. We will let u know as soon as we r ready", to which Jin replied, "Good. No hurry. Just do it right!"

I received a text message from Jin on the **18ᵗʰ** stating, "Tom. Just let you know ahead of time. I'm going to LA next month for a couple of months. I'm set up new store down over there. But we keep in touch."

I replied, "Ok. Just so you know, we may get into the welding business. We have an old shed on some family property that used to be used for a welding shop. It is perfect. On family property, we won't disturb the neighbors with our welding. It is heated, insulated, and has power and water. It is right behind Tina's sister's house."

Jin asked, "Rent?"

"Tina's real dad owns it. He is not well and needs full-time care. The shop sits right now. But I guess we would pay Tina's sister. We will work that out", I responded.

Jin wrote back, "Perfect How big?"

I answered, "I think so. I think it is about 30' by 40'. Or 1200 square feet. Good for a first one, huh?"

"Can be 80", Jin responded.

I wrote Jin back with, "Ok. I will measure it on Monday. What date do you leave for LA?"

"Will be 01 Sept", Jin responded.

I answered, "Ok. We will talk this coming week. Take care, my friend."

On the **21ˢᵗ**, I texted, "Jin: our shop is 32 by 40. We have it cleaned up and ready. Power will be done tomorrow night. How do we get equipment from you?"

Jin replied, "How many plant will be fit in?"

"You are the expert there, but I would guess 100", I responded.

305

Jin replied, "Good. I need to talk to my people for all equipment. I will get back to you tomorrow".

"Sounds good. Our goal is to have some weight for you when you get back from LA. We wanna make you proud and prove we can do this!" I answered.

Jennifer and I were supposed to "freshen up" as many of our "top eight" cases as possible towards the end of August and early September. The Franklin/Parker/Backster crew made this easier for us, as they had all been calling and emailing us separately, asking us to come and buy from them. Jim Backster was the only one in the group who was still in the same house as our last visit, while Kyle and Tanya had moved again. I agreed to meet with Tanya Franklin on the 27th.

Tanya Franklin was now living with Tanya Larson in a house that suited both of them perfectly. I arrived at the twin-Tanya house on the **27th**, and Franklin immediately told me she didn't have all of her items and explained that some other women had stolen them and were "holding them hostage." Franklin said these women accused her of owing them money and had taken her eagle and hawk feather items. They were either going to sell them on eBay or to me. Franklin said she had spoken to these women that day, and they wanted to bring the items over and sell them directly to me. I told Franklin I didn't like doing business with people I didn't know. Franklin said she did have a few items left in the house. I followed her into the house to see four new items (two pipes decorated with Rattlesnake skins and feathers, and two natural wood bases with single eagle feathers). She told me a woman named Pam Sterns had the stolen items and would bring them over for me to look at if I wanted her to. I told Franklin to call Pam

306

and tell her to bring the items over quickly, but only her. Franklin said her (Franklin's) "very best friend," Ronny, would have to drive Pam over. I told Franklin that was fine, but nobody else. Franklin called Ronny (using her cell phone) and told him to bring Pam and the eagle feathers over. This was becoming even more bizarre than usual.

While waiting for Pam's arrival, I told Franklin I would take the four new items for $160. Tanya agreed. Inside the house, she showed me two trays (sitting on a footstool) of what she identified as "baby hawk feathers." She said she had way more hawk feathers, too. I asked her if she lived at this house now, and she said she still had some of her stuff in the camper at the Trail Road address but was living at this house (the Livengood Road address) with Larson and another male roommate. Franklin stated she intended to stay at the Livengood address since Pam lives at the Trail Road address. During our conversation, Tanya Larson came out of one of the side rooms and entered the conversation. Larson offered to sell me a large dreamcatcher (decorated with what appeared to be raptor feathers). She said she still had the two bobcats and bear hides if I wanted them. Larson said she lives full-time in this house and has a boyfriend (from Moses Lake) who lives with her, too.

To gather some updated info, I asked Franklin if Kyle was doing a lot of meth. She said they both used meth, but she didn't do much anymore. She said Kyle was totally out of control and had recently broken into a woman's freezer and had stolen several pounds of her marijuana. Kyle had used a chainsaw to cut a hole in the wall to get to the freezer containing the marijuana.

307

At about noon, a white Ford pickup arrived in the driveway. I followed Larson to the vehicle, where I met "Ronny" (driving) and Pam Sterns. Pam brought out a nylon zippered bag and produced four smudge fans. She said the feathers on at least two of the fans were eagle feathers, while the feathers on the other were turkey feathers. I asked Pam whose they were, and she said Tanya owed her a lot of money, so they had agreed she (Pam) could sell them and keep the money. Pam told me she had more hawk and eagle feathers at her house. I told Pam that since the eagle and hawk feathers are illegal, my market was very small. I asked her the price for the four items, and she said, "$150 each". I told her she could keep them, and I wouldn't pay more than $200 for them. Pam, of course, agreed to $200 for all four items. I paid her $200 in cash and placed the items in my truck.

I returned to the house and offered Larson $80 each for the larger bobcat and the dreamcatcher. She accepted, and I paid her $160 in cash and got the hell out of there as quickly as I could. I was thankful I would never have to return to that nuthouse again!

It was time to refresh the Wilson and Craig cases. The next day, on the **28**[th], I called each of them and asked if they would be around on the 29th. Each, separately, of course, said they would be around and welcomed me to come up. I specifically asked Wilson if he had any claws for sale. He said he would be there and had lots of birds, claws, and teeth to sell me. He also said he had a lynx and a huge bull elk for sale.

On the morning of the **29**[th,] I met with (recently promoted) Detective Julie Cook, who provided me with ten hatchery steelhead. I cleaned and photographed the fish. I called Mike Craig, who told me to bring them to the restaurant anytime after 3:30 p.m. I arrived at the Cascade Crest Restaurant at about 3:30 with the ten steelhead, quoting him a price of "Eight dollars each, just like last time." He handed me a check for $80 and placed the fish in a cardboard box in his truck. As I was driving away, I saw him carry the fish into the restaurant. Goodbye, Mike!

That afternoon, I arrived at Wilson's taxidermy shop and found he was all alone. He showed me a mounted lynx with a ptarmigan, which he offered me for $800 for the mount. I said I would ask around and see if anyone was interested in it. I took two photos of the mount using my cell phone.

He opened a plastic tackle box and began showing me bear claws and teeth, and opened a black plastic bag with a bear hide inside (paws attached). He asked if I would buy the claws from this bear, stating the hide was wet (fresh), so the claws hadn't been cleaned yet, and I said I would take them. Next, he showed me cougar claws and asked if I was interested in buying some. I selected ten cougar claws, 47 bear claws, and 13 bear teeth for $415.

Wilson told me to buy a few ducks, and I said I had limited funds but would buy a canvasback for $100. I owed him $515 for everything, which I paid in cash. He said to come back, and he would have more similar stuff for me. I silently told Wilson I wouldn't be back, but a bunch of my friends would be.

The last call of the month was from Steve Stuart on the **31st**. Steve asked if I remembered him, and I said I did. He asked if I was still in the "same business," which I said I was, and the business was doing very well. Steve said the bear hunting season was opening up this coming weekend, and he and six of his friends were going hunting. He asked if I remembered what we had talked about "from bear" (gallbladder), and I told him I remembered. He wondered if we were still interested in buying, and I verified we were. He said that with seven of them hunting, they should come up with a couple of bears.

I was tempted to be honest with Stuart and tell him we wouldn't buy from him, no matter what he came up with, because he had not made the "top eight" list (even though he was trying like hell). No matter what, he would still be charged, but I couldn't buy anything more from him, no matter how bad he really was. But I couldn't directly tell him "no" either, so I left him hoping we would come over with a wad of cash.

"Good luck, and see ya soon," I said as I ended our conversation.

Like all the other suspects who had contacted us since February 29th, Stuart just hadn't timed it right (actually, their timing had worked out well <u>for them</u>).

CHAPTER 25- SEPTEMBER 2012

This was it; only 18 days until the take-down day. Jennifer and I had the warrants pretty much ready to go, other than updating any further contacts we would have before we took the warrants to different judges all across the state. The Feds were ready to go, we had communicated to all the other involved states about our plans (so they could execute their take-downs simultaneously), and Julie Cook had been assigned full-time to assist with the case files and follow-up. Jennifer and I met and split the "top eight" cases right down the middle, with each of us in charge of four cases (writing the warrants, picking the officer teams to execute the warrants, and conducting the briefings). We had already scheduled conference rooms to brief the multitude of officers on their specific cases and warrants.

Everyone was on board and ready for the September 18th takedowns except for the DEA, who wanted to extend the operation long enough for us to get our equipment and starter plants from Jin or his brother. I was stuck in the middle, having absolutely no say in the decision process. In the end, the DEA's request for an extension was denied by our command staff, and we were told to forget the grow operation and attend to the warrants as scheduled.

Because we had only been allowed to continue to work the "top eight" cases (actually nine with the Russians), those were the only cases we had any chance of obtaining search warrants for (so we could search for other evidence and links to other poachers and traffickers). Frustrating as it was, we knew that as of the 18th, we would lose a ton of valuable evidence when suspects who were not on the "top eight" list heard about all the warrants. Through Hobbs, we had pleaded to

Cenci not to conduct media releases on the warrant services until we had a chance to have all the suspects rounded up (which would take a couple more weeks), but we knew there was no chance of keeping that dog on a leash. Even though Cenci didn't care much about deer and elk, I was certain he would plaster this operation all over the news. I knew he would do so if for no other reason than to fire one more torpedo at our operation.

As the take-down date neared, Jennifer and I wondered about the odds of retaliation against us personally from some of the more dangerous suspects we had worked with. Sgt. Hobbs had also expressed concern over this issue and had even requested the agency to purchase electronic security systems for our houses to protect us as much as possible. The agency had denied the request, but the Rocky Mountain Elk Foundation had come to the rescue and had generously written a check to buy top-quality electronic monitoring equipment for both our homes, an act of sheer kindness for which we will always be thankful.

Jennifer and I wanted to refresh our cases as much as possible (so our warrants would be approved). In early September, we started contacting several of them one by one, but Dusty Hilton must have been reading our minds.

I received a text from Dusty on the 3rd, "We shot two elk, and they both got away bro im srry I was using a 308 and it just didn't put them down. Is next Saturday to late"

I replied, "You are shitting? Saturday is better than nothing. What does your buddy shoot?"

312

"A 7mm but he sucks at it he didn't even fire a shot…it sucks I screwed u over they were right on the road", Dusty answered.

I wrote back, "Shit happens my friend. Can't say I haven't lost anything I shot. Let's make it next Saturday!"

Dusty replied, "The one broke its back I dnt even know how she got up"

"That really sucks cause it's just gonna be coyote food. They are really tough critters sometimes", I answered.

Dusty replied, "Next Saturday I will have my 7 mm no fuck ups. Yep I know Both cuse the other is hit threw the lungs"

"Ok. We will see ya next Saturday", I wrote back.

Dusty answered, "Ok Srry again I tied my hardest. Im realy disappointed in my self my brother keep asking me qfter that what r u gona do. I was like theres nothing I can do".

I answered, "I know. I'll catch up with ya later. I am not pissed".

On the 5th, I texted Liev, "Any word on when you might have some fish and/or caviar?"

Liev replied, "I have black now…Yuli is here."

"Ok. I'll talk to ya tomorrow. I am sick. Going to bed", I answered.

Yuli replied, "Get well….Talk tomorrow."

313

The next day, I texted Liev, "Still not feeling too good. What time would someone be around tomorrow afternoon?"

Liev replied, "Any time, Yuli will be home."

"Great. Is this the same paddlefish black from Oklahoma? How old is it?" I asked.

Liev replied, "Last may. Same"

"Ok. I will take 5 pounds". What is Yuli's phone #? I will call him when we are getting close. We have to go to eastern WA in morning", I said.

Liev replied with the phone number, and I wrote back, "Thanks."

Finally, on the 7th, I sent Yuli the following text message: "Yuli: this is Tom Davis. Will around 11 today work for you?"

At 10:03, I received a call from Yuli, who stated he would meet me at the Chevron station on 164th Street in Lynnwood. Yuli asked me how many pounds I wanted, and I told him five.

I arrived at the Chevron station at about 10:20. At 10:24, I saw Yuli driving into the parking lot in a blue Mitsubishi. He produced a grocery bag containing five jars of black caviar. I handed Yuli $500 in cash and asked him how long he was going to be around. He said he would be here for three more weeks. I asked when they would get me some fish, and Yuli said: "We are going fishing tomorrow." Within an hour, I turned the caviar over to Agent Andrews and was reimbursed for the $500.

314

Later that same day, I received a text from Glen Sullivan, offering four deer, which I turned down. Although we were allowed to work Glen because he was a tribal member, he was still not on our "top eight" list.

I received a text from Dusty Hilton on the **8**th, "we got a big doe"

I replied, "I will head your way now."

I told Dusty I should arrive at his place at about 2:30 pm.

"You whack it with your 7mm?" I asked Dusty.

He replied, "no my buddy shot it.308"

Since Jennifer had her hands full taking her Sergeant test on this date, I headed east alone, arriving at Dusty's house at about 2:30. I drove to the backyard of his house, where Dusty and Janet met me. He said his neighbors (across the street) were watching him, and his landlord had been "an asshole." His landlord had jumped all over him about all the elk antlers, asking where Dusty got them. His landlord also complained about his hanging deer and elk in the shed.

Apparently, Dusty's landlord hated his poaching, but not enough to turn him in, or maybe he was scared.

I asked if he rented the shed/shop, to which Dusty replied, "No, that's the landlord's, and I am not supposed to use it."

He went into the house to retrieve the deer carcass (I suppose it was in the bathtub again), which he carried out in two pieces. He loaded the deer into my truck, and I paid him $200 in cash. Dusty said

315

"they" had killed the deer on the Indian reservation. He also said their elk hunting had been screwed up because someone had locked the gate up to the area they usually elk hunt. He said he likes to hunt on the reservation because "We don't get fucked with by state game wardens." He asked when we would want more meat, and I told him we would hold off for a while until it cooled down. I said I would be in touch, which was kind of true.

On my way back, I had an idea. Since we hadn't done any business with Bourey in five months, I knew we had to refresh our case with him if we were to have any chance of searching his house. I knew he was one of the top traffickers in Washington's history, and the thought of not getting a chance to search his house concerned me greatly, so I decided to see if Bourey was willing to go from supplier to buyer. I called Bourey and told him I had just purchased some deer and had one extra. I said I had purchased two deer for $250 total, and one was pretty small, and I wanted to keep the large one, but would sell the smaller one to him for $100. Bourey said he would call around to see if anyone wanted a deer. I told him that if he didn't want it, to say so, and that was fine, but if he wanted it, to tell me now. Bourey said to bring it to his place, and he would take it. I told him I would be at his house at about 6 p.m. The deer I had purchased from Hilton was a small doe in poor condition. Since I knew I would never see that deer whole again, I pulled over, photographed it, and took a DNA sample.

I arrived at Bourey's residence in Tacoma at about 6:00 p.m. and noticed around 25 cars parked in front. I walked through his open garage and found a large party (including a live band) going on in the backyard. I found Bourey and talked to him while men conducted cock-fights adjacent to us in the backyard. I asked him how I was supposed to carry a dead deer through all these people.

Bourey said, "Don't worry about it, I will have my soldiers carry it in for you" (Apparently, he had promoted a few of his "monkeys" to "soldiers").

Bourey spoke with a "soldier" in Cambodian and sent the man with me to get the deer. The "soldier" and I carried the two separate deer halves from my truck through the garage to a freezer in the backyard. Bourey came over, looked at the deer, and began making room in the freezer for it. Bourey's men put the deer in the freezer while he offered me food and booze. He asked where Tina was and why I didn't bring her, and I said she was home, cutting up the other animals. I turned down the alcohol, and he fixed a plate of food for me to take home to my wife and paid me $100 in cash for the deer. I told him we would talk about business later (or at least he would be talking with someone soon).

I called Jennifer when she was on her way home from her sergeant interview, filled her in, and her only question was, "Well, where's my food?" I smiled, thinking about the plate of mystery food, which was now sitting in a dumpster at a gas station.

Early morning on Monday, September 10th, Jennifer and I took off on our last road trip, knowing neither of us would ever work undercover again and would never work together again (except for court cases, which would likely result from the Operation Cody cases). I had set my retirement date as December 17th, which I believed should leave Jennifer, Julie Cook, and me time to complete all the case files, get all the evidence processed, and allow the uniformed officers to scoop up over 100 suspects we had identified. Altogether, for the "top eight" cases, we had 14 search warrants to present to judges for service later. A couple of the cases had only one place to search, while others, such as the Parker/Backster/Franklin cases, had multiple search locations requiring separate warrants (and warrant teams) for each location.

On this last road trip, we had lined up judges across the state whom we would meet with before conducting the briefings for each of the search warrant teams in those areas. We also intended to refresh the cases on Backster/Parker and Duck Song while we were running around getting warrants signed and conducting briefings.

Monday found us in Spokane for a morning meeting with a Spokane County Superior Court judge. On Monday afternoon of the 10th, Jennifer and I met with the judge, and Jennifer presented her search warrant affidavit. As is typical, the judge went through the affidavit and warrant slowly and thoroughly, then swore in Jennifer. With the first warrant signed and sealed, we drove to the Spokane WDFW regional office to make copies of the warrants for the search teams. We worked through much of that night, making last-minute preparations for the remainder of the week.

We conducted our first briefing at the Spokane regional office on Tuesday, the 11th. Since this region only had to deal with the search warrant for Kent Rousch, we only had a handful of officers and federal agents in attendance. Jennifer took about an hour and a half to run through a PowerPoint used to bring the officers (none of whom knew anything about Operation Cody) up to speed on the case. She covered the safety plan, the backup plans, and the search details. She advised the group to decide among themselves who would take on what role (search, photographing, security, evidence, and interrogation). Jennifer told the group we had split the cases, and this one was hers, so on takedown day, if any questions arose, they should call her first, as I would be busy answering questions on my assigned cases. At the end of the briefing, we answered all the questions and walked outside to get six fresh pheasants from Detective Lenny Hahn.

Our first stop in Tri-Cities was at Duck Song, which we needed to refresh, so with the backseat full of search warrants, we pulled into the restaurant at about 11:30 a.m. We were again met by Tou Liu, who asked, "Do you have fish?"

Jennifer showed her the six pheasants. Tou Liu asked Jennifer if they were fresh, and I answered, "We just killed them yesterday and have kept them refrigerated."

Jennifer proposed a price for the pheasant, which Tou Liu accepted and paid. As we drove to the courthouse to get a warrant signed for this restaurant, I looked in the rearview mirror and watched Tou Liu carry the feathered birds into the restaurant's kitchen.

We drove from Duck Song to the Benton County courthouse, where Jennifer presented her search warrant for Duck Song. As the judge read through the warrant affidavit, he let out a "holy expletive." Apparently, "His Honor" eats (or used to eat) at the Duck Song fairly often. The judge swore Jennifer in and told us he would never eat there again.

After leaving Benton County, we traveled down to Walla Walla County to have the Walla Walla County judge review Jennifer's warrant affidavit for Jin Dong's home, restaurant, and vehicles. It was no surprise to either of us when that judge also said he had eaten at Dong's restaurant. He was more than happy to sign the warrant and wished us luck as we went out the door.

We spent the night in Yakima and readied ourselves for our appointment with a Yakima County judge first thing in the morning.

At 8 a.m. on Wednesday, the 12th, we walked into the office of one of the Yakima County Superior Court judges. Since we had a large number of warrants to present in this county, Jennifer and I had made arrangements to email the affidavits to this particular judge the previous week, so he would have time to read them. The judge had read through the four warrants for the Parker clan (one for Parker's house, one for Backster's house, one for the Tanya twins' house, and one for Pam Sterns' house), as well as the warrant for Hilton's house and truck. He reviewed the warrants, signed them, and congratulated us on an exceptional case.

With warrants in hand, Jennifer and I headed out on one last undercover contact to Backster's house. Earlier in the week, Jim Backster had called us saying he had a whole elk and a whole deer for us hanging in his new walk-in cooler. So for the first time in my career, we drove to a suspect's house to make an undercover contact while we had a signed search warrant, in our backseat, for that very same property.

On our way there, I texted Backster, "We will be there around 10:20. Work for you?"

"We are here. Got my friend Kyle on a clean roll, so he is here now and looking forward to seeing you, to," Backster replied.

On the way to the Backster property, Jennifer recorded the serial numbers from the eight $100 bills and photographed the bills, just in case the bills were still in their possession when the search warrant was served. At about 10:20, Jennifer and I arrived at the Backster residence to purchase our elk and deer. We were met by Jim Backster, who took us into a walk-in cooler where he produced a quartered elk and a quartered deer. We agreed to a price of $800 for both critters. Jennifer paid Jim Backster $800 in cash after Jim and I had loaded the meat in our truck. Jim took us to his house to see Kyle Parker. Both Kyle and Jim said Kyle had shot and killed the elk, and Jim had killed the deer. Kyle told us he was back living at his parent's house in Naches and is "off meth now." He also said he still has his .22 Hornet rifle "at home" and would never give that one up (I was pretty sure he would be giving that up).

We left the Backster household and headed to the Yakima WDFW office to offload our deer and elk and prepare for our next briefing. Months before, Jennifer and I had been given total administrative authority by the chief to hand-pick whichever officers we felt were best suited for each warrant team. Jennifer had picked the teams for her warrants, and I had done the same for mine. We emailed our chosen officers, asking them if they were willing to participate in warrant services on the 18th, but we didn't give them any details of where they would be searching. We also asked them to set aside the date of their respective regional briefings. As a courtesy, we cc'ed their supervisors and asked them to contact Sgt. Hobbs, if they had any questions or concerns, but nobody did. Lastly, we asked the captains from each region to please reserve their conference rooms for our briefings. We were set and had all the necessary paperwork (copies of the warrants, safety plans, etc.) set aside for each team.

Our only stumbling block came from the Yakima region. Just before our briefing, we learned that Sgt. Grant and his Captain (Mann) had thrown a tantrum about us directing their subordinates without getting their permission. These two were joined in their campaign by Sgt. Jewell and Captain Anderson. When these four joined hands and cried to the DC, Cenci changed course and allowed them to make the final call on what officers they wanted at each warrant service, but nobody bothered to tell us. As a result, when we arrived at the Yakima regional office, we no longer had any idea which officers were on which team (or even how many officers were allowed to come out and play), which made our warrant package preparation a bit confusing.

As Jennifer and I were making copies of the search warrants, Captain Mann came into the copy room and told us the briefing was no longer going to be held at the WDFW office, but had instead been moved to a local sheriff's precinct office, and he didn't know the address. We scrambled around trying to find out where "our" briefing would be held until we finally got the answer. Once we had the search warrant packages completed, we headed to the new meeting location, while I called Hobbs (who was on his way over) to tell him about the change and to express my frustrations. Being the intelligent man he is, Hobbs could tell I was in the mood to rip someone's ass and kindly

322

asked me to have Jennifer conduct the entire briefing. I agreed that was a good idea, as I was in a very hostile mood and had nothing to lose by blowing up on these clowns (as I was retiring soon anyway), and while Jennifer was just as frustrated, she is generally a lot more subtle.

When we arrived at the briefing, we had to wait another ½ hour for everyone else to arrive, which was difficult since nobody seemed to know who was supposed to be there; it's hard to take roll-call when you don't have the list of attendees. While this was supposed to be my briefing, I (mostly) sat quietly and listened to Jennifer fill everyone in on the various warrants, suspects, and cases. While she was talking, I took a headcount and came up about eight officers shy of what we had initially planned. Still, I guess the two captains figured they could cover the eight locations to be searched in the region with the dozen or so officers they had invited. Jennifer explained we had two warrants in Walla Walla, one in Tri-Cities, and five in the Yakima area. She went on to tell the group what time of day they could expect the suspects to be home (we wanted the suspects home when we executed the warrants so that they could be immediately interrogated), which varied from 8 a.m. to 7 p.m., depending on each suspect. She explained that while we wanted the warrants, all served on the same day, there was no way we could serve them simultaneously, so it was imperative the media didn't learn of the warrants, or our officers and evidence would be jeopardized.

At the end of Jennifer's presentation, the officers had many good questions, which we answered to the best of our abilities. Once completed, we left to meet with our last judge of the day in Skagit

County. On our way back over the mountains, Hobbs called and thanked me for not starting World War III and laughed as he told me the two captains had approached him after the meeting and said it was apparent they needed to bring in more officers for the Yakima region warrants........hell, why didn't we think of that?

On my way home, I dropped Jennifer off before I continued north to meet with a Skagit County judge, who had generously agreed to meet after hours in her home to sign the warrants I had for her. I presented her with three warrants: the Cascade Crest Restaurant, Mike Craig's home, and Wyatt Wilson's taxidermy shop. Again, I had arranged for her to receive the affidavits a few days in advance to speed the process up. As she signed the warrants, I asked if she had ever eaten at the Cascade Crest restaurant, and we were both pleased she had not. That night I got to sleep in my own bed, which was really nice.

The next morning, the **13**[th], I drove to the Snohomish County judge to get the Smirnov warrant signed, followed by the region four briefing. I conducted the WDFW Seattle regional briefing, which went off without a hitch. Since both Jennifer and I lived and worked in Region 4, we knew everyone there, which, along with much more reasonable supervisors, made the whole process much smoother.

After another night in my bed, on the morning of the **14**[th,] it was on to Pierce County Superior Court for the Bourey warrant. As we were driving down to Tacoma, Jennifer said she should hear any day now about whether or not she got the sergeant position. I told her it was inconceivable anyone could beat her out, as she was well respected, knowledgeable, and had spent her entire life in that area

324

(and therefore knew it like the back of her hand). That, coupled with the fact that WDFW had zero female or minority supervisors, made me believe she was unbeatable. However, we had all long ago given up trying to predict how this administration came to its decisions.

The Pierce County judge read Jennifer's affidavit, complimented her on its quality, and signed off quickly. We were now on our way to the last of our briefings. For the Bourey warrant, Jennifer had chosen to have the Tacoma Police Department SWAT team do the entry, as we were more than a little concerned it might not go so smoothly if he had a house full of "soldiers." It's always a good idea to have the men in black do their thing when there is any chance of the entry being dangerous. We met at the Tacoma P.D. station, where we prepared search warrant packages for the team members. As we waited for everyone to file in, I wondered if DC Cenci would attend the briefing since it was only about 40 minutes from our headquarters office and would be a great opportunity for him to put on a show. When Hobbs entered the room, I instantly knew something was wrong by looking at his face. I figured the DC was only a couple of steps behind him, but instead, he asked Jennifer, "Can I talk to you in the hall?" As they walked out in the hallway, I knew it wasn't Cenci's appearance that Hobbs was so somber about. It was Jennifer's promotional hopes.

With only about half our warrant team members in the room, Jennifer returned with the same look on her face that Hobbs had displayed moments before and asked me to come outside with her.

When we got outside, I turned and asked, "You didn't get the promotion, did you?"

325

Her answer confused me, "I don't know. Hobbs said the chief has determined Bill Franklin and I are tied."

After I yelled "bullshit" loud enough to be heard inside the building, I asked, "What now. How do they break the tie, arm-wrestling?"

Jennifer said they had not decided yet. Since Jennifer and her husband were entrenched in the area, they had always lived in, moving was out of the question, so this sergeant position would likely be her only shot at promotion. I calmly assured her that no matter what tie-breaker they were to come up with, she would prevail. I was pretty confident that was true unless the administration manipulated the system (which had certainly been done before).

We went back inside and put on a professional search warrant briefing without being encumbered by the DC's presence. Soon we were done, and the wheels were in motion. Tuesday the 18th would be a bad day for a lot of bad guys. Hopefully, we could keep the DC from making a media circus out of this, so in the following two weeks (after the 18th), we would be able to ruin the days of a multitude of other suspects. Jennifer and I had told everyone at the briefings that we would be sitting in a room (our little command center) with our phones, computers, and case files ready for any questions that might arise. Since we had warrants scheduled to be served from 5 a.m. to 7 p.m. on the 18th, it would be a long day, but the two of us weren't encountering any of the risks our co-workers would face.

The weekend was pretty relaxed at my house as my wife and I got re-acquainted. For the last 22 months, I had been on the road one hell of a lot and owed my wife a great deal of actual quality time when this was all over. When I first began considering retirement, I was nervous, even scared at the prospect, wondering if I was making the right decision. But that weekend at home, I knew I was too tired of being away so much to continue working. Long-term operations take their toll on undercover officers and their families. It was time to move on, and I was finally totally comfortable with my decision.

On Monday, the **17**[th], Hobbs called to confirm what I had expected; Cenci had invited a television crew to cover the Bourey search warrant service. The warrant was scheduled for pre-dawn on Tuesday, and Hobbs said the news crew would be there. He went on with more good news; he (Hobbs) was assigned another news crew to go with him on the Cascade Crest warrant. Oh well, as long as they didn't release the story until all of the warrants were completed, we wouldn't lose any evidence or endanger the safety of the search teams for the "top eight" cases. Still, the other 85 or so suspects would be moving and dumping evidence faster than a speeding bullet.

I explained to Hobbs that if the searches were shown on television, we would lose most (if not all) of the evidence on our remaining suspects and asked if there was anything to do to stop this. Hobbs just said. "I know, and I am sorry, but I can't stop him. The media will be there."

CHAPTER 26- THE WARRANTS

Just as with our business, Jennifer and I had planned on our "marriage" failing. This day, September 18th, 2012, was the first day of our legal separation and was soon to be followed by our imminent divorce. Like some couples, we had agreed to remain friends, despite the fake divorce of our fake marriage, so early on the morning of the take-down day, Jennifer and I drove to our office for the last time. We immediately moved into the conference room, spreading out all our case files and dodging the extra-large coffee cups.

At about 6:30, we heard back from Detective Golden on the Bourey warrant. Without a hitch, Bourey had been taken into custody by SWAT, and they had cleared the house with no real issues while all of it was captured by the television crew, with Cenci leading the charge of WDFW uniformed officers. Cenci was too busy to attend our pre-search briefing but was right there leading the team when cameras were rolling.

As the morning moved on, our phones were flooded with calls from the various search teams, all asking legitimate questions, which we answered as fast as they came in. All was going well, and by 10 a.m., several other warrants were in the process of being served with no problems.

Everything had gone as planned until around noon when I received a call from a friend (not involved in the search warrants) who asked if I had anything to do with the statewide fish and wildlife search warrants "they" were talking about on the radio and television. I immediately jumped on the internet and found Deputy Chief Mike

Cenci proclaiming the charge against wildlife traffickers everywhere I looked. Cenci gave details, including "Two undercover fish and wildlife detectives using a phony website to lure in poachers....". As I looked on the internet, I learned the headline, "**Major Wildlife Trafficking Busts Across Washington Today,**" was the lead story and had first gone public at 10:30 that morning!

**King-5 Seattle, television report (filmed live at Bourey's house).
Posted on the internet on September 18, 2012, <u>at 11:15 AM (hours
before most of the warrants were to be executed)</u>.**

This set the benchmark for stupidity and irresponsibility for any officer, but as the second in command, I thought Cenci should have faced immediate termination and arrest for obstruction of law enforcement due to his actions. Because of his love for himself and the cameras, Cenci had just crossed the line and jeopardized our cases and his officers' safety! We immediately began calling the search teams, who hadn't yet served their warrants, to warn them that their suspects might know they were coming. We advised the search teams to go early, if possible, and exercise caution because our deputy chief certainly hadn't.

One of the suspects I was most concerned about, now that our search warrant plans had been made public, was Hilton. In the briefing, we told the search team members that Hilton had a job that kept him away from home until about 6 p.m., so we advised them to hit his house at about 7 p.m. With Hilton's size, aggressive behavior, and criminal history, he was to be taken seriously, and now, he likely knew he would be having unwelcome company very soon. I called that particular search team and told them to "Go now! Search the house now, even if he isn't home, but be very careful." That team went ahead and executed the search warrant within an hour of my call and later called us back to say Hilton was already at home when they arrived (we don't know why he was home, and not at work). The search team found the house was void of evidence, no drugs, none of the firearms we wanted, no wildlife, and he had tried to delete all of the contacts and text messages from his cell phone.

The remainder of the warrants had gone reasonably well, with valuable evidence seized at most locations. Vehicles (seized for forfeiture) had been towed, Bourey was sitting in jail, confessions had been recorded, and tons of evidence had been seized. Most importantly, none of our officers had been in any physical confrontations, and everyone was going home safely. Because we had to speed up the search warrant executions, everyone was clear of the warrant searches by 6 p.m., and we all headed home.

As Jennifer and I wrapped up for the day, I sincerely thanked her for everything she had done. I reminded her that while I had been paid to do undercover, she had volunteered and gone well above and beyond the call of duty. I asked her to thank her husband, Robb, for putting up with all her long hours and trips away from home, and went on to tell her she had been a great partner and friend, and I owed her. I dropped her off that night, knowing I wouldn't see much of her from then on, as I had firmly decided it was time to move on to the next chapter of my life. Back to civilian life.

The remainder of the week, Detective Julie Cook and I waded through the reports, statements, and evidence that the warrant teams had obtained. We quickly assigned the remaining 32+ cases (with over 70 suspects) out to the uniformed officers for follow-up, warning them all the suspects would likely know their day was coming (some probably didn't get too much sleep on the night of the 18th, wondering when their doors would come busting down).

The follow-up was a tremendous task. We had the remaining suspects to contact, we had to explore every lead we had gained from interviews and evidence to the end, and we had to prepare complete case files for all the prosecutors. The video evidence alone was voluminous. By way of the covert video placed on Bourey's residence, we had identified not only the Indian who had delivered elk and deer (Ellen Buck) but many of the buyers, suspects who would need to be contacted and charged as well.

Throughout my career, I have found it's easy to get officers to volunteer to go on search warrants, but a lot more challenging to get those officers to write reports and get their paperwork completed, so a great deal of our time was spent nagging the officers to submit their documentation.

Sometime that week, Jennifer called and told me the powers-that-be had decided how to break the tie for the sergeant promotion. The two tied officers were to take an "online personality profile," which would not be graded. Instead, it would result in a written assessment to be provided to the chief to decide which of the two officers' personality traits best suited them for that particular position.

When I was done laughing, I told Jennifer, "Look, since it is an online test, they won't know who is sitting at the computer answering the questions, so I'm willing to help you. I'll sit down and take the test for you."

It was then Jennifer's turn to break into laughter as she said, "Thanks, that's just what I need, an assessment that comes back stating I'm a psychopath with delusions of blowing up the headquarters office. I appreciate the offer, but I think I'll take this on my own."

I answered, "Remember if you change your mind, I'm here for ya."

As I got off the phone, I thought about this tie-breaker and considered the reality. In my opinion, Jennifer and Bill (the officer she was "tied" with) couldn't be more polar opposites. She is a total type "A" personality, driven and serious about work, but open and funny away from work, and Bill is more a type "B," very relaxed and almost unconcerned with work, much quieter and sensitive. This should be interesting. At least I couldn't see another tie coming out of this test.

As the case reports trickled in, we learned Bourey had partially confessed but had not given up anyone other than his Indian supplier (whom we had already identified). Hilton had confessed to trafficking but had lied about many of the details. Rousch had called his attorney and had two attorneys present during the search and refused to answer any questions, although he was found to have a treasure trove of illegal wildlife in his home. At Duck Song, Liu apparently forgot she could speak English and had not answered any questions. The entire Parker group had all fully confessed, turned on each other, and had given up valuable information about other suspects (likely a result of the illegal firearms and meth which had been found during the searches). Jin Dong, who the Feds arrested in L.A., had thrown his cell phone in a nearby pool and clammed up, wanting his lawyer. Wilson started to confess and give up other suspects, but had a change of heart and shut down, even though a multitude of illegal wildlife had been seized in his shop. Mike Craig was belligerent and refused to cooperate in any fashion. Smirnov and Ivanov told their versions of the truth, but lied about most details.

The confessions (or lack thereof) didn't matter as we had video evidence of every transaction, but what we hoped to gain was intelligence leading to other suspects. There was more than one way to skin a cat, and what the suspects didn't tell us, the evidence would. We had seized computers, documents, cell phones, and bank records, and with that, we would be able to tie in a lot of other suspects.

CHAPTER 27- CLOSING SHOP

On October 1st, Julie Cook and I drove to Olympia (my least favorite place) to attend <u>Sergeant</u> Jennifer Maurstad's promotional ceremony. She and Brian Fulton (Tri-cities) had both won out in their bids for promotions, and I couldn't have been more proud of each of them. Both had worked extremely hard throughout their whole careers and were very deserving of their promotions. For once, virtually the entire workforce agreed with the promotional decisions.

As Jennifer settled into her new role as a detachment sergeant, Julie and I dove headlong into the arduous task of putting together the final case files. Each separate case required comprehensive case files which contained proposed criminal charges, suspect backgrounds, the undercover officer's case reports, a list of all evidence, evidence chain of custody, evidence identification (DNA reports, expert identification, or chemical analysis), photos, covert videos, phone/email, and text records, search warrants, written statements (both witness and suspect), certifications of licenses (or certification of no license), supporting officer's reports, and any other materials related to the investigations.

We prepared three identical case files for each case/group of suspects. We retained the original, a copy for the prosecutor, and a copy for the defense. Normally, the prosecutor makes a copy for the defense counsel. Still, experience had shown me that by taking a little extra time to make the copy ourselves, prosecutors were more likely to go forward with charging in a timely fashion, as they didn't have the burden of getting the reports copied. An additional burden for us was that we had several suspects who we had done business with in more than one county, or they had also violated federal laws, thus requiring us to make even more sets of files.

Julie and I discovered just how screwed up the operation's evidence was early into the case file process. Many of the items we believed had been sent in for testing/identification long ago were still sitting in the evidence room and had never been submitted. A few items of evidence were missing entirely. When we asked for photos of the evidence, we found much of it had not been photographed. The most troubling evidence problem was our discovery of several serious breaks in the evidence chain of custody.

Evidence needs to be secured (only accessible by the evidence custodian, in this case, Detective Clarke) and accounted for every step of the way. On one particular set of evidence items, Detective Clarke had left the evidence on top of a desk in an unlocked office, open to anyone. On another set of evidence, he had allowed a civilian friend (with a serious criminal history) to handle and photograph the items while unsupervised.

We had a severe problem, which, long before, I had warned Sgt. Hobbs might be the case. It made me sick to think we might lose some of our cases, which we had worked so hard on, due to sloppy evidence procedures. In Clarke's defense, he had been tasked with far too much work to complete in the allotted time (which explained why some of the evidence hadn't been submitted for identification), but that certainly didn't excuse the absolute breaches in the protocol that had occurred.

After determining the number and degree of evidence protocol breaches, I called Deputy Prosecutor Charlie Silverman to see what we needed to do about it and just how screwed we were. I detailed the situation to Charlie, who patiently took it in, occasionally releasing an expletive. In the end, Charlie's opinion was that we would lose some evidence (very little, actually) but would need to attach a report detailing every violation of proper evidence handling protocol to all of the case files, not just the cases involving the compromised evidence. It was his opinion that these breaches were severe enough to fall under the Brady Exculpatory Evidence rules. Exculpatory evidence is evidence that would harm the prosecution's case and must be disclosed to the defense just as the evidence that helps is disclosed. This is part of the discovery process, a procedure in which the prosecutors are required to share their information before trial. Charlie felt, and I certainly agreed, that it is better to disclose your screw-ups from the start than to have the defense find them later, as the latter would be perceived as hiding something.

Charlie referred me to another prosecutor, who was an expert on exculpatory evidence, for a second opinion. When I called for a second opinion, I got virtually the same answer, so there was no doubt in my mind about what we had to do. I passed this information on to Sgt. Hobbs, who also spoke to two attorneys about our "situation," and the answers were consistent. Hobbs briefed the DC on our issues. Hobbs called me back and said Cenci had told him we would not disclose the breaches in evidence protocol except for those cases directly related to the tainted evidence. This was one time I failed to follow directions from my command (ok, I confess I may have done so a few other times in my career), as I not only included the notifications

336

of evidence breaches in each case file I sent forward, but I instructed Detective Cook to do the same. Law trumps command directives (or even orders) every time in my book, and I wasn't going to have any part of being accused of withholding exculpatory evidence. Additionally, I hadn't been ordered not to include the exculpatory notice; I had been told that was Cenci's position. I never heard the word "order" in the conversation anywhere.

Sgt. Hobbs, Julie, Jennifer, and I reviewed the evidence with Clarke on several occasions to make sure everything was submitted for identification and had been photographed and accounted for, and all in all, we came out pretty good. The evidence still needing identification was prioritized by the USFWS forensics laboratory as well as by WDFW's lab, and the results came back fairly quickly.

As we put together the case files, the WDFW uniformed officers and USFWS agents were busy following up on additional suspects gained from suspect information and seized evidence. We executed several more search warrants for phone, email, and banking records, which further solidified potential criminal charges on these additional suspects and identified new suspects. As a result of this follow-up, we passed the 100-suspect mark (including Washington and out-of-state suspects) by mid-November. Most Operation Cody suspects faced multiple state and/or federal felony charges. Topping the charts were the Franklin/Parker/Backster crew, Jin Dong, and Bourey. These three cases alone accounted for well over 100 criminal charges.

By the end of November 2012, most of the legwork was done, and the cases were in the hands of the various state and federal prosecutors. Agent Andrews was still busy pursuing the potential federal evidence to the end, but WDFW's efforts had subsided. It was evident that all I had left to do was testify in court, which I could certainly do from retirement, so I set my retirement date and turned in my papers. December 17th, 2012, would officially be my last day working for the Department of Fish and Wildlife.

The 17th of December rushed upon me, and before I knew it, I was saying goodbye to my colleagues for the last time. After 34 years, my career had come to an end, and despite the hurdles we had faced, I still believe I went out at the top of my game. Now, as I write this, I find my pre-retirement prediction was accurate. I don't miss the job, but I do miss some of the people.

CHAPTER 28- THE AFTERMATH

As Operation Cody progressed, very few people knew what we were up to (for security reasons), but several of those who were aware told me, "You should write a book about this case." At first, I was strongly opposed to the idea of writing a book on our operation because I was concerned such a book might educate the criminal element (if they could read it) and therefore jeopardize undercover officers and their cases. Three realizations changed my mind: 1) I knew, despite our pleas, that the WDFW administration would make a media circus out of all this and release more details than I would ever consider releasing in a book. 2) The real story needed to be told to educate the public on what is happening to our wildlife and to educate fish and wildlife enforcement administrators across North America about the pros and cons of such an operation. 3) I was retiring, and Jennifer had moved onto a uniformed supervisor position. Therefore, neither of us would be jeopardized any worse (the criminals already knew our true identities from court documents), and neither of us would ever work undercover again.

I felt, and still feel, I could produce a book detailing Operation Cody without releasing "secrets of undercover work" (procedures or specific techniques used by undercover fish and wildlife officers) that could put people in harm's way. As I have always been most concerned about the safety of our men and women fighting against poachers, I did, however, struggle with my decision to write and release this book.

On February 13th, 2013, Sgt. Hobbs called, stating, "You are going to be really pissed."

He went on to tell me he had been ordered, by Cenci, to conduct an interview with a Seattle television station regarding Operation Cody.

I answered, "As long as they didn't release our undercover videos or details about the website, then I'm ok with it."

Hobbs quietly responded, "That's why you are going to be pissed. I was ordered to show the TV crew the website, and they were provided with all of your covert videos. Sorry, but I wasn't given a choice."

I'll never know why, after four months, our administration decided to conduct another television segment on our operation. As I watched the television report that night, I was shocked again. The report featured Sgt. Hobbs (the man in charge of a covert unit) in full uniform showing our website up close and personal, including the covert videos of several of our transactions.

The one thing about the news story that made me laugh was that they didn't show our faces. Hobbs told me the media had first to agree not to show Jennifer's or my face before the videos would be released to them.

I told Hobbs that was the exact opposite of what I would have done. "Both Jennifer and I are done with undercover. Showing our faces now would allow the wildlife criminals out there to know who to look out for. By not showing our faces, they won't know who might be an undercover officer. If the news story had shown our faces, it would have made things a little bit safer for anyone else working undercover in the future. The bad guys could look at the face in front of them and realize, "That ain't them."

The only good news was that I was no longer concerned about proceeding with this book.

Sometime after, Sgt. Hobbs called me in February 2013, he was promoted to the Region 4 (Seattle region) captain's position. After promoting Hobbs to captain, Chief Bjork moved Lt. Steve Crown to head up SIU. While Steve is a nice guy, he had very little time in the field as an officer before taking an office job in headquarters, a position most officers call an "empty holster position."

Unfortunately, Lt. Crown had earned a reputation as being non-responsive in his position as training/hiring lieutenant. He rarely responded to questions or concerns in a timely fashion and seemed to deal with his workload by either ignoring it or delegating it to someone else. I questioned how well he would do at SIU. It seemed like another foolish decision on the chief's part, or maybe he didn't have anyone else interested in the position.

Before the trials and forfeiture hearings (suspects who had vehicles or other property seized for forfeiture have an appeal opportunity) started coming up, I asked the logical question, "Will WDFW at least pay for my travel expenses to attend these mandatory proceedings?" The answer was, again, just what I expected: "No." WDFW was willing to spend thousands of dollars to catch wildlife criminals, but was unwilling to pay my travel expenses to testify in court against the suspects. Perhaps they knew my dedication to this operation wouldn't allow me to blow off the hearings and trials. In essence, they could get something for nothing and/or have one last dig at me personally. As predicted, Jennifer and I ended up testifying in various proceedings. She was paid for her time and reimbursed for travel expenses, and I was not (although some of the prosecutors' offices offered to pay my mileage). Unfair as it was, I knew when I submitted my retirement papers, I would never see another dime out of my former employer, yet I would have a lot of "gratis" work left to accomplish.

In the months following my retirement, I still attempted to keep track of Operation Cody and the criminal proceedings. I very much wanted to see all our hard work culminate in the most successful outcomes possible. Knowing it is not uncommon for overworked prosecutors to simply sit on case files without actually filing the charges, I hounded Hobbs and Crown in an attempt to ensure someone kept on top of these cases.

A couple of months after Crown took over SIU, I checked in on the status of the cases. That's when I discovered nobody was monitoring most of the cases' progress. At least one of the cases had gone beyond the statute of limitations (the time in which a case must be charged), and many others were sitting there waiting for their time limit to expire. I sent Crown an email pleading that he would have someone monitor the cases so that the time, money, effort, and risk Jennifer and I had endured wouldn't all be for nothing.

A couple of emails back and forth ended in some severe hostility on both our parts, at which time Crown quit communicating with me entirely. It seemed that Crown and his bosses couldn't have cared less about Operation Cody. Once they got their media time out of the operation, they pushed it to the bottom of their priority list.

While Jennifer, Julie, Lenny, and Detective Willette were still working to push the cases through, it appeared to me they had no direction or support from the administration to do so. I found myself on the outside, trying to fix things on the inside (even though I couldn't fix too much when I was on the inside). In an effort to get these cases through the court, I contacted every prosecutor in Washington who had Operation Cody cases. I also went so far as to contact the other states/jurisdictions for the same reason. I learned many of these prosecutors had asked WDFW for more information or clarification on certain aspects of the cases, but had not received any response.

By mid-July 2013, six months into adjusting to and enjoying retirement, I realized I was still spending a great deal of time on Operation Cody, with the same supporting cast and the same opposition from the WDFW administration.

I reflected back on one of my first conversations with Sgt. Hobbs, when I was bringing him up to speed on Operation Cody. I remembered him telling me he had first been assigned to "fix the G&R shellfish case," which he did (after months of work). It was clear that Lt. Crown hadn't received any such direction, from the Chief or Deputy Chief, regarding Operation Cody, a disparity I pointed out to Crown in one of my unanswered emails.

As the cases moved forward through the judicial system, I anticipated most suspects would accept a plea bargain rather than face a judge or jury. It is very common for overworked prosecutors to offer suspects a deal in which the majority of their criminal charges are dropped in exchange for a guilty plea on one or more charges. All our transactions had been video-recorded, and in about 75% of the contacts, there were two of us present (now available to testify), so there wasn't much hope for any suspects to win at trial.

I also didn't hold any false hope of extraordinary sentences for the various wildlife crimes. I knew most courts viewed them as "victimless" and didn't give these serious crimes the attention most Americans feel is needed. Sometimes, as a game warden, you must learn to somewhat adopt the attitude, "We just catch them, we don't cook them." It is, however, always a hard pill to swallow when you witness a major poacher or trafficker getting off with only a hand slap.

This experience also showed me that the larger the county, the less likely the prosecutor's office would take our cases seriously. No county illustrated this better than King County. I was amazed to learn that King County had refused to prosecute one of our cases (one in which I had purchased an illegal mountain goat). The deputy prosecutor who "handled" the case said it would not be prosecuted because it did not meet King County's minimum threshold of $1,000 (even though it was still a felony by state law). In that particular case, in addition to not charging the suspect, by their inaction, they also allowed him to keep the proceeds (cash I paid him) from an illegal sale!

When we began Operation Cody, we had no idea what we would accomplish in a relatively short time. As I look back, I'm most proud of these statistics:

344

1) In addition to Washington, we developed cases and intelligence in Oklahoma, Idaho, Oregon, California, New York, Illinois, Montana, South Carolina, Florida, China, and B.C., with offers from several other states/provinces.

2) We spent less than $50,000

3) We received (to be forfeited) well over $10,000 in cash from the suspects.

4) We developed probable cause for the arrest of over 100 suspects.

5) We developed probable cause for arrest on the suspects with over 1,000 counts of state and federal criminal charges (most are felony level).

6) We successfully worked into the underground world of illegal trafficking markets for sheep, bear (claws, gallbladder, teeth, and meat), cougar, eagles, caviar and sturgeon meats, hawks, owls, deer and elk meat, game birds, mountain goat, and African wildlife.

7) We seized over ten vehicles for forfeiture.

8) We drove over 50,000 miles in our undercover truck.

9) Jennifer and I conducted an unprecedented number of undercover contacts- over 600!

I know readers would very much like to hear what the individual criminal suspects received for sentences for their crimes, but in the interest of not disclosing anything that might endanger officers or ongoing cases, I simply can't list the individual sentences. Many of the suspects arrested in Operation Cody were offered reduced sentences if they would fully cooperate and provide information, which would result in the apprehension of even more serious wildlife

345

criminals. Most suspects turned down the offer, but a few took full advantage of it, resulting in investigations of new suspects. Those state and federal cases are ongoing as I write this. If I were to list the individual sentences in this book, it would be easy to determine who cooperated and who didn't.

The sentences handed down to the suspects varied widely from zero jail time and $500 fines to long prison sentences and $30,000 in fines. Some sentences I agreed with, while others frustrated me rather severely, but that's the nature of the beast.

Our initial goal was to identify and arrest some of Washington's worst illegal wildlife traffickers and deter others from their illegal activities. Despite the hurdles we encountered, there is still satisfaction in knowing we far exceeded our expectations and have been true to our mission of preserving and protecting our wildlife resources.

In writing this book, I also hope that the public can begin to understand the magnitude and sheer volume of these poaching crimes and become more aware and involved in the issues surrounding wildlife protection.

Please support anti-poaching efforts by insisting the courts and legislatures take these crimes seriously. If or when you meet a uniformed game warden, please take the time to thank them for their service, let them know you appreciate everything they do, and ask what you can do to help them.

While the majority of poaching crimes go unseen, poachers almost always commit their crimes for two reasons: bragging rights (to show off their trophies) or for-profit (the whole "to feed my family" argument is largely a myth). It is then that you may witness or hear about these crimes. Please take the time and effort to turn this valuable information into your local game warden! The phone numbers to report poaching crimes can easily be found in all hunting and fishing regulations pamphlets or on the internet. Always insist that an officer personally call you back. If you see something suspicious- call!

Game wardens are few in number and (as this book illustrates) need your support and help!

AN UPDATE ON WDFW PERSONNEL

Captain Jennifer Maurstad was promoted to sergeant for several years, then became the first female in WDFW history to be promoted above the rank of sergeant.

Sgt. Hobbs was promoted to the region four captain position, then to deputy chief, and then later resigned.

Detective Julie Cook retired and now lives in eastern Washington.

Detective Lenny Hahn continues to work in the SIU.

Detective Clarke was moved to a uniformed officer position (under Sgt. Maurstad's command), then back to SIU as a detective.

Officer Dave Jones was terminated shortly after becoming the officer's guild vice president. He successfully sued WDFW for wrongful termination and, as a result, won a substantial cash settlement and his job back with seniority, wages, and all benefits reinstated.

Chief Bruce Bjork announced his retirement, effective August 31, 2013.

After an intensive, wide-sweeping, grueling, and thorough 23-day "nationwide search," a replacement was found for Chief Bjork. It was decided that the best candidate in the whole country was right there in the very same office. In late July 2013, Lt. Crown was awarded the WDFW enforcement chief position. Later, **Chief Steve Crown** resigned from WDFW and now works in a city police department in eastern Washington.

In August 2013, **Deputy Chief Cenci** demoted to marine division captain, and then Chief Crown put him right back in as a deputy chief, in charge of the marine division and SIU detectives. He retired shortly after WDFW had selected a new enforcement chief (from Alaska).

THANKS

First, I want to thank my wonderful wife, **Judy**, whom I put through hell on this operation. If the long hours, time away from home, worry about me being hurt or killed, and the risk of retaliation (against our family) were not enough, she also had to listen to my constant complaining about the WDFW administration. Judy was asked to tolerate an awful lot, with absolutely no support or recognition from my former agency. Without my wife, I would indeed be nothing. She has been my best friend and the love of my life for more than the 45 years of our marriage.

I also want to thank our daughter **Beth**, who put up with much of the same but was always supportive of her "Big Bro." I have no doubt she was always as proud of me as I am of her.

Needless to say, I want to thank my partner, **Captain Jennifer Maurstad**. Her total commitment to the job, coupled with her intelligence, courage, family values, ethics, and strong character, made her not only a great partner but a great friend. Without her involvement in Operation Cody, there would be little to write about in these pages.

I also want to thank Jennifer's husband, **Robb**. Robb spent numerous nights alone, worrying about his wife's safety. I appreciate his sacrifice, and I am sure he is very pleased that Operation Cody is finally over.

My admiration and appreciation goes out to the numerous **citizens** who showed the courage to come forward with information regarding poaching and illegal wildlife trafficking. Many people know of these crimes, but few step up and actually do something about them. Thanks!

My gratitude also goes out to the **Rocky Mountain Elk Foundation** for their generous financial support to keep my partner and me as safe as possible.

I have had the honor of working, off and on, with **Deputy Prosecutor Charlie Silverman** (San Juan County) throughout my career. Charlie has more legal knowledge stored away in his brain than anyone I have dealt with, and he can be trusted with secrets. He spent countless hours helping us through the legal hurdles in this operation, and I am very grateful.

Special thanks to **Julie Cook, Dave Jones, Lenny Hahn, Paul Golden, Karen McManus, Wendy Willette, Rich Phillips, and the USFWS Agents**. Without their assistance, our operation would have failed before we ever got off the ground. This was indeed a team effort, one in which several officers often had to work "under the radar" to avoid being caught (by our administration) helping us out on this operation.

Finally, I want to thank my extended family, the Washington Department of Fish and Wildlife officers. Many of you had a valuable part in Operation Cody, and (as with the others listed above) we couldn't have done it without you. I had the honor of working with a number of you and have a great deal of respect for many more. I am very proud to have been a member of this elite group. Remember, I'm just retired, not dead. If you ever need me, just call.

IN MEMORY

Right in the middle of Operation Cody, I was devastated to learn of the death of a very close friend. Deputy Rob Breland was one of the best all-around cops I have ever worked with. I worked, hunted, fished, laughed (a lot), and generally goofed around with Rob for many years, and miss him to this day. Losing a close friend is never easy, but it's always worse when it happens at such a young age. I will never forget the times we shared.

ABOUT THE AUTHOR

Todd Vandivert grew up in the Washington D.C. suburbs of northern Virginia until his love of the outdoors led him to the northwest. He attended Washington State University, and in 1978, he graduated with a Bachelor of Science degree in Forest Management, hoping to start a career working in the outdoors. While in college, he met Judy, whom he married just after graduation. A few years later, Todd and Judy had their daughter, Beth.

Todd began his career with the Washington Department of Game in 1979 and has been stationed in three of the state's six regions. During his career, he started the agency's FTO (Field Training Officer) program and has trained around 50 new officers. Todd was the first game warden in the world to design and build a radio-controlled (robotic) deer decoy, now being used in almost every state in the country. He was a Defensive Tactics Instructor, as well as a Critical Incident Peer Support Counselor. He has taught classes on ballistic forensics, recognizing false identification, clandestine methamphetamine labs, and wildlife investigations.

Todd was also a union shop steward and the Washington Game Warden Association magazine editor.

He is one of only two officers who have received the WDFW Statewide Officer of the Year award twice. His other awards include; the NWTF Officer of the Year award, the WDFW Case of the Year award, WDFW Detective of the Year award, the Shikar-Safari Club Officer of the Year award, the American Police Hall of Fame award, the Legion of Honor Award, the US Forest Service Award of Merit-Outstanding case, and the NAWEOA (North American Wildlife Enforcement Officers Association)- Outstanding officer award.

Todd, his wife Judy, and their yellow lab now live in western Washington, where they enjoy hunting, fishing, and camping in their spare time. More than anything, they enjoy having spare time together.

Amazon also offers these other books by Detective Todd Vandivert (retired)